ʉmayamada™

SAMURAI CHEF

CREATED & WRITTEN BY: MAYAMADA

ILLUSTRATED BY: PINALI (A L JONES)

EDITED BY: LARA-LEE GREEN

INTRODUTION GRAPHIC BY: NIKKI DAWSON

KICKSTARTER CREDITS BY: POSOLA KARUNWI

EMAIL US: CONTACT@MAYAMADA.COM
VISIT US ONLINE: WWW.MAYAMADA.COM

PUBLISHED BY MAYAMADA
SAMURAI CHEF © 2014 MAYAMADA LTD
ALL RIGHTS RESERVED

ISBN: 978-0-9931121-0-2

THIS COMPLETE PRINT EDITION OF SAMURAI CHEF (VOLUME 1 & 2) WAS MADE POSSIBLE
THANKS TO SUCCESSFUL INDIEGOGO AND KICKSTARTER FUNDRAISING CAMPAIGNS.

SAMURAI CHEF IS ONE OF THE SHOWS WITHIN THE FANTASY TELEVISION NETWORK
WORLD OF MAYAMADA. THEY ARE NOT ANIMATED SHOWS
...YET.

MAYAMADA   SOUTHWARK LIBRARIES   AND MANGA,
FO   K.

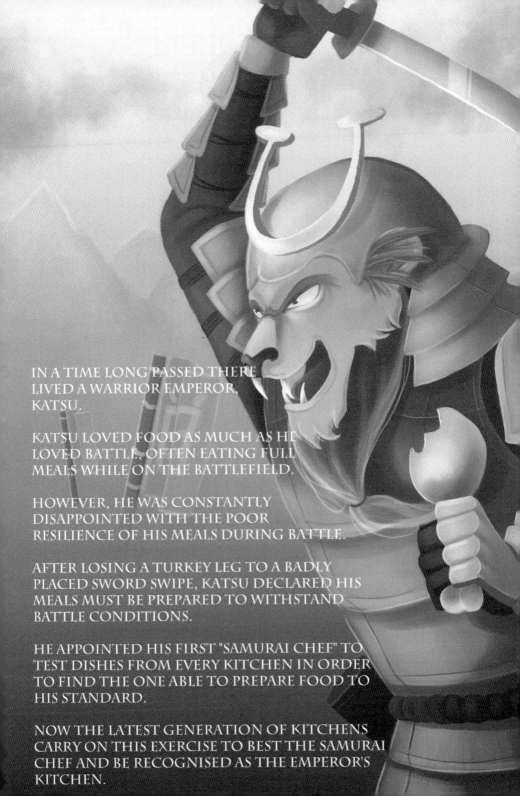

IN A TIME LONG PASSED THERE
LIVED A WARRIOR EMPEROR,
KATSU.

KATSU LOVED FOOD AS MUCH AS HE
LOVED BATTLE, OFTEN EATING FULL
MEALS WHILE ON THE BATTLEFIELD.

HOWEVER, HE WAS CONSTANTLY
DISAPPOINTED WITH THE POOR
RESILIENCE OF HIS MEALS DURING BATTLE.

AFTER LOSING A TURKEY LEG TO A BADLY
PLACED SWORD SWIPE, KATSU DECLARED HIS
MEALS MUST BE PREPARED TO WITHSTAND
BATTLE CONDITIONS.

HE APPOINTED HIS FIRST "SAMURAI CHEF" TO
TEST DISHES FROM EVERY KITCHEN IN ORDER
TO FIND THE ONE ABLE TO PREPARE FOOD TO
HIS STANDARD.

NOW THE LATEST GENERATION OF KITCHENS
CARRY ON THIS EXERCISE TO BEST THE SAMURAI
CHEF AND BE RECOGNISED AS THE EMPEROR'S
KITCHEN.

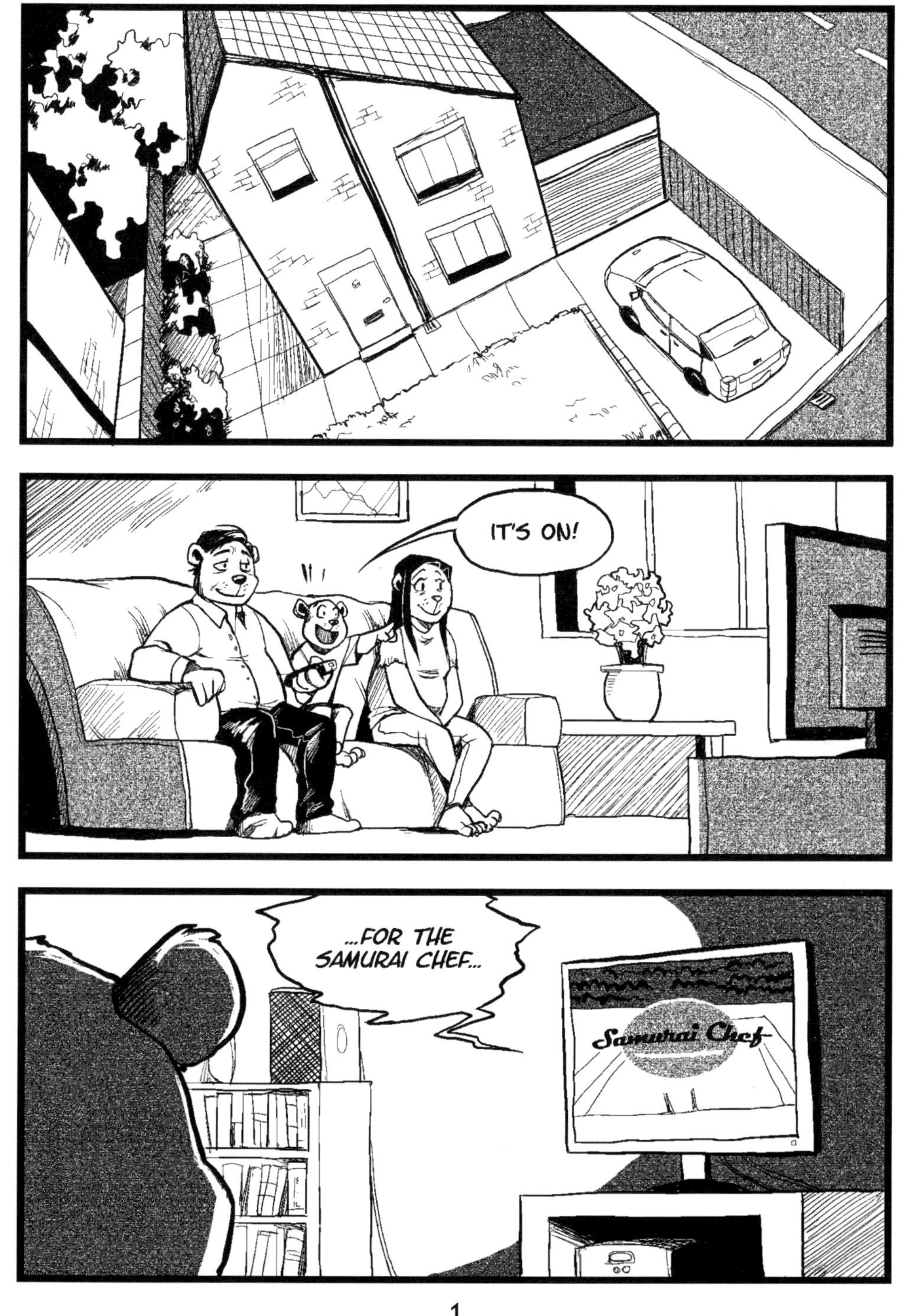
IT'S ON!
...FOR THE SAMURAI CHEF...
Samurai Chef

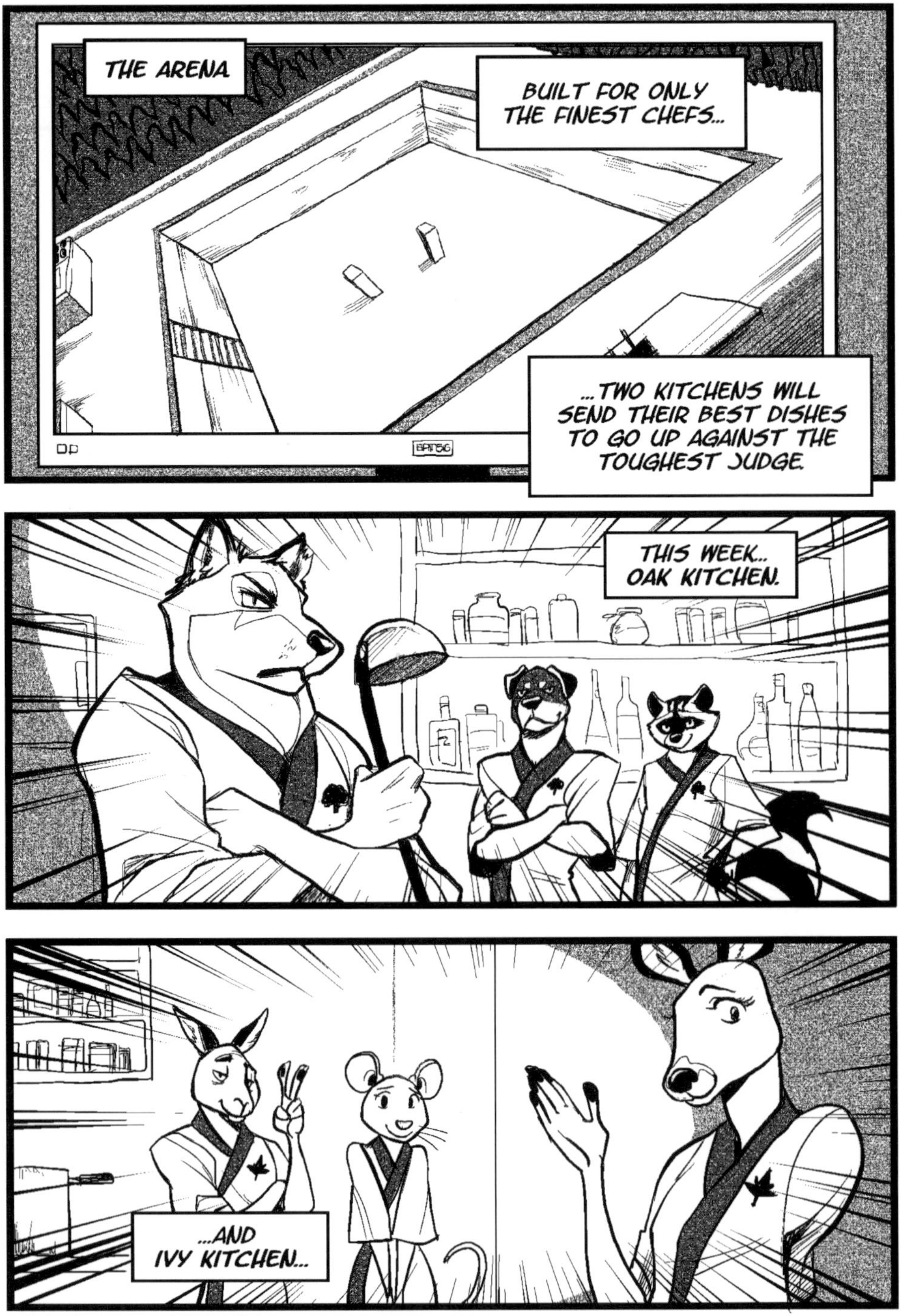
THE ARENA
BUILT FOR ONLY THE FINEST CHEFS...
...TWO KITCHENS WILL SEND THEIR BEST DISHES TO GO UP AGAINST THE TOUGHEST JUDGE.
THIS WEEK... OAK KITCHEN.
...AND IVY KITCHEN...

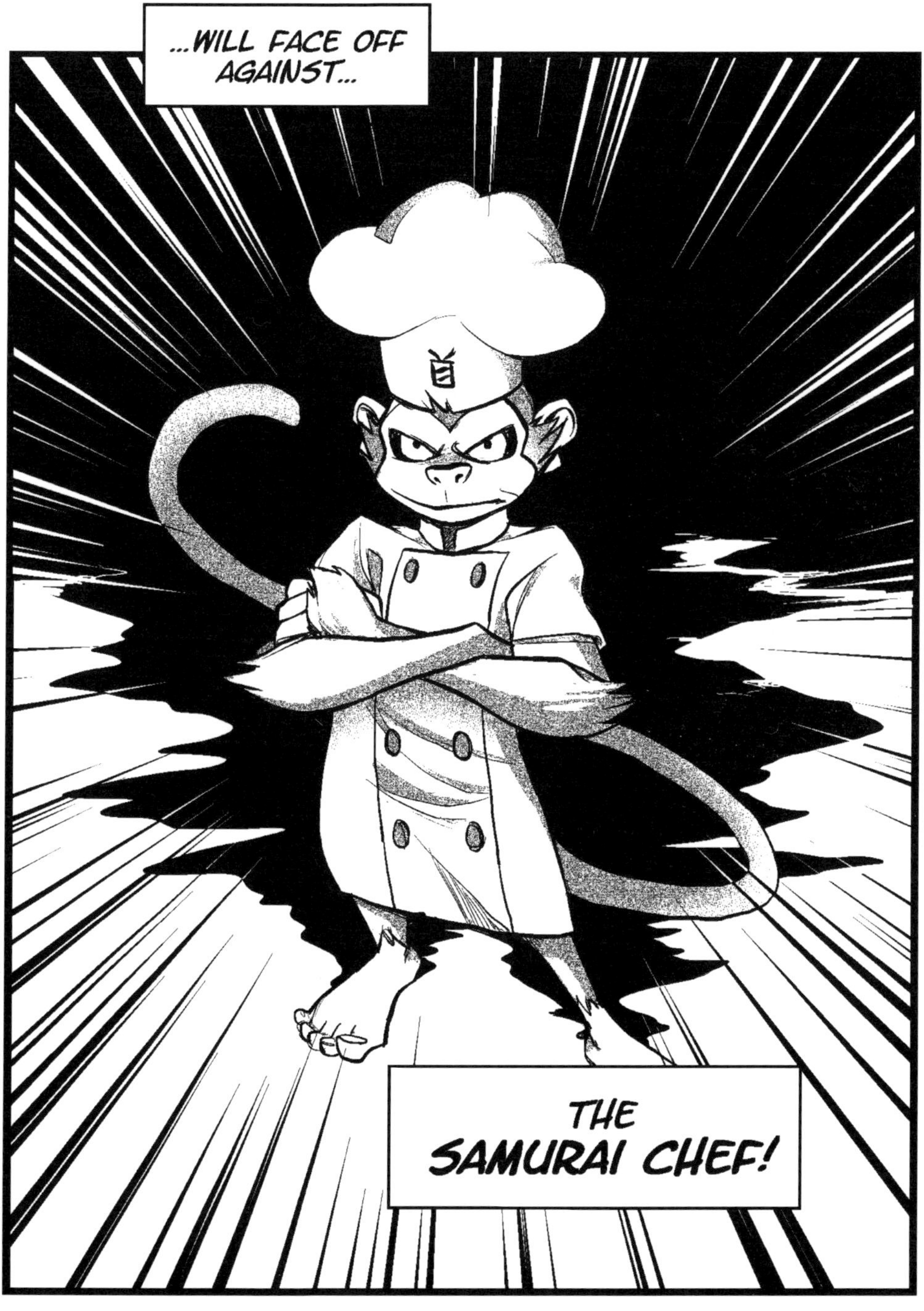
...WILL FACE OFF AGAINST...
THE SAMURAI CHEF!

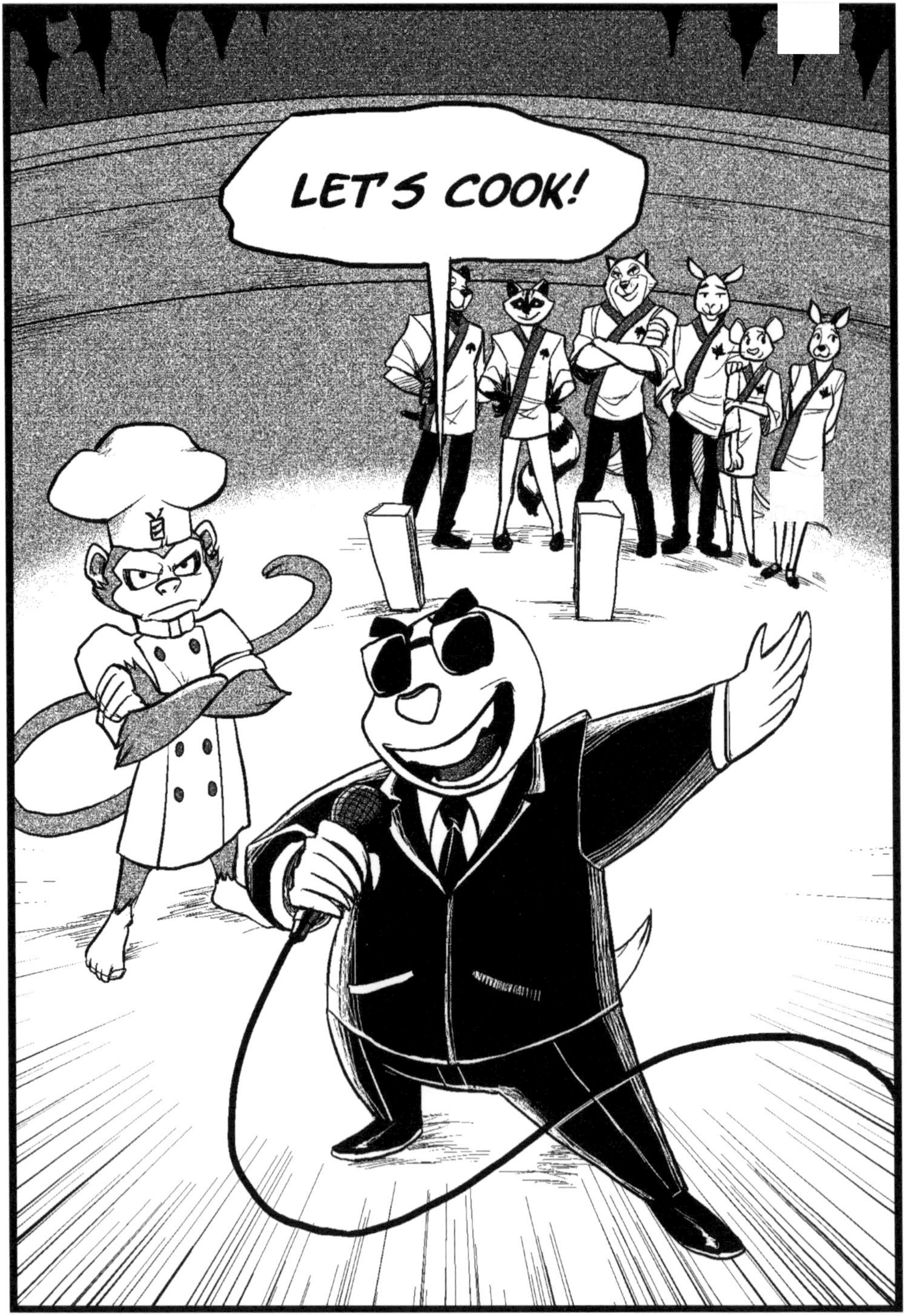
LET'S COOK!

CHOP
CHOP
CHOP

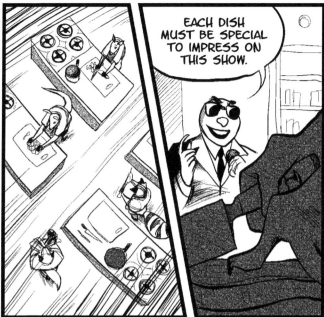

EACH DISH MUST BE SPECIAL TO IMPRESS ON THIS SHOW.

WE'LL BE MAKING KOBE BEEF FILET MIGNON

AND SAUTEED VEGE-TABLES.

SHIN
OAK KITCHEN

IT WILL GO DOWN WELL WITH THE JUDGE FOR SURE.

SSS SSSS SS

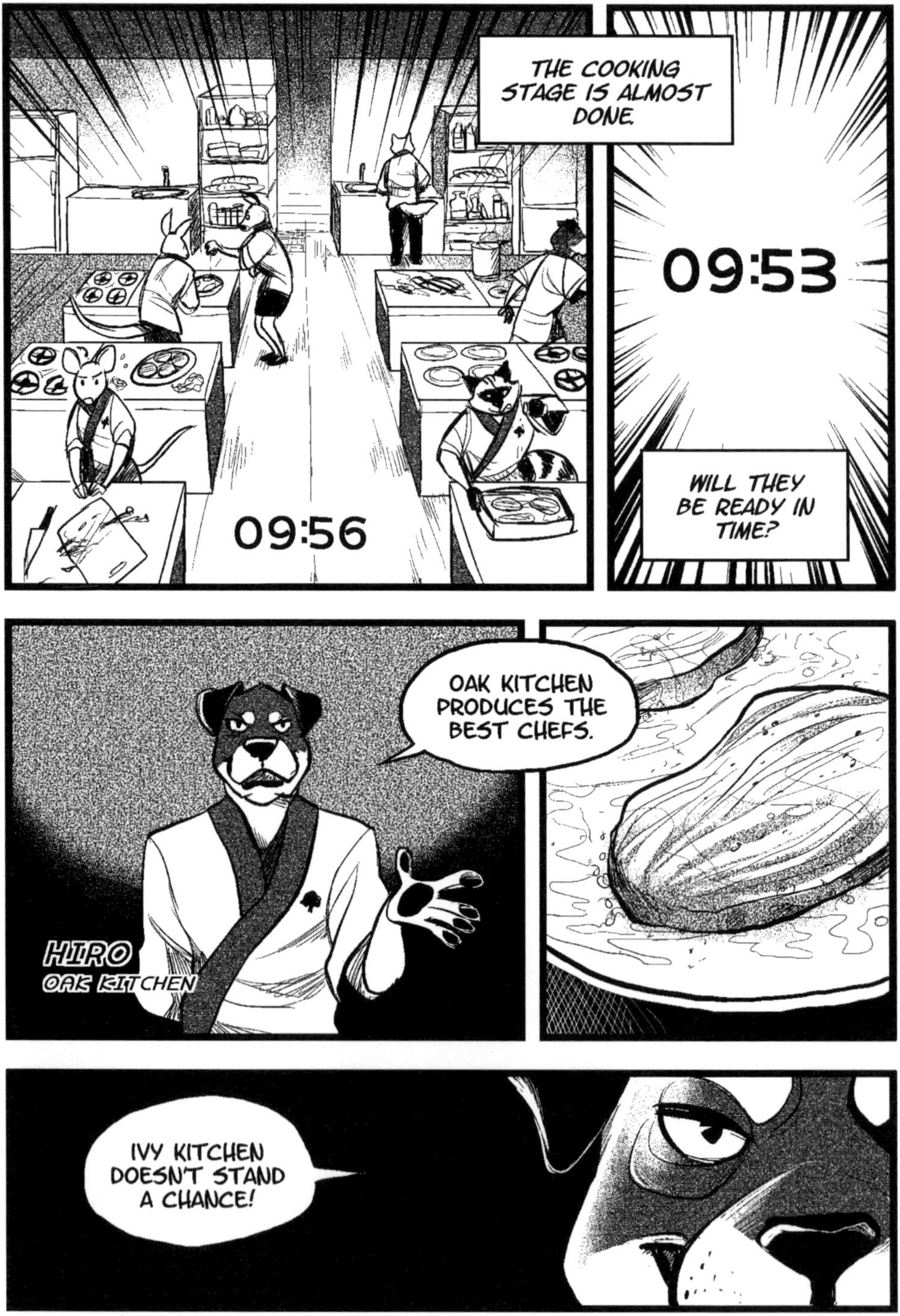
THE COOKING STAGE IS ALMOST DONE.
09:56
09:53
WILL THEY BE READY IN TIME?
OAK KITCHEN PRODUCES THE BEST CHEFS.
HIRO
OAK KITCHEN
IVY KITCHEN DOESN'T STAND A CHANCE!

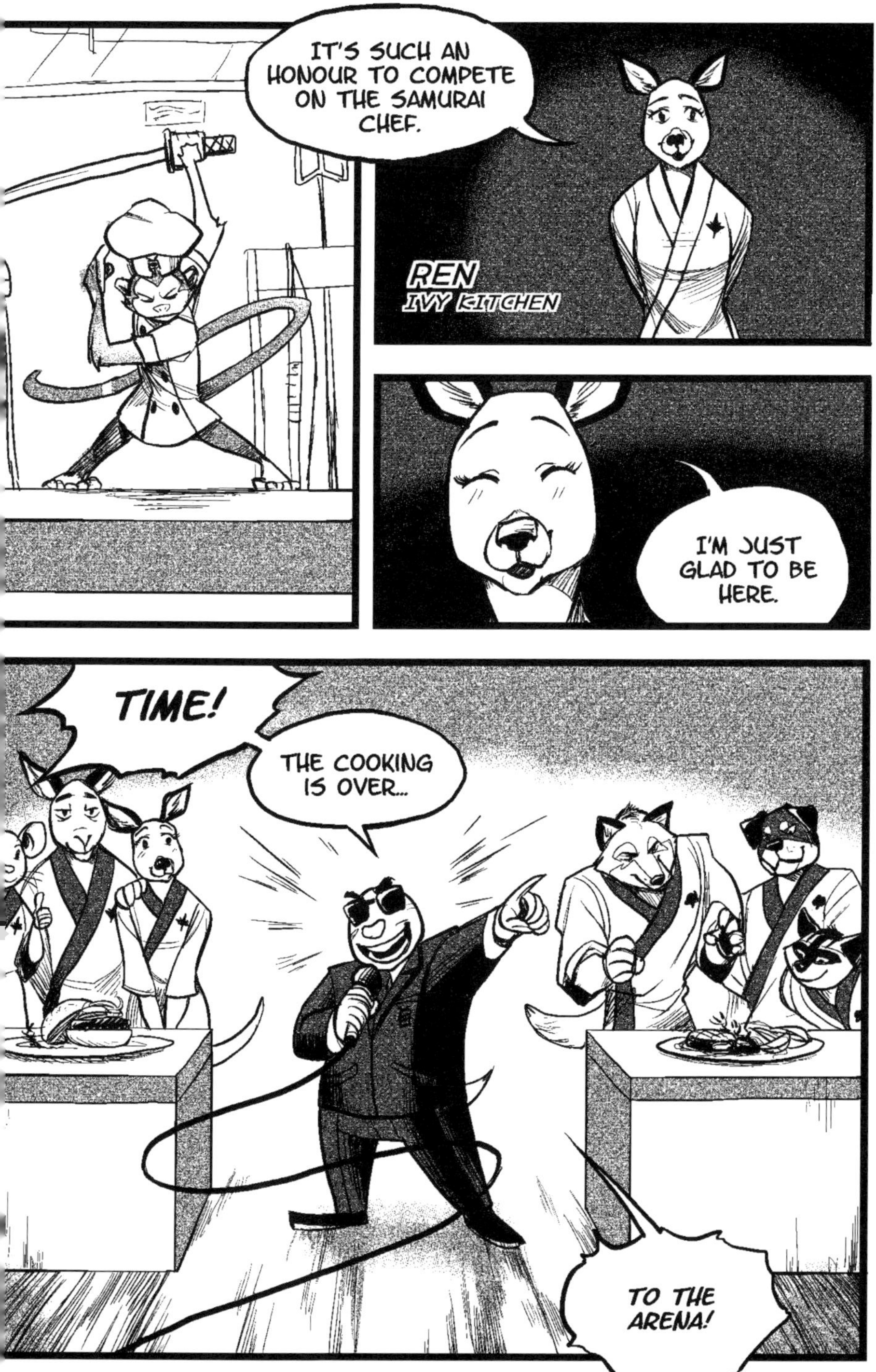
IT'S SUCH AN HONOUR TO COMPETE ON THE SAMURAI CHEF.
REN
IVY KITCHEN
I'M JUST GLAD TO BE HERE.
TIME!
THE COOKING IS OVER...
TO THE ARENA!

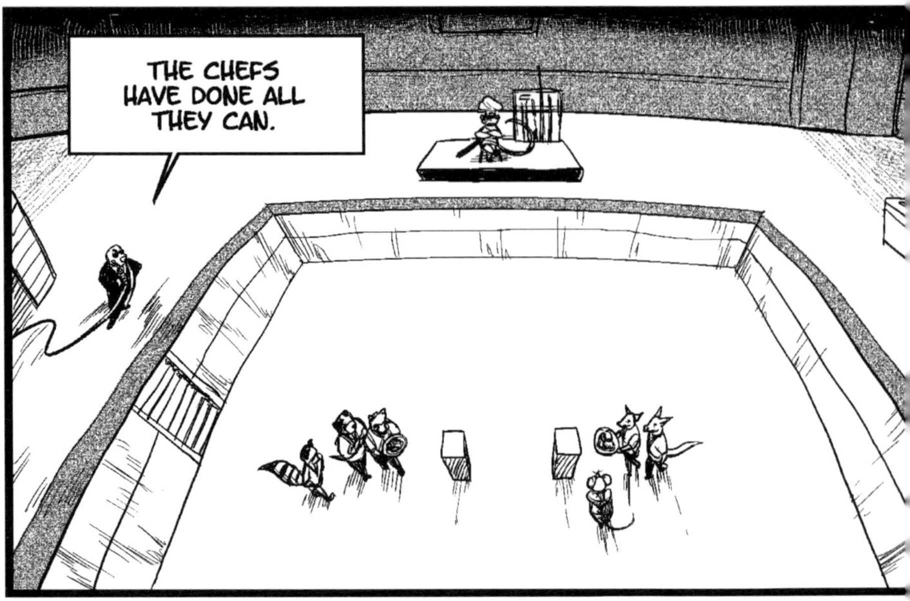
THE CHEFS HAVE DONE ALL THEY CAN.

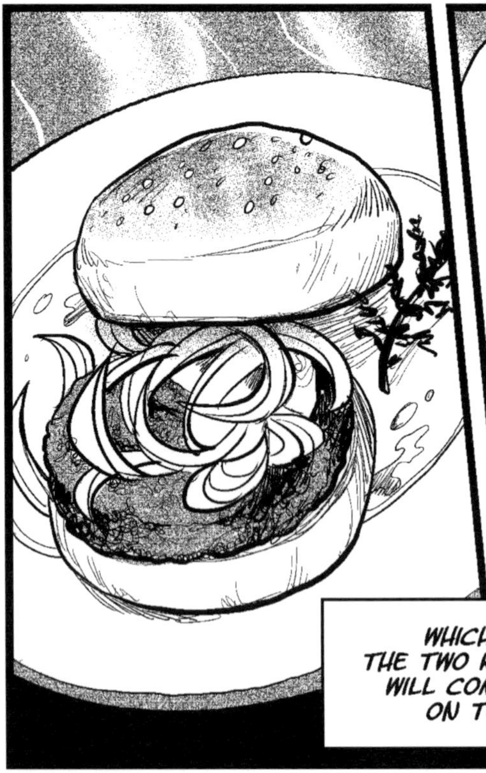

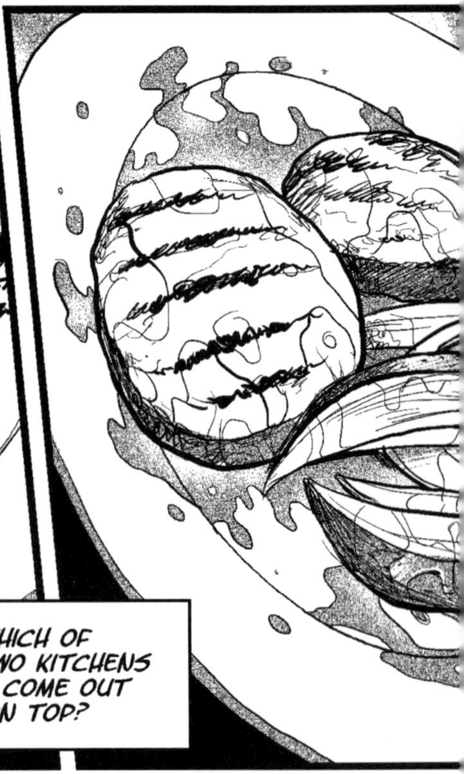
WHICH OF THE TWO KITCHENS WILL COME OUT ON TOP?

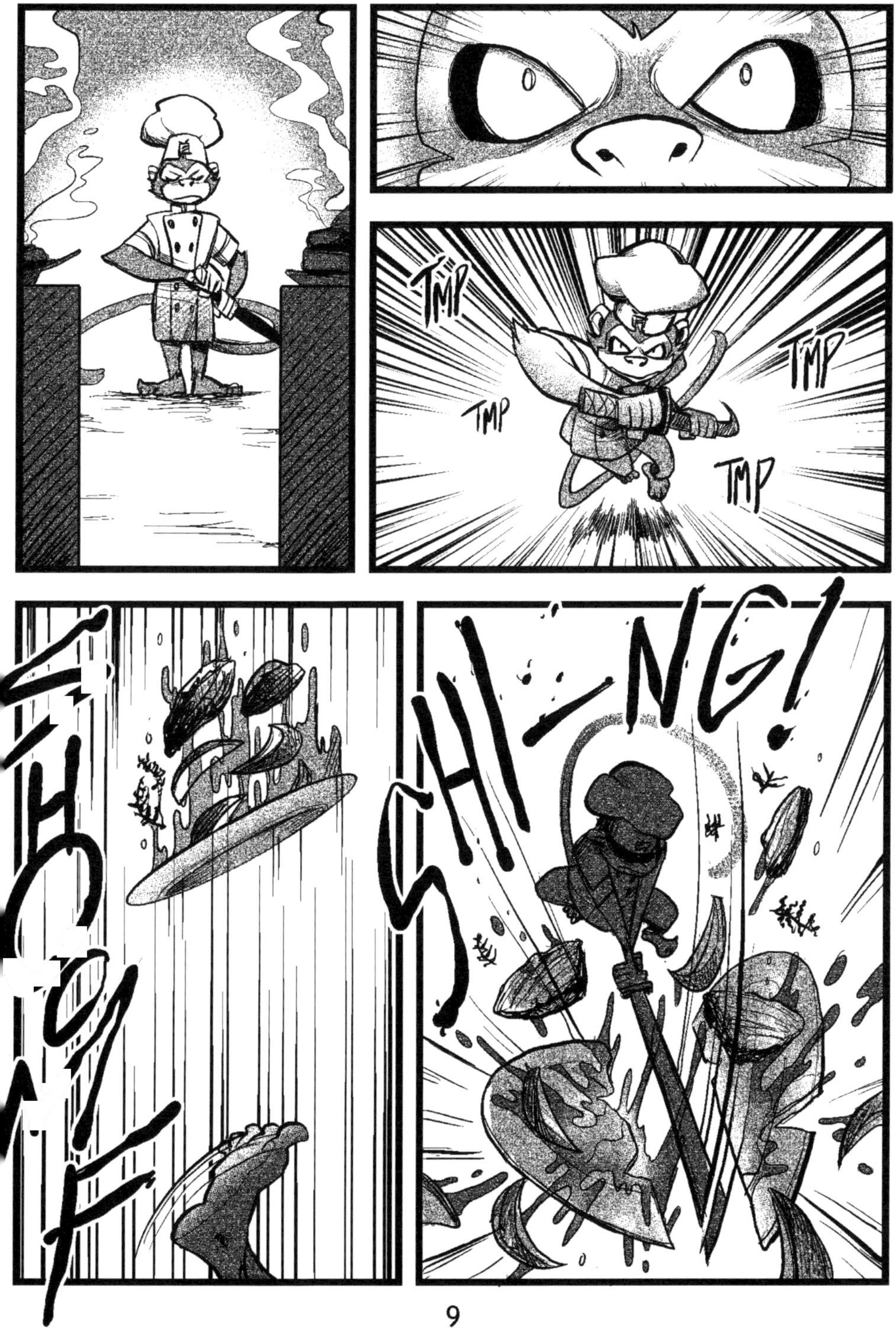
TMP
TMP
TMP
TMP
SHI—NG!

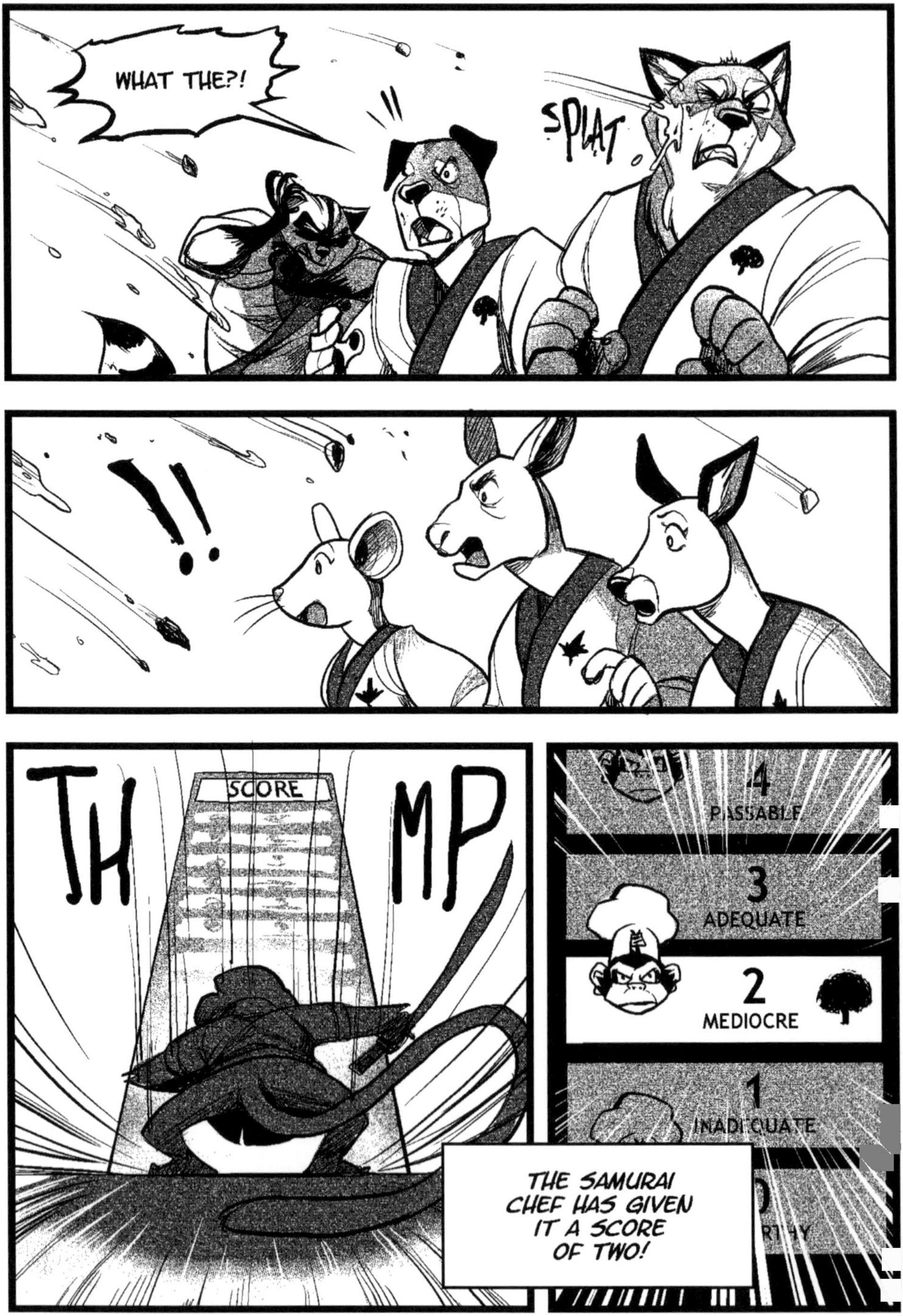
WHAT THE?!
SPLAT
!!
TH
SCORE
MP
4
PASSABLE
3
ADEQUATE
2
MEDIOCRE
1
INADEQUATE
THE SAMURAI CHEF HAS GIVEN IT A SCORE OF TWO!

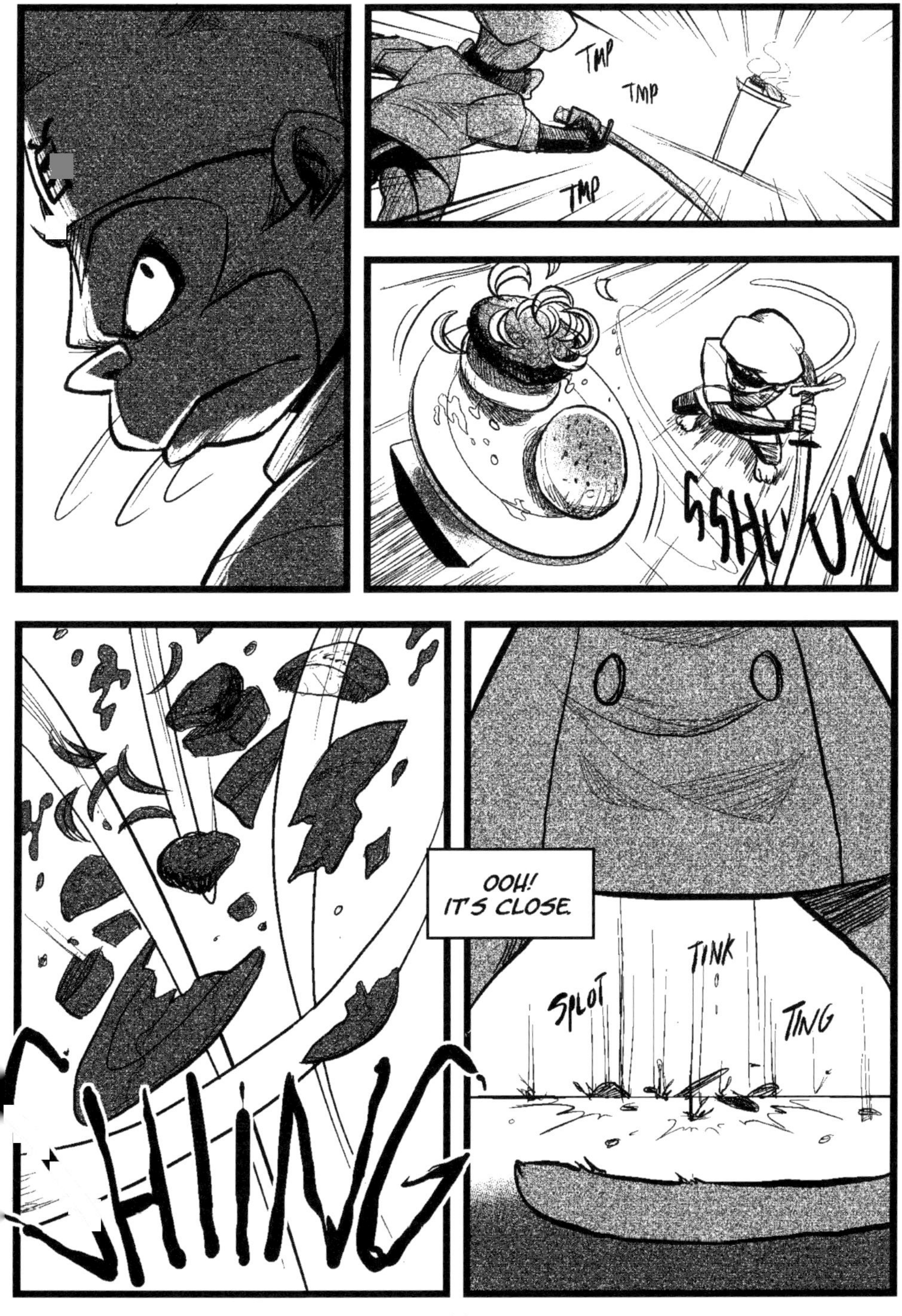
TMP
TMP
TMP
SSHUUU
CHIING
OOH!
IT'S CLOSE.
SPLOT
TINK
TING

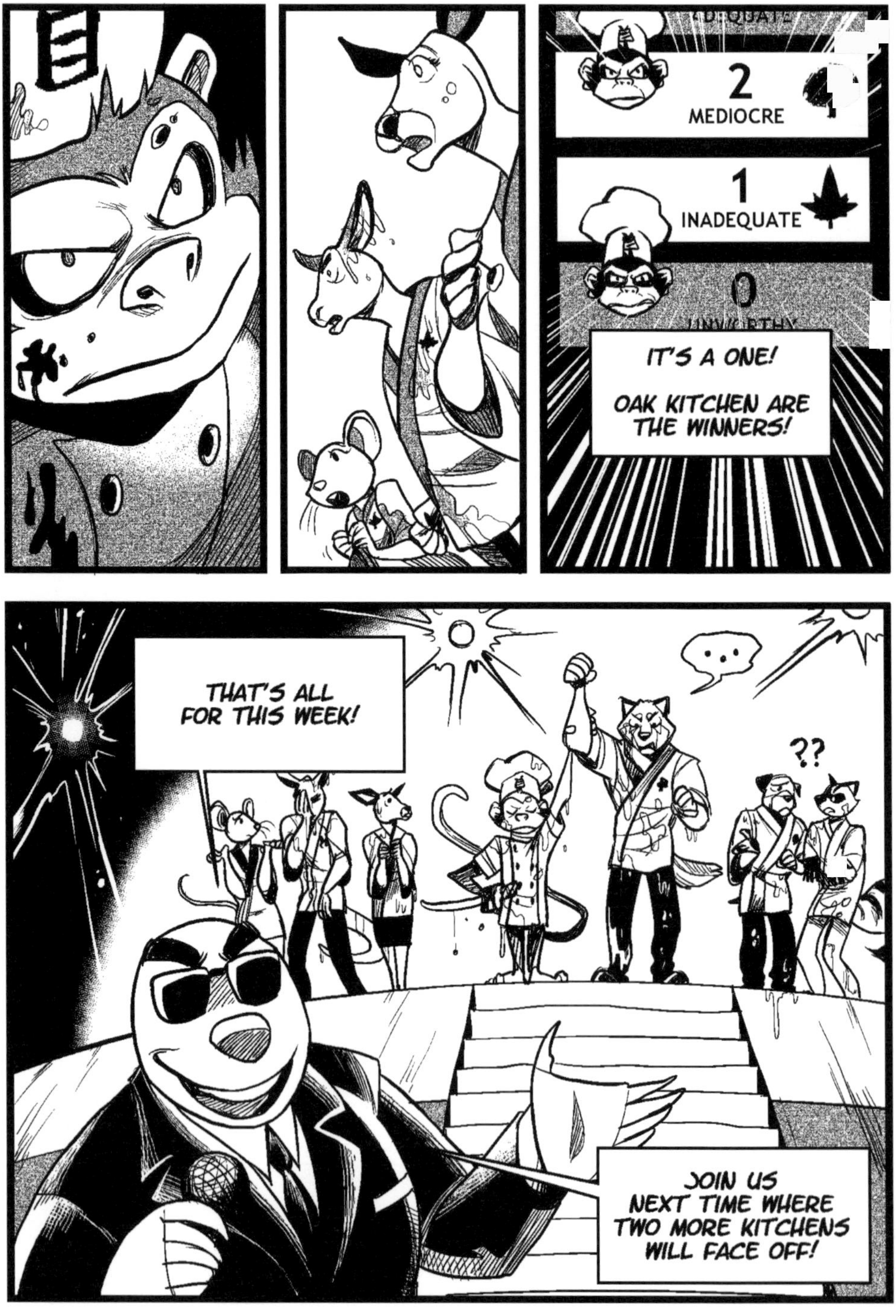
2
MEDIOCRE
1
INADEQUATE
0
IT'S A ONE!
OAK KITCHEN ARE THE WINNERS!
THAT'S ALL FOR THIS WEEK!
...
??
JOIN US NEXT TIME WHERE TWO MORE KITCHENS WILL FACE OFF!

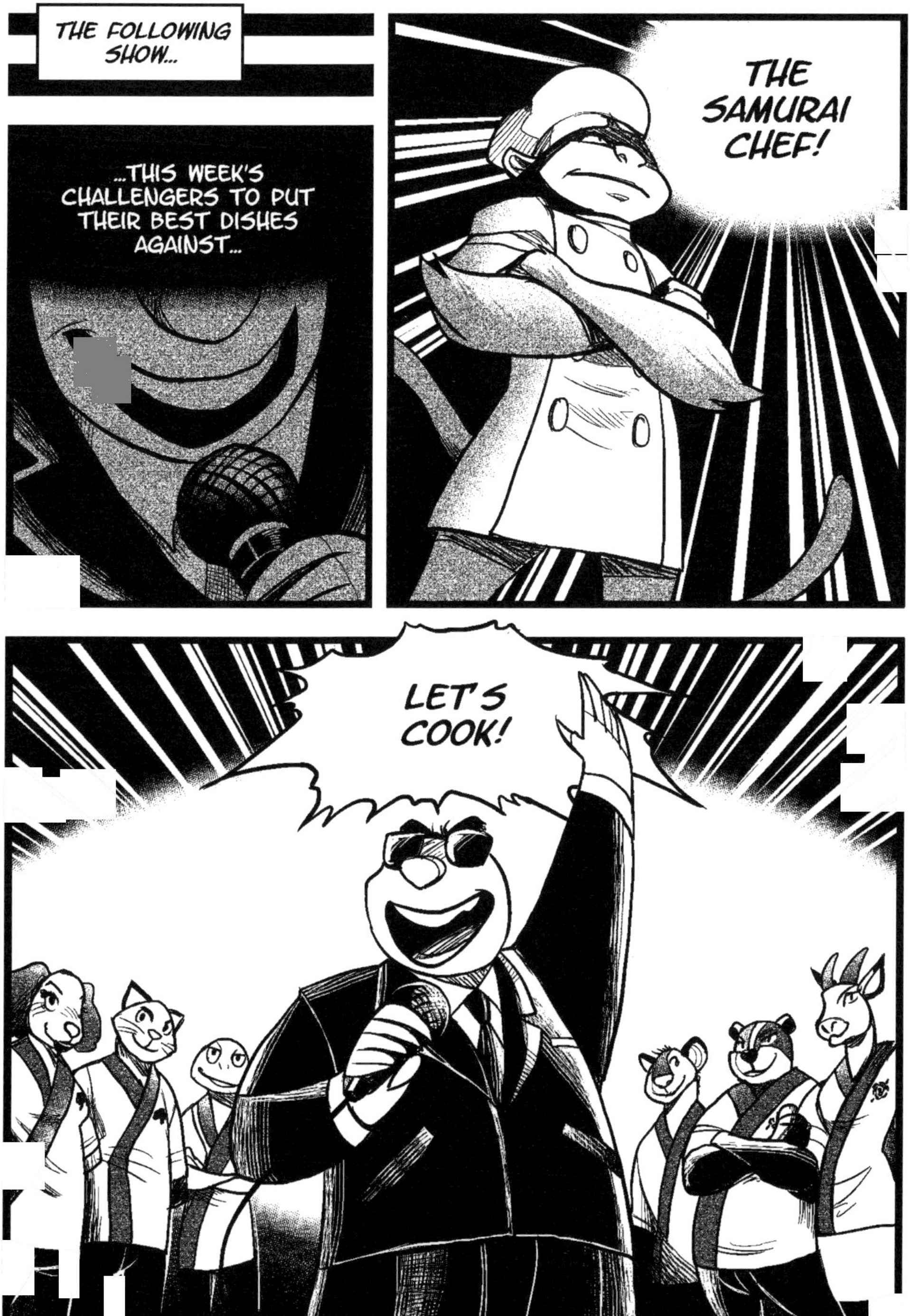
THE FOLLOWING SHOW...
...THIS WEEK'S CHALLENGERS TO PUT THEIR BEST DISHES AGAINST...
THE SAMURAI CHEF!
LET'S COOK!

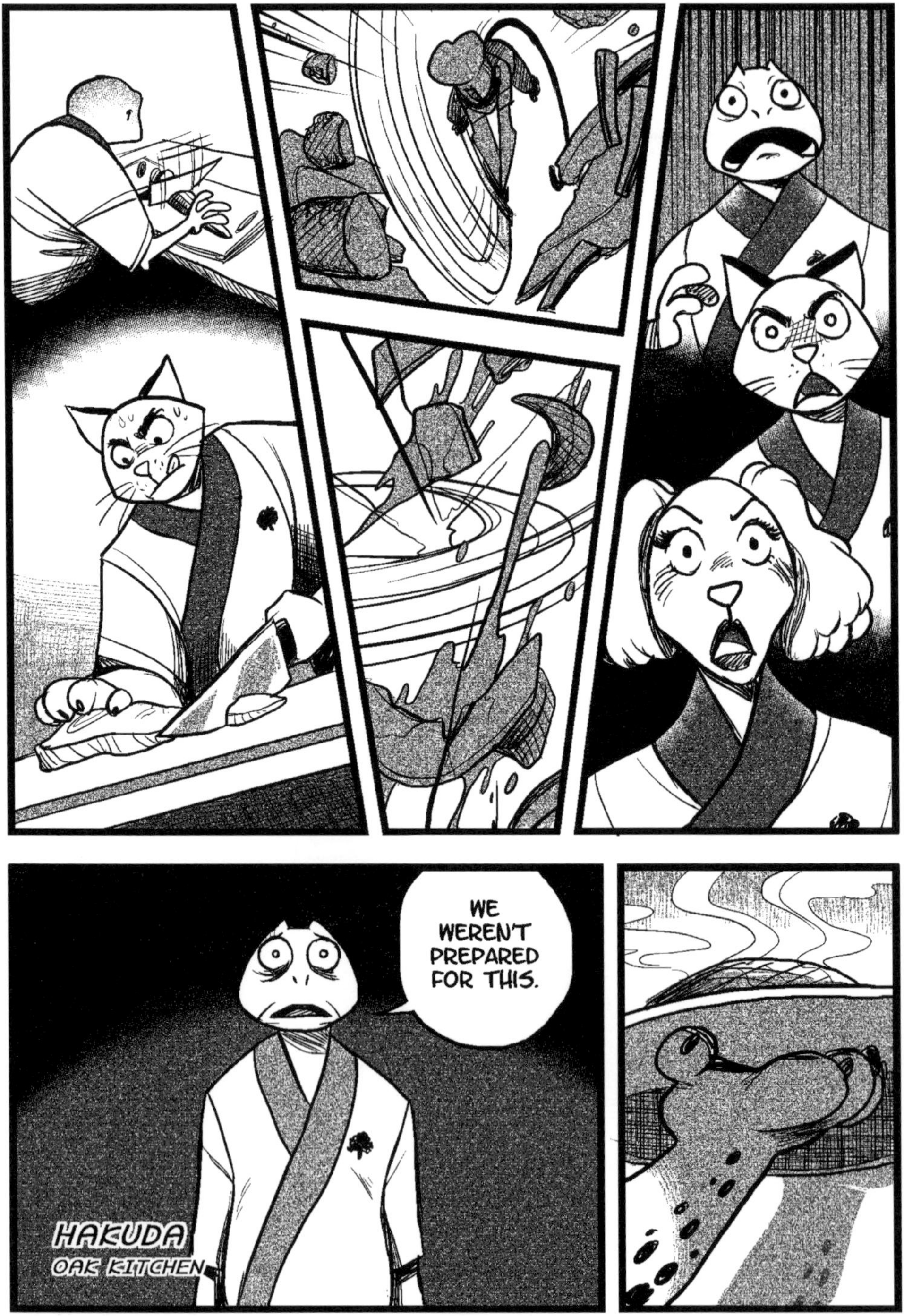
WE WEREN'T PREPARED FOR THIS.
HAKUDA
OAK KITCHEN

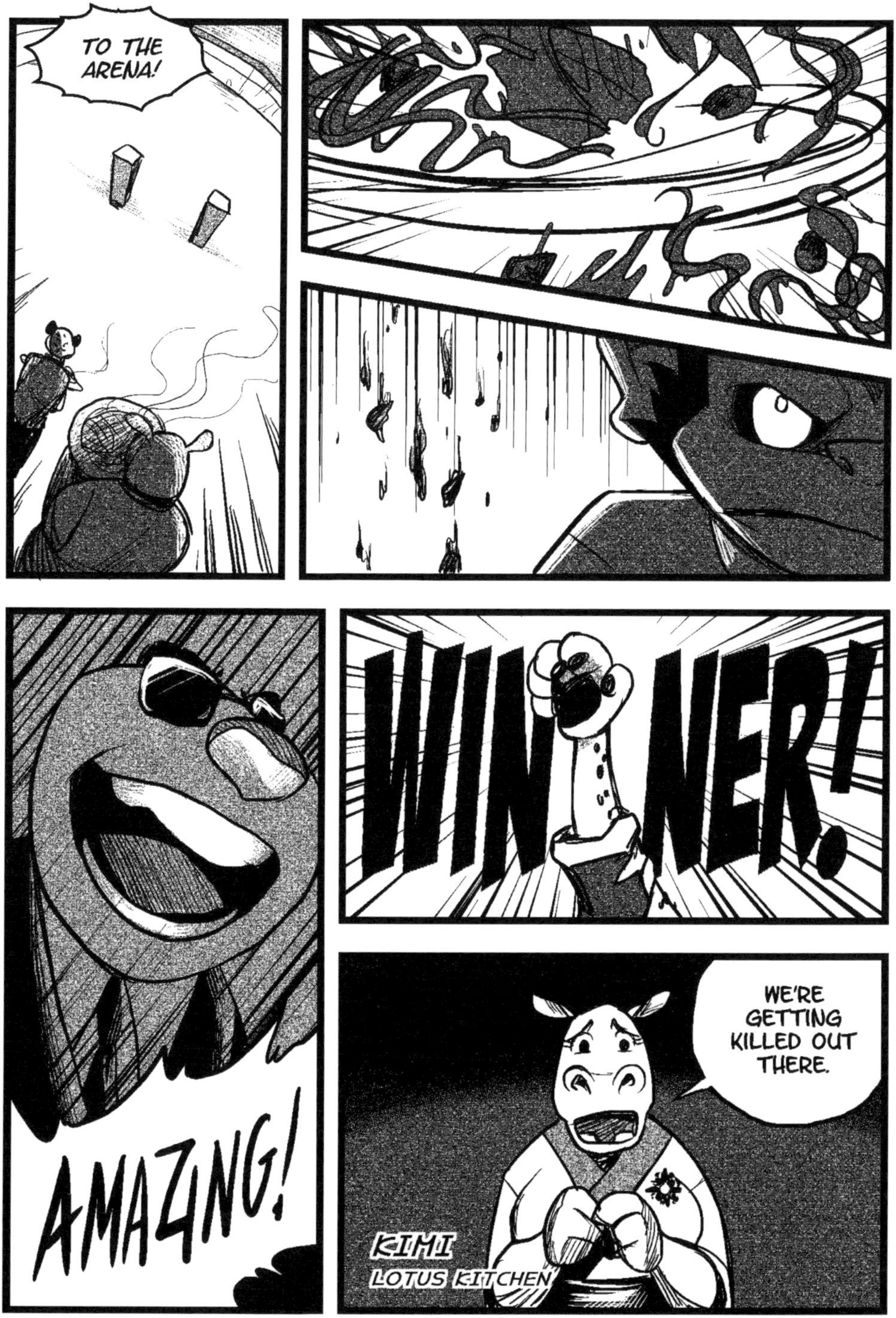
TO THE ARENA!
AMAZING!
WIN NER!
WE'RE GETTING KILLED OUT THERE.
KIMI
LOTUS KITCHEN

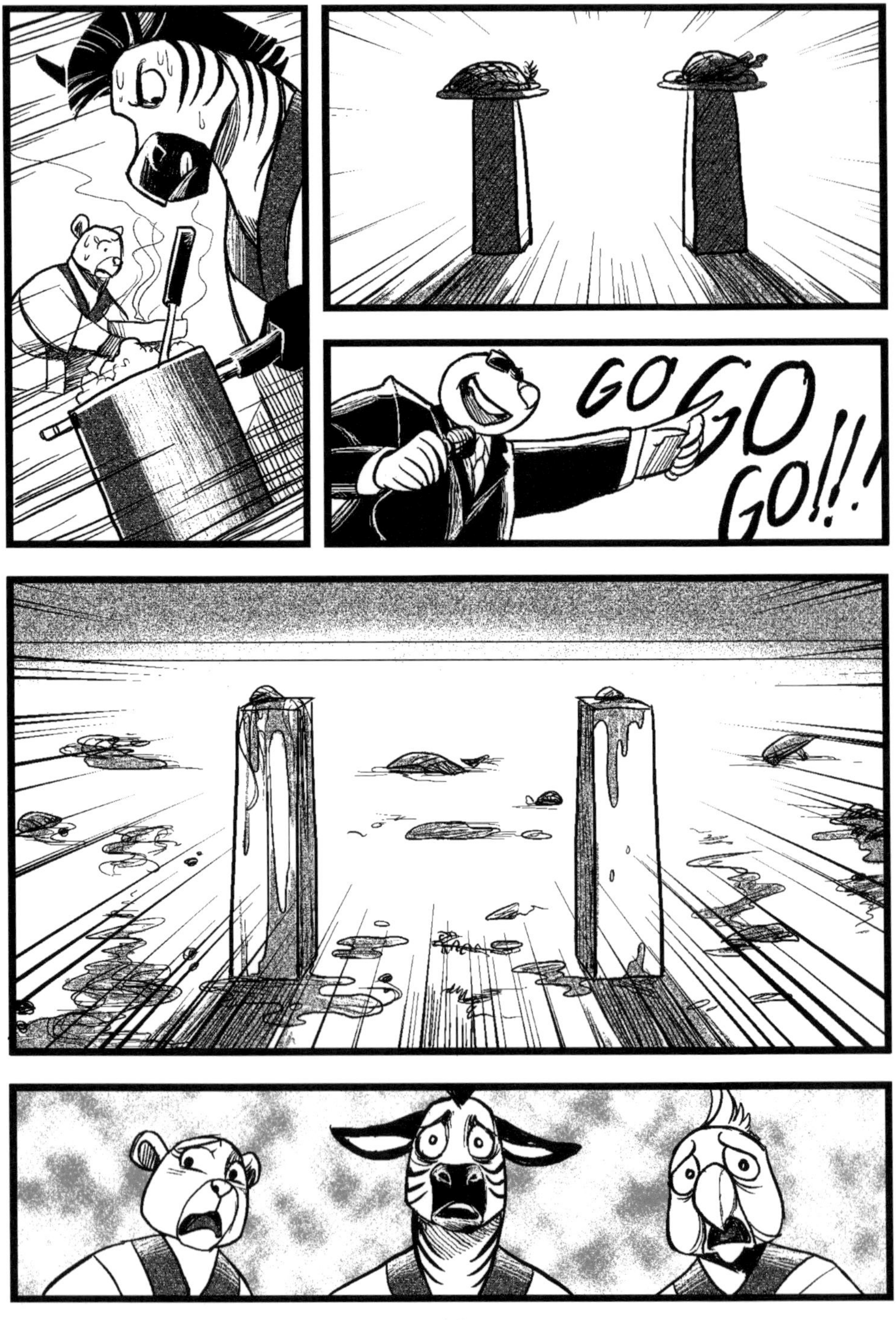
GO GO GO!!!

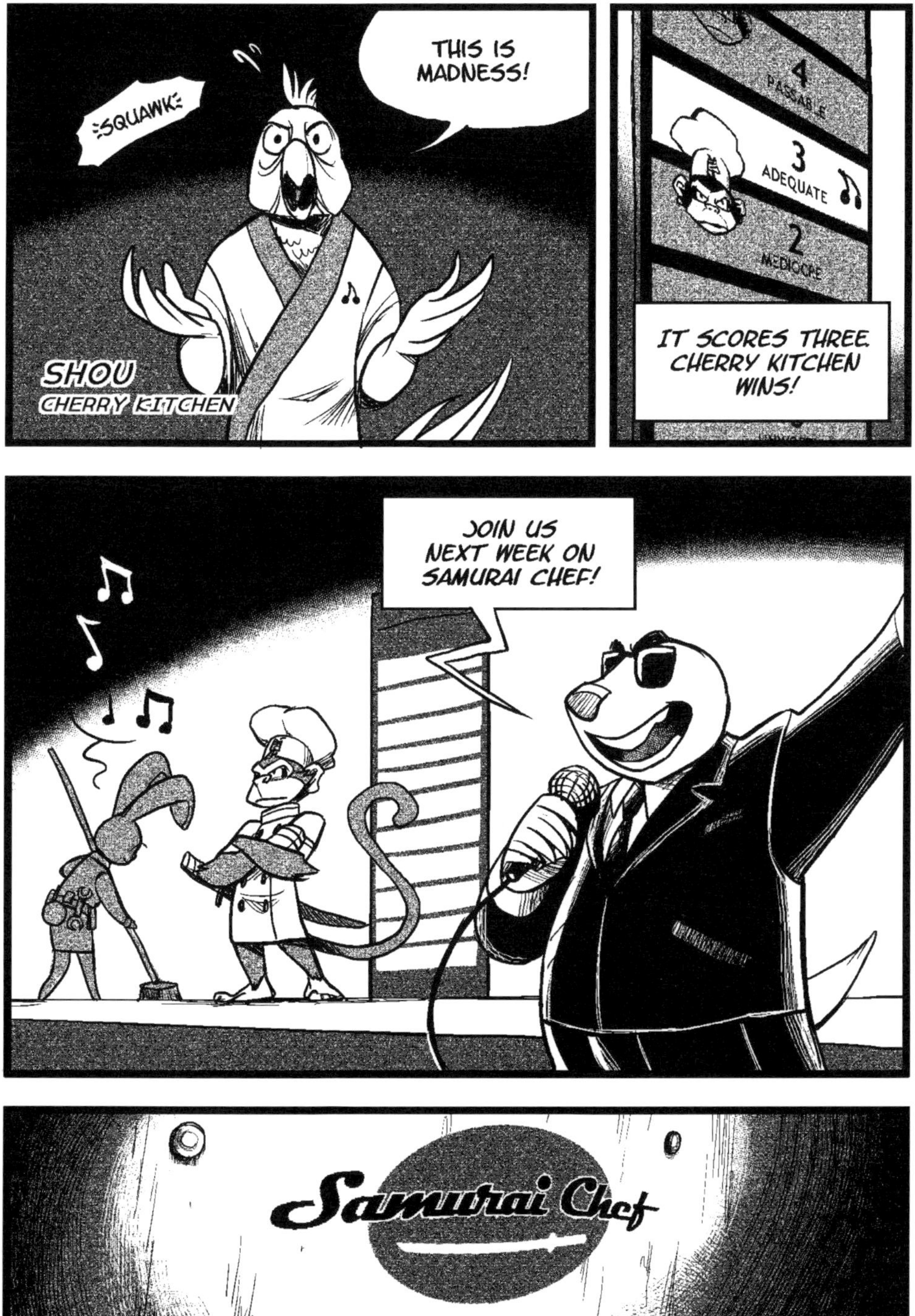
SQUAWK
THIS IS MADNESS!
SHOU
CHERRY KITCHEN
4 PASSABLE
3 ADEQUATE
2 MEDIOCRE
IT SCORES THREE. CHERRY KITCHEN WINS!
JOIN US NEXT WEEK ON SAMURAI CHEF!
Samurai Chef

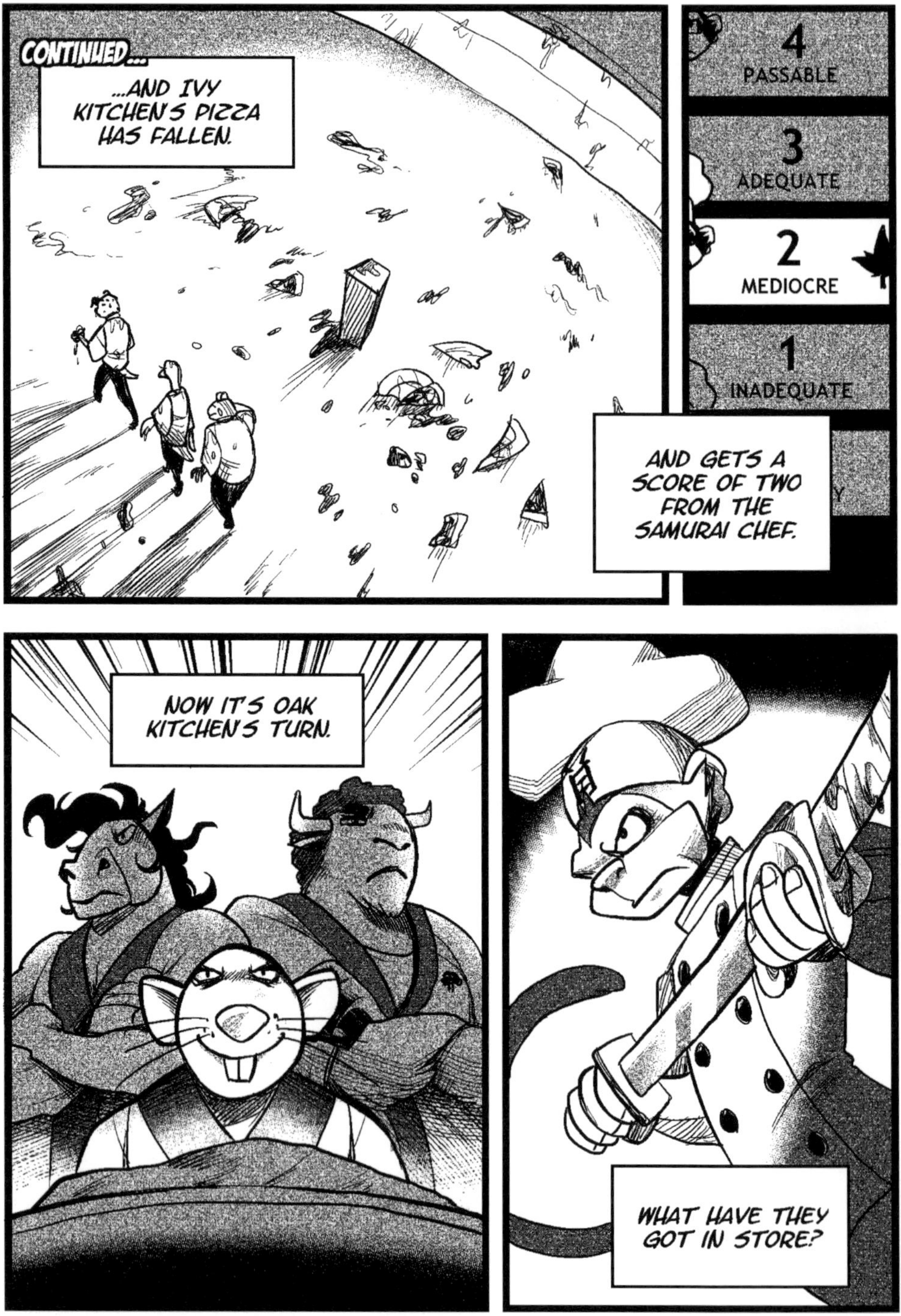
CONTINUED...
...AND IVY KITCHEN'S PIZZA HAS FALLEN.
4
PASSABLE
3
ADEQUATE
2
MEDIOCRE
1
INADEQUATE
AND GETS A SCORE OF TWO FROM THE SAMURAI CHEF.
NOW IT'S OAK KITCHEN'S TURN.
WHAT HAVE THEY GOT IN STORE?

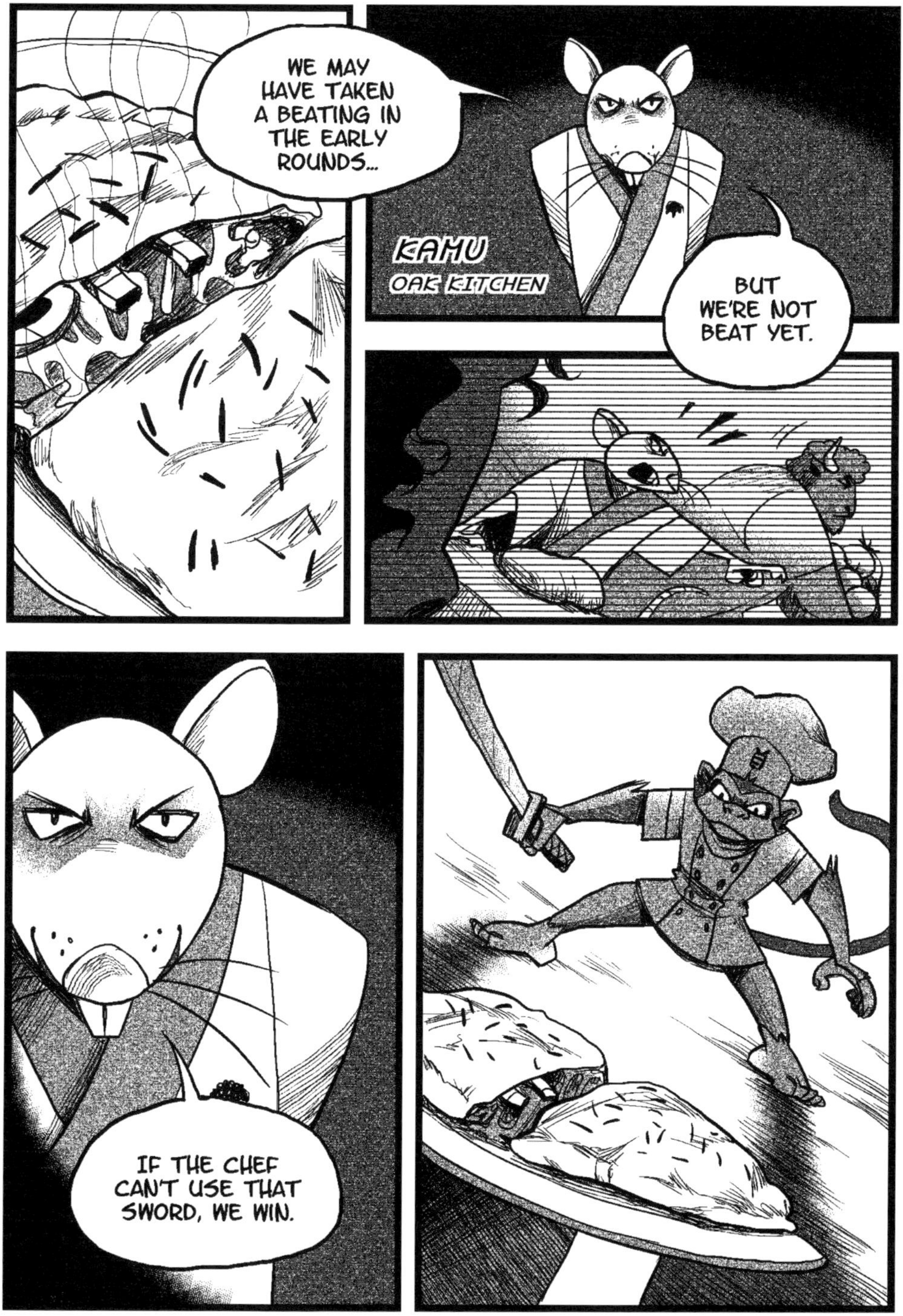
WE MAY HAVE TAKEN A BEATING IN THE EARLY ROUNDS...
KAHU
OAK KITCHEN
BUT WE'RE NOT BEAT YET.
IF THE CHEF CAN'T USE THAT SWORD, WE WIN.

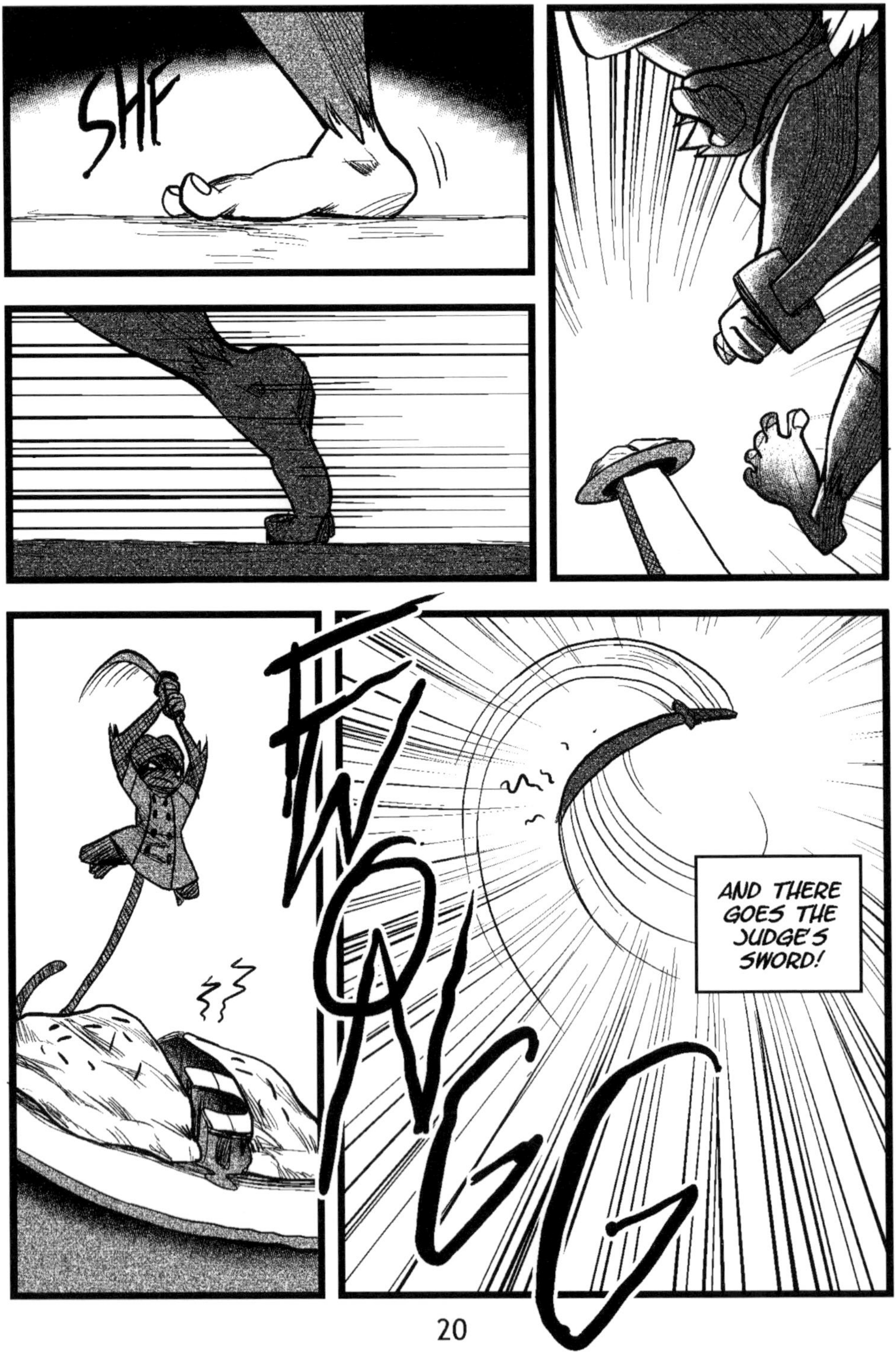
SHF
FWANGG
AND THERE GOES THE JUDGE'S SWORD!

TWAANG

OOH! THAT WAS A CLOSE CALL.

WE DID IT! THE PLAN WORKED.

WITHOUT HIS SWORD HE'S NOTHING!

IT LOOKS LIKE OAK KITCHEN HAS COME PREPARED.

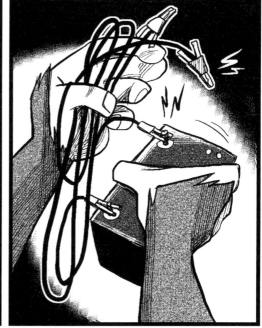

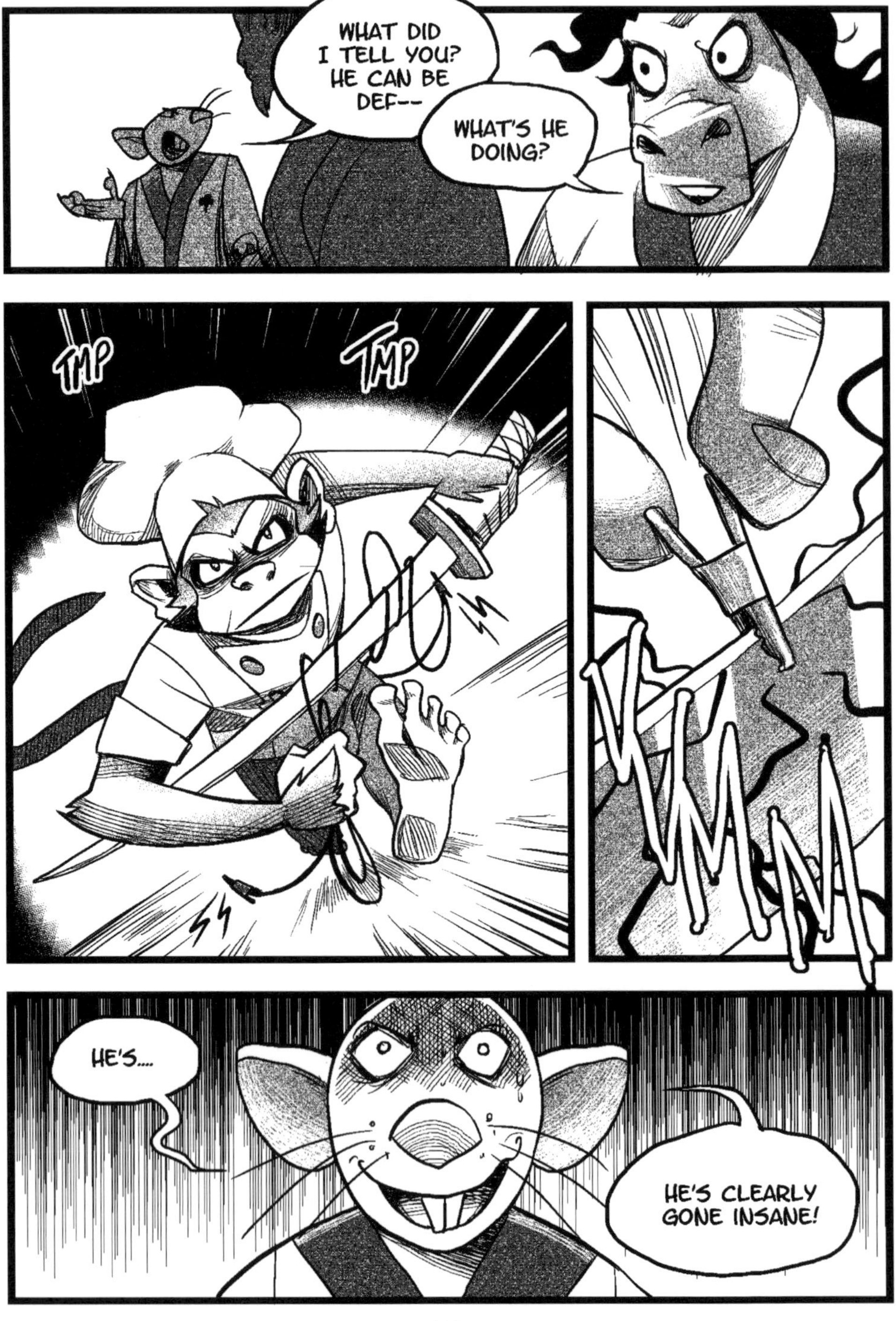
WHAT DID I TELL YOU? HE CAN BE DEF--
WHAT'S HE DOING?
TMP
TMP
HE'S....
HE'S CLEARLY GONE INSANE!

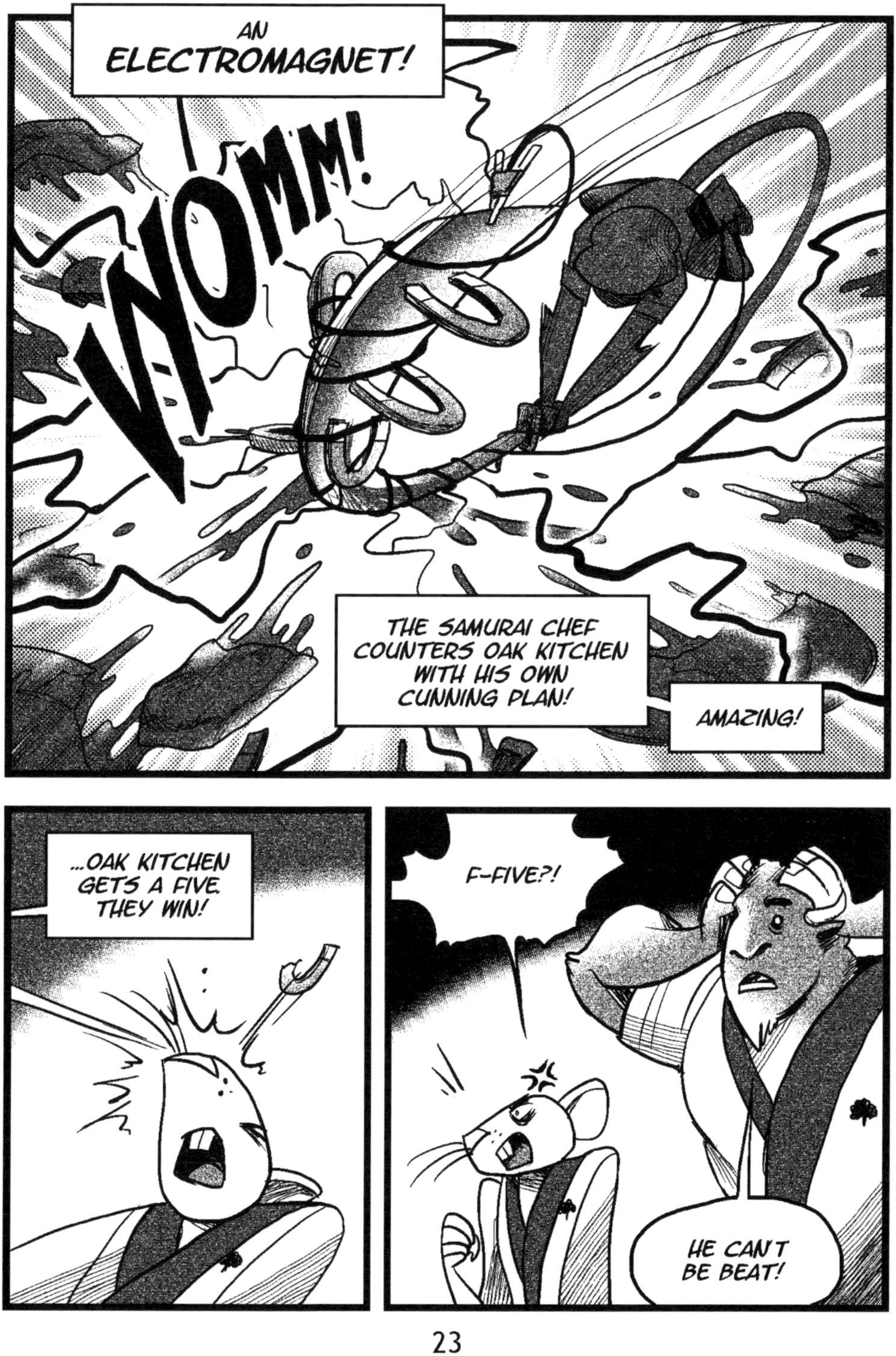
AN ELECTROMAGNET!
VVOMMM!
THE SAMURAI CHEF COUNTERS OAK KITCHEN WITH HIS OWN CUNNING PLAN!
AMAZING!
...OAK KITCHEN GETS A FIVE. THEY WIN!
F-FIVE?!
HE CAN'T BE BEAT!

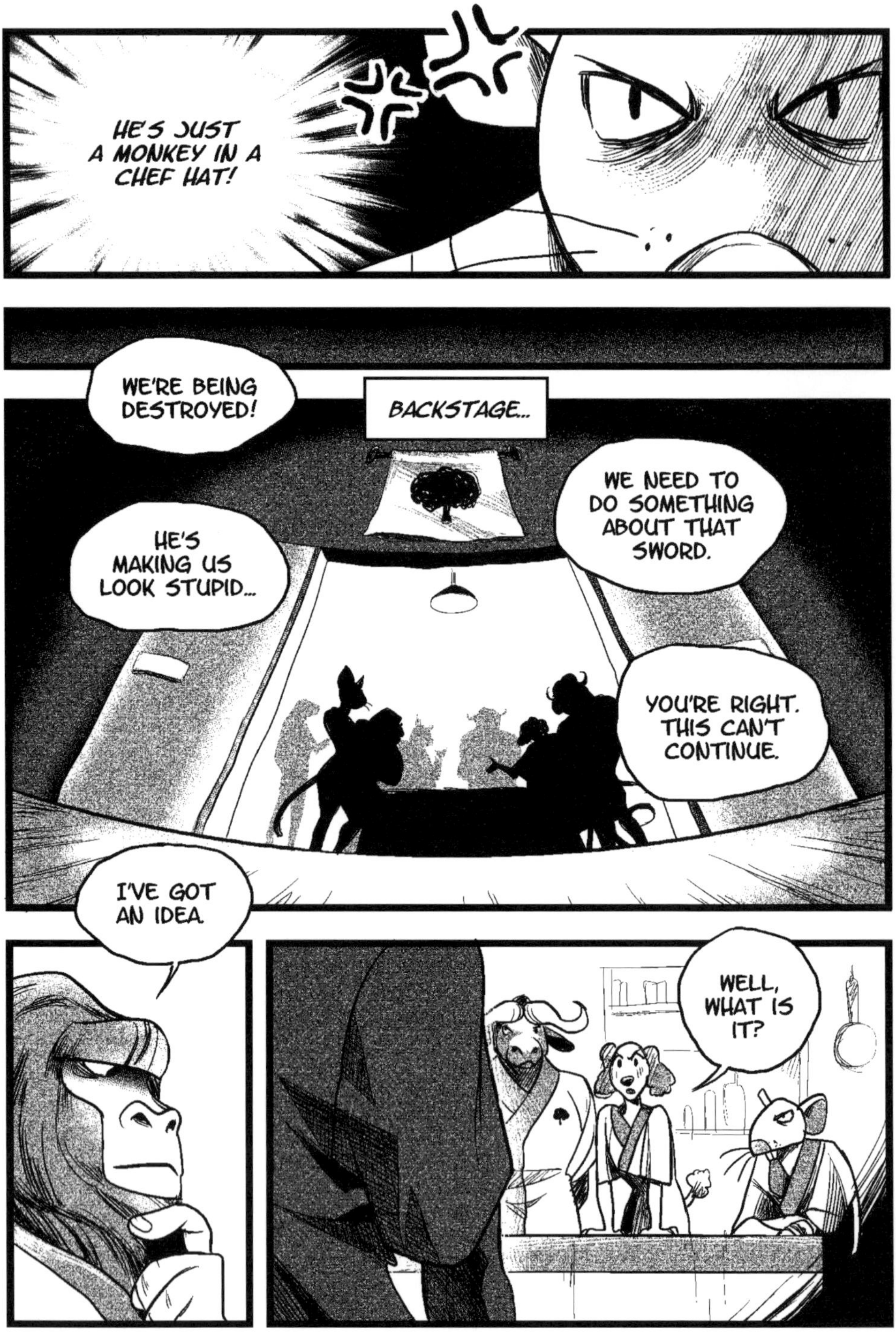
HE'S JUST A MONKEY IN A CHEF HAT!
WE'RE BEING DESTROYED!
BACKSTAGE...
HE'S MAKING US LOOK STUPID...
WE NEED TO DO SOMETHING ABOUT THAT SWORD.
YOU'RE RIGHT. THIS CAN'T CONTINUE.
I'VE GOT AN IDEA.
WELL, WHAT IS IT?

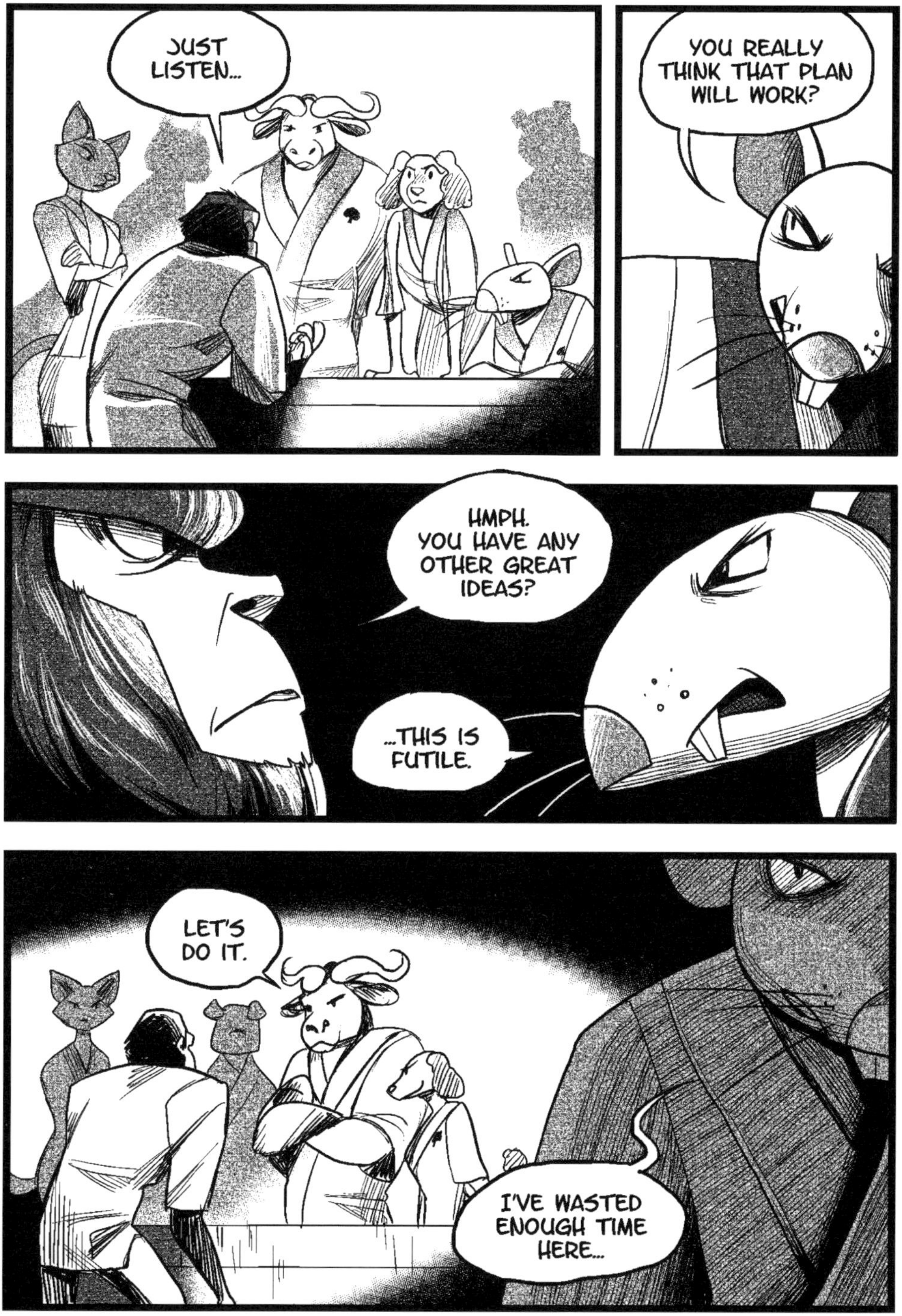
JUST LISTEN...
YOU REALLY THINK THAT PLAN WILL WORK?
HMPH. YOU HAVE ANY OTHER GREAT IDEAS?
...THIS IS FUTILE.
LET'S DO IT.
I'VE WASTED ENOUGH TIME HERE...

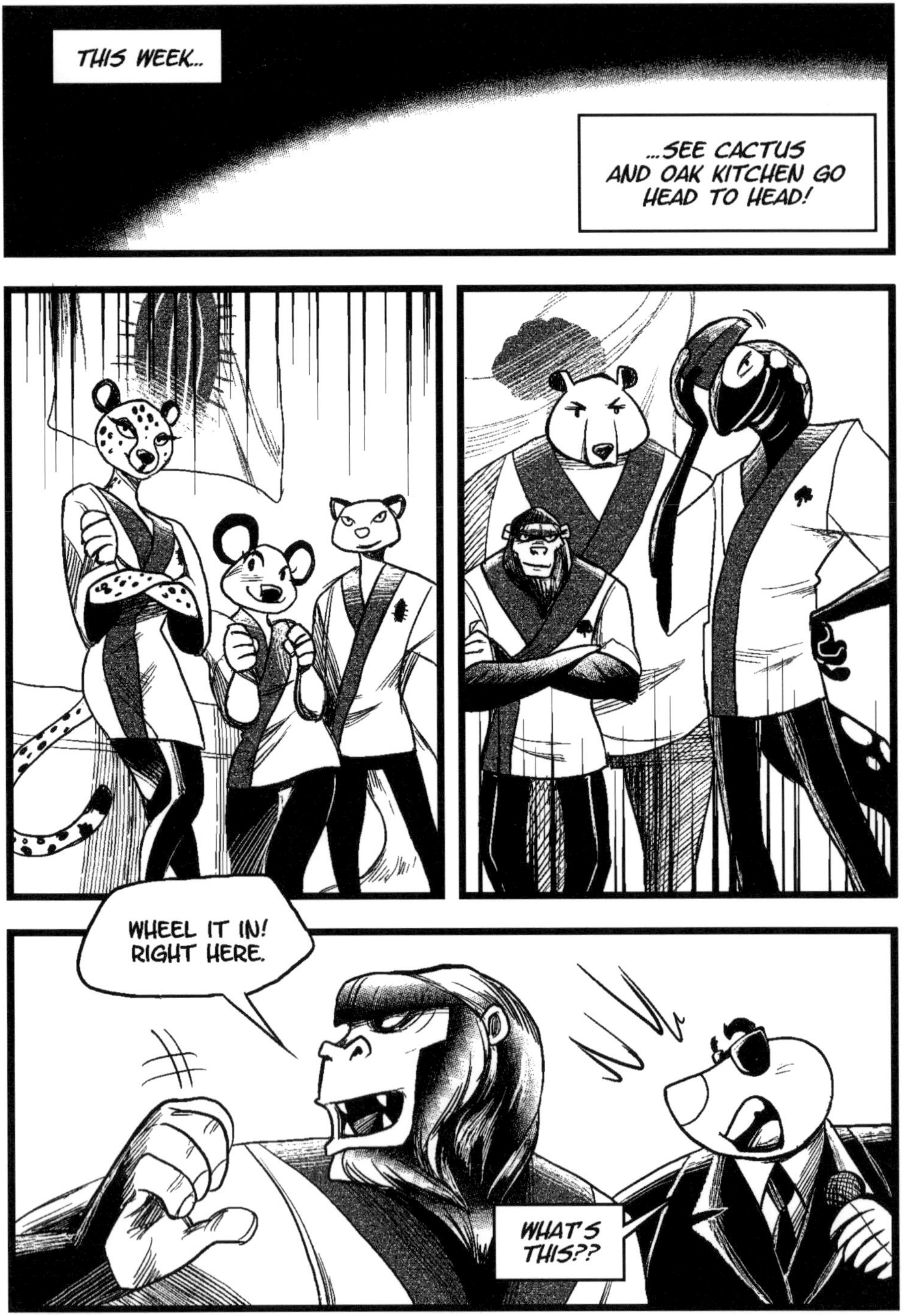
THIS WEEK...
...SEE CACTUS AND OAK KITCHEN GO HEAD TO HEAD!
WHEEL IT IN! RIGHT HERE.
WHAT'S THIS??

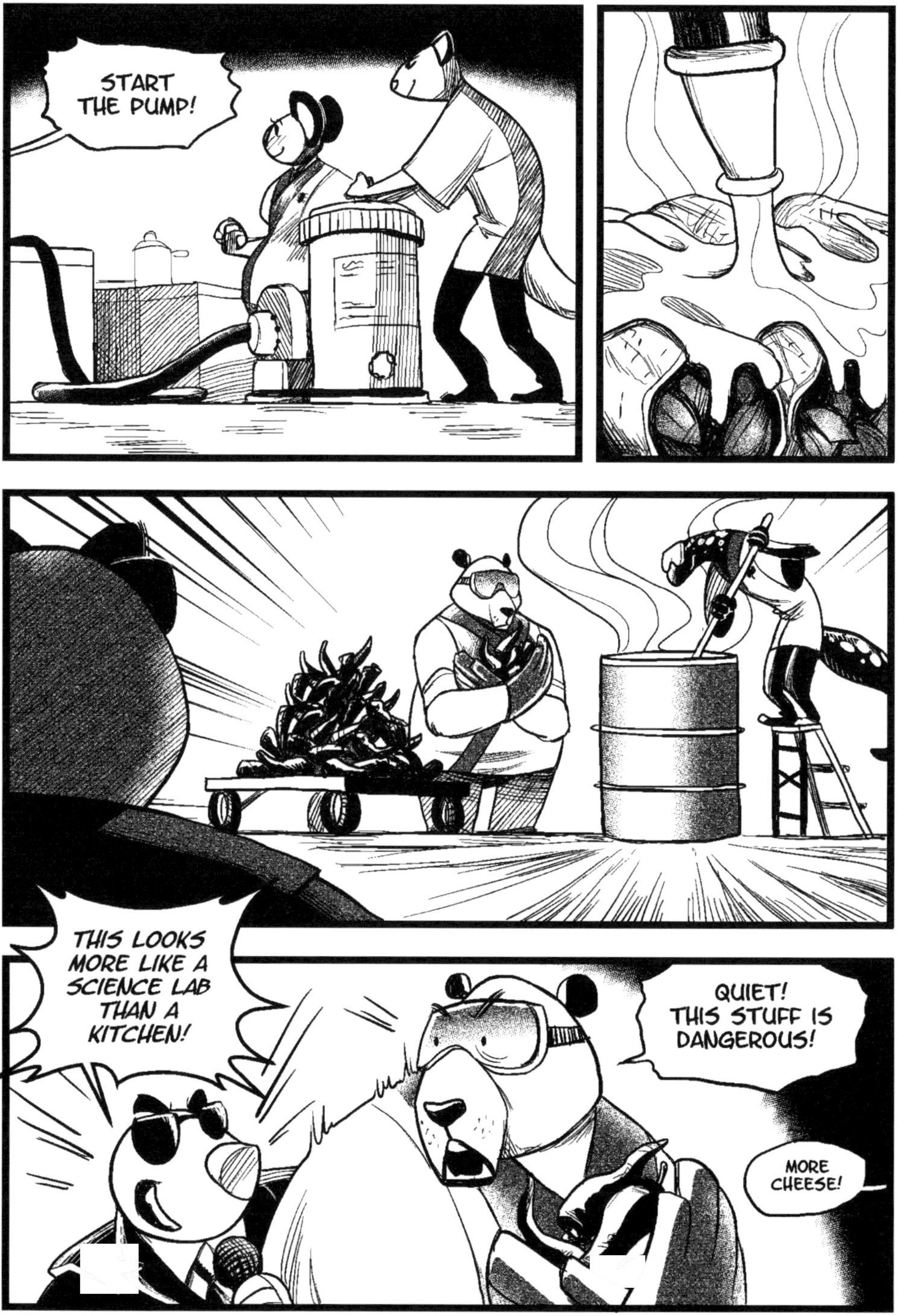
START THE PUMP!
THIS LOOKS MORE LIKE A SCIENCE LAB THAN A KITCHEN!
QUIET! THIS STUFF IS DANGEROUS!
MORE CHEESE!

CACTUS KITCHEN IS UP FIRST.

TNK

TNK

TNK

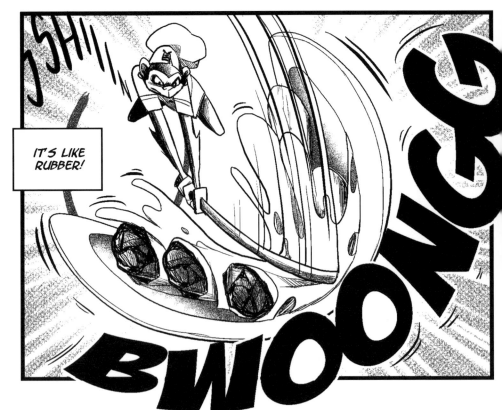

SSHIII

IT'S LIKE RUBBER!

BWOONGG

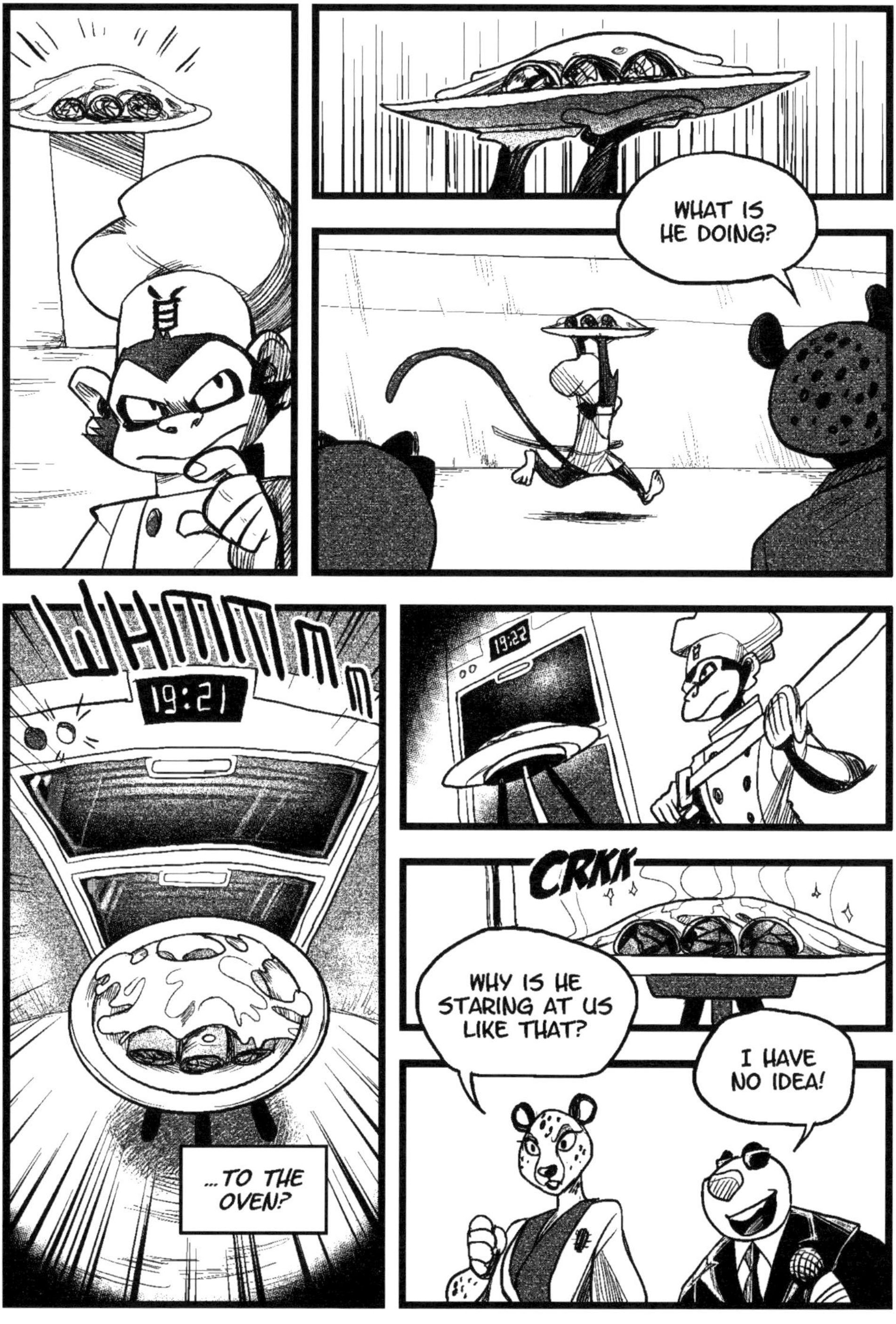
WHAT IS HE DOING?
WHMMMM
19:21
...TO THE OVEN?
19:22
CRKK
WHY IS HE STARING AT US LIKE THAT?
I HAVE NO IDEA!

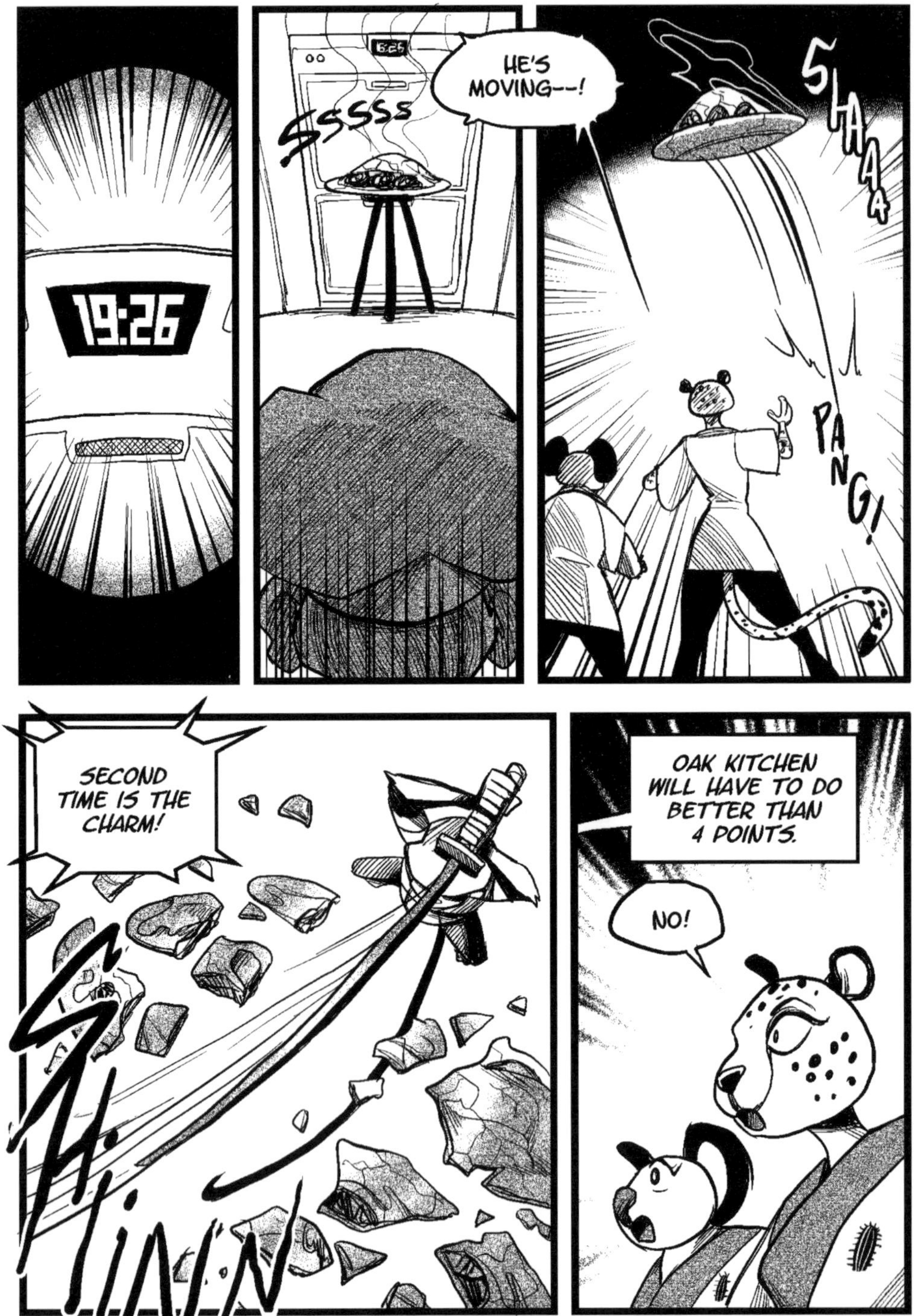
19:26
HE'S MOVING--!
SSSSS
SHAAAA
PANG!
SECOND TIME IS THE CHARM!
SHINN
OAK KITCHEN WILL HAVE TO DO BETTER THAN 4 POINTS.
NO!

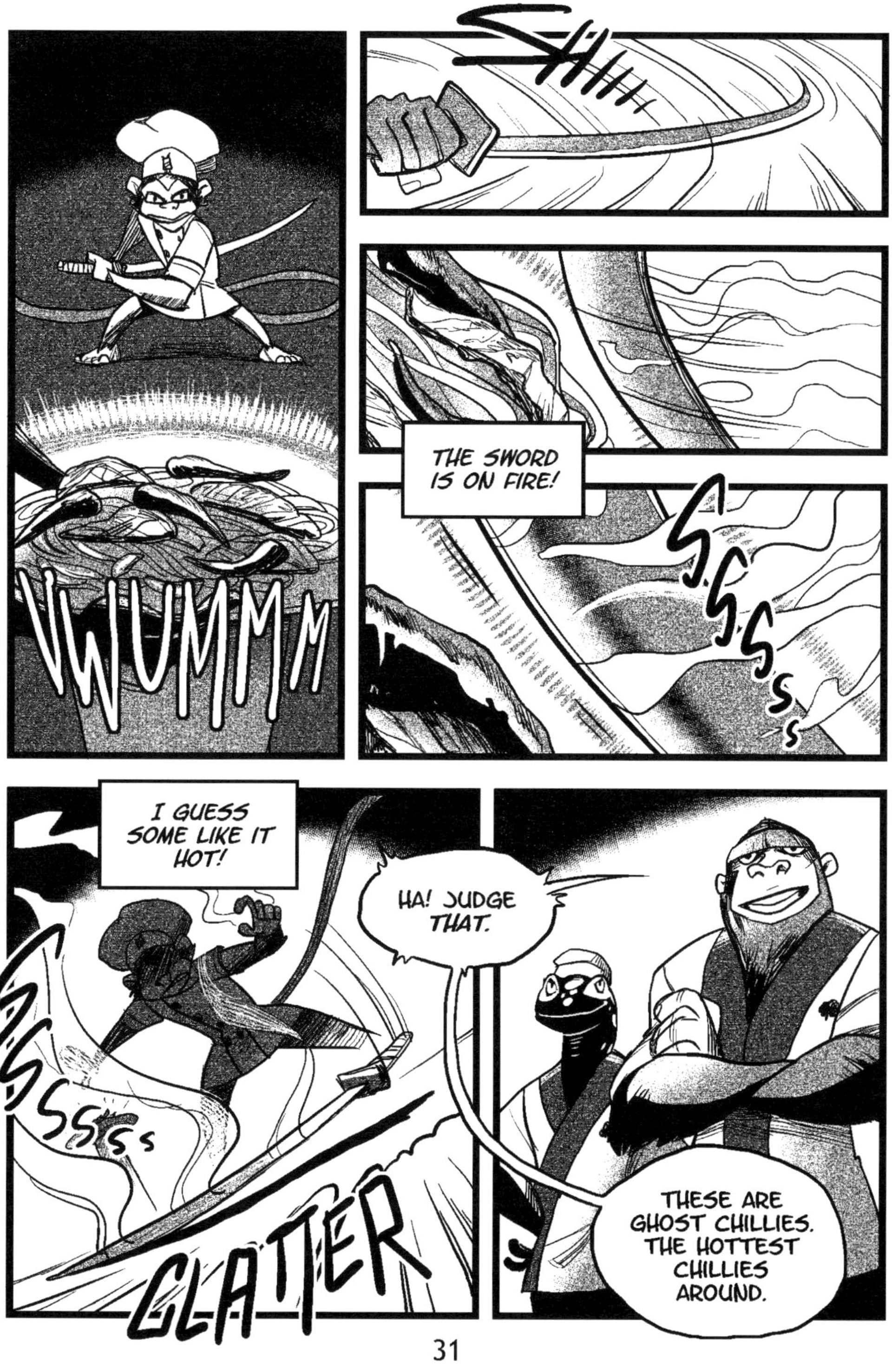
VWUMMM
SHHH
THE SWORD IS ON FIRE!
SSSSSs
I GUESS SOME LIKE IT HOT!
HA! JUDGE THAT.
SSSSSSs
CLATTER
THESE ARE GHOST CHILLIES. THE HOTTEST CHILLIES AROUND.

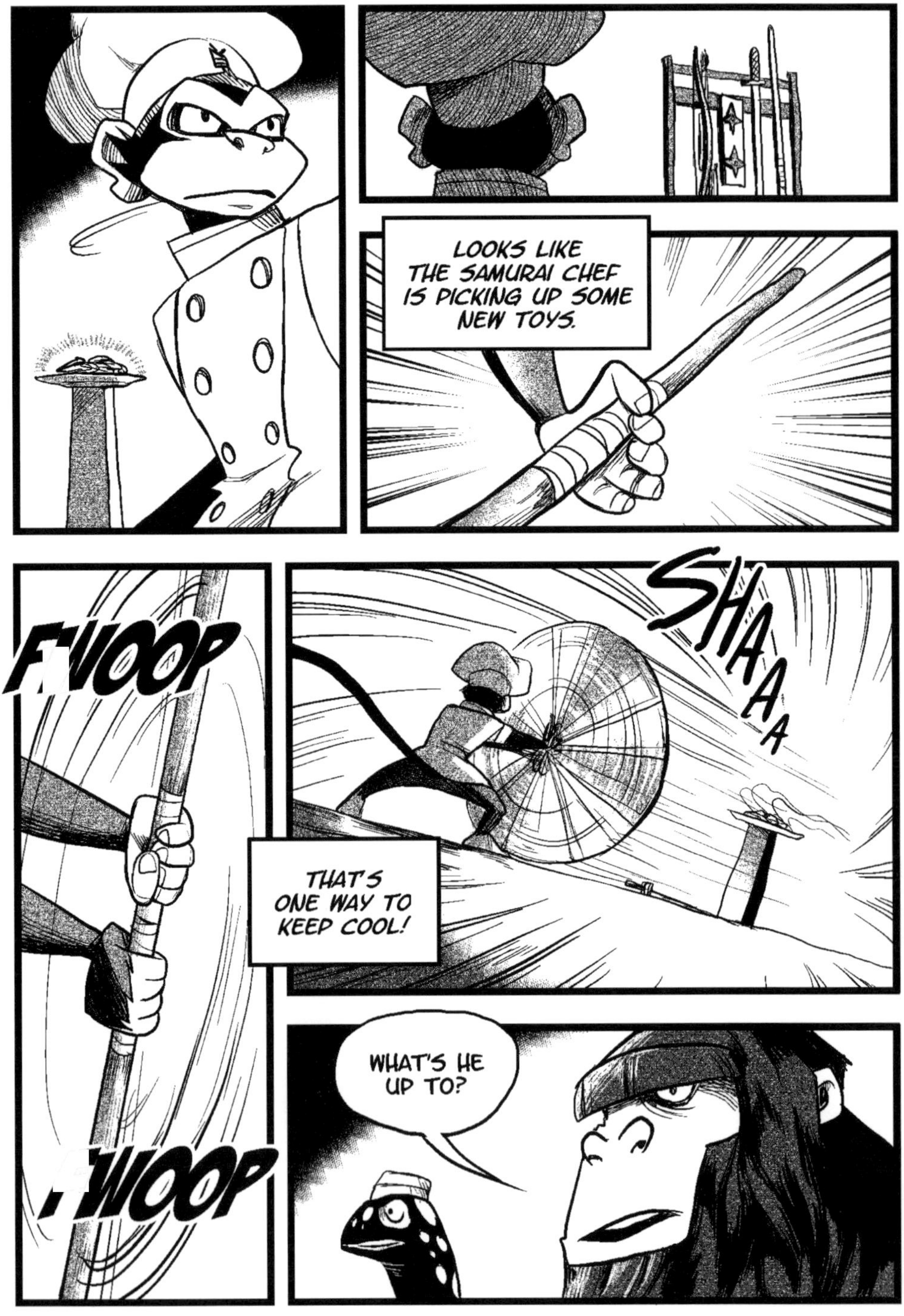

LOOKS LIKE THE SAMURAI CHEF IS PICKING UP SOME NEW TOYS.
FWOOP
WOOP
SHAAAA
THAT'S ONE WAY TO KEEP COOL!
WHAT'S HE UP TO?

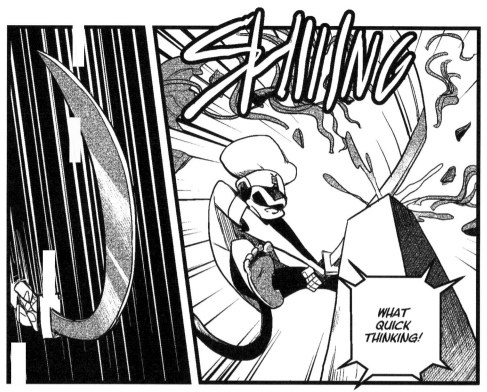

WHAT QUICK THINKING!

7
ABOVE AVERAGE

6
RESPECTABLE

5
SUFFICIENT

4
PASSABLE

HE GIVES IT A 5.

2

OAK KITCHEN IS THE WINNER!

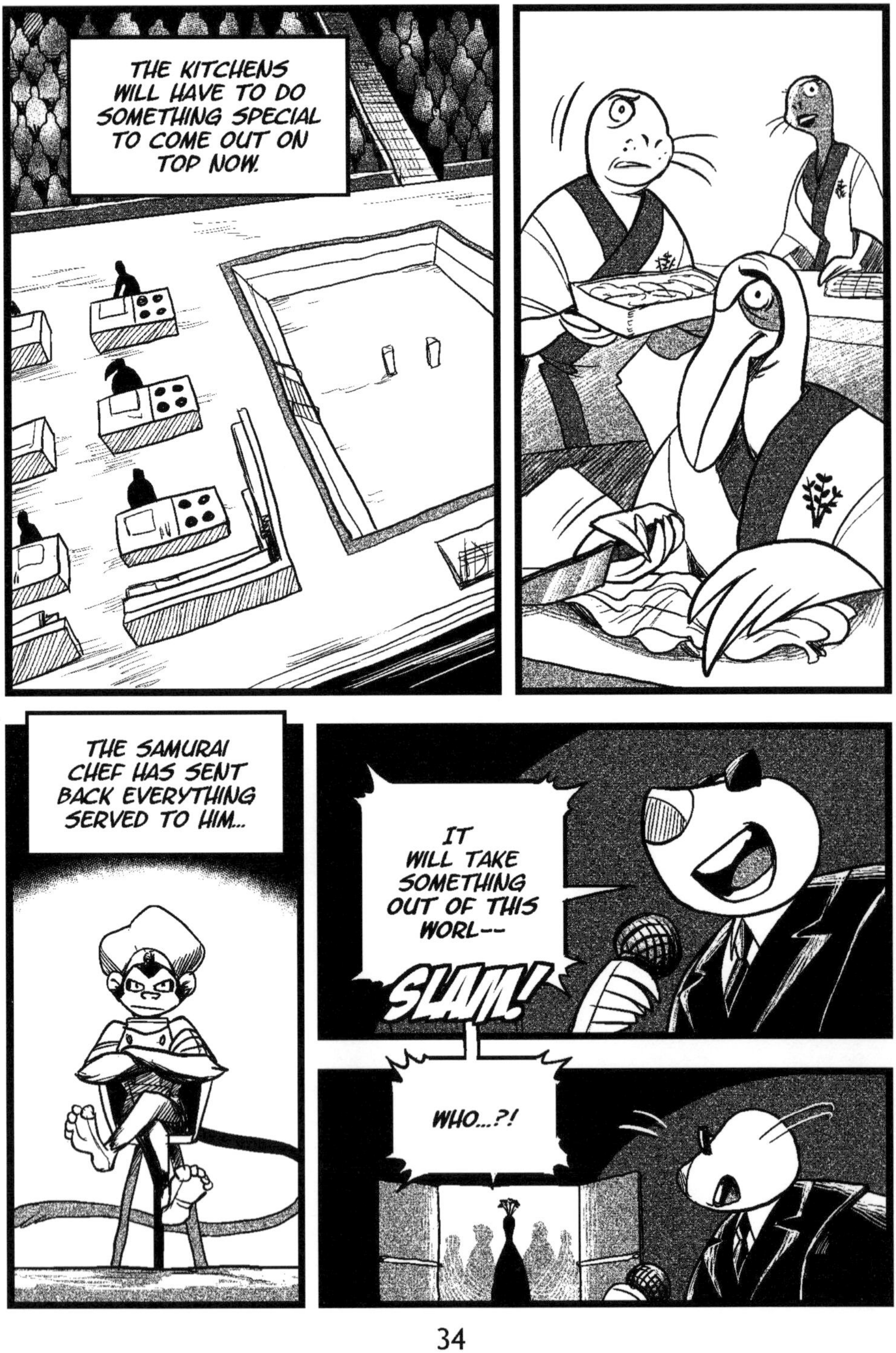
THE KITCHENS WILL HAVE TO DO SOMETHING SPECIAL TO COME OUT ON TOP NOW.
THE SAMURAI CHEF HAS SENT BACK EVERYTHING SERVED TO HIM...
IT WILL TAKE SOMETHING OUT OF THIS WORL--
SLAM!
WHO...?!

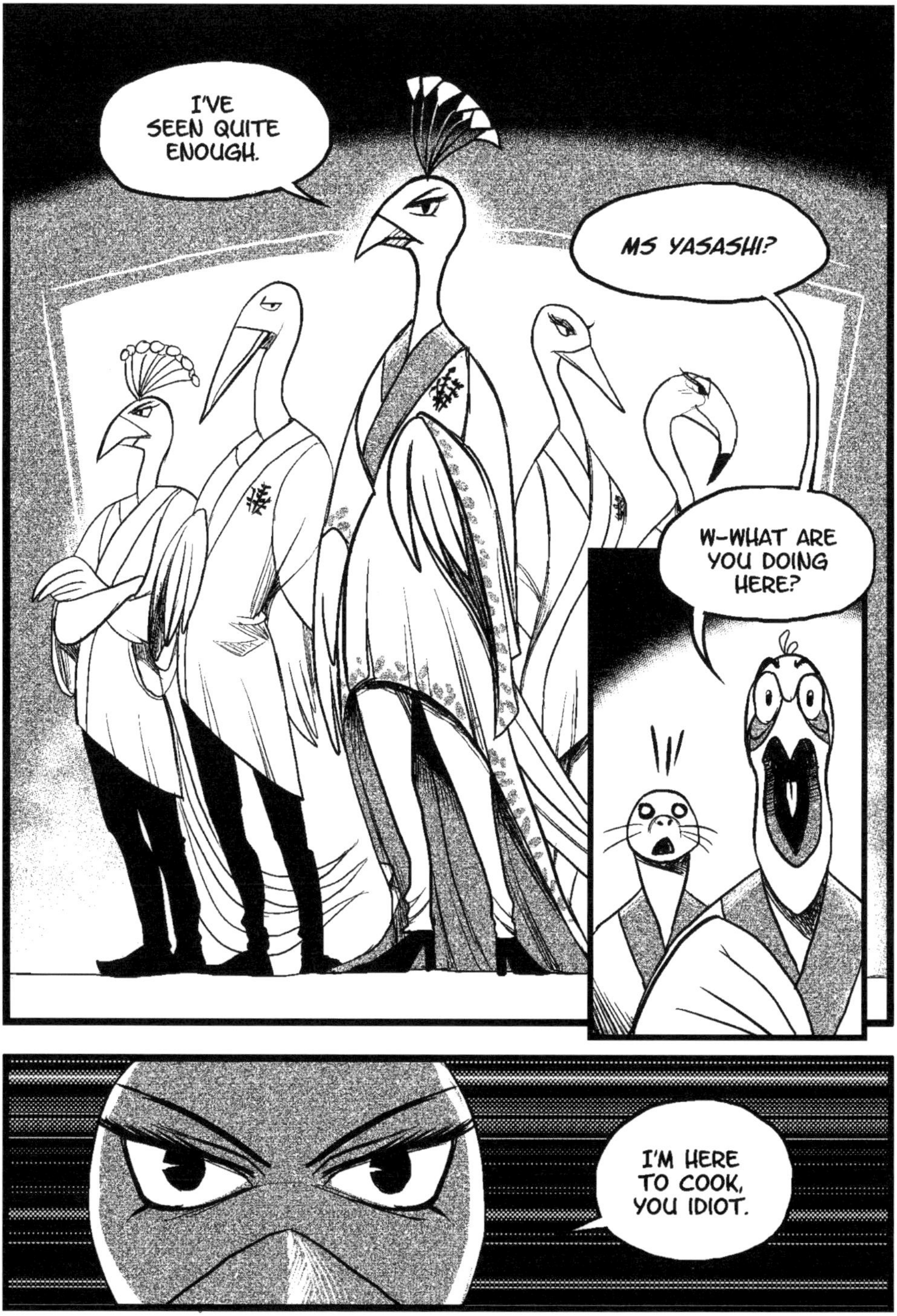
I'VE SEEN QUITE ENOUGH.
MS YASASHI?
W-WHAT ARE YOU DOING HERE?
I'M HERE TO COOK, YOU IDIOT.

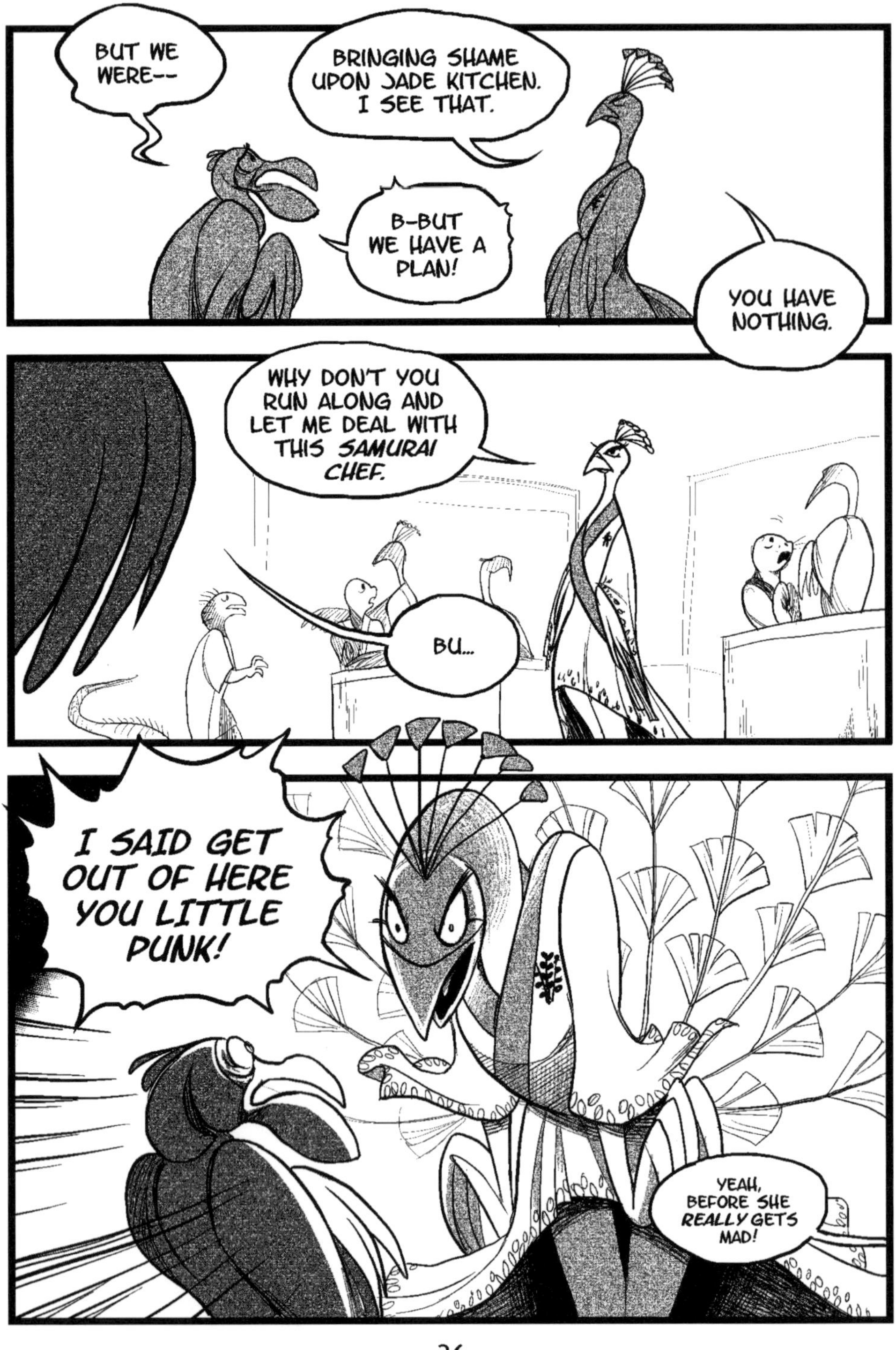
BUT WE WERE--
BRINGING SHAME UPON JADE KITCHEN. I SEE THAT.
B-BUT WE HAVE A PLAN!
YOU HAVE NOTHING.
WHY DON'T YOU RUN ALONG AND LET ME DEAL WITH THIS *SAMURAI CHEF.*
BU...
I SAID GET OUT OF HERE YOU LITTLE PUNK!
YEAH, BEFORE SHE *REALLY* GETS MAD!

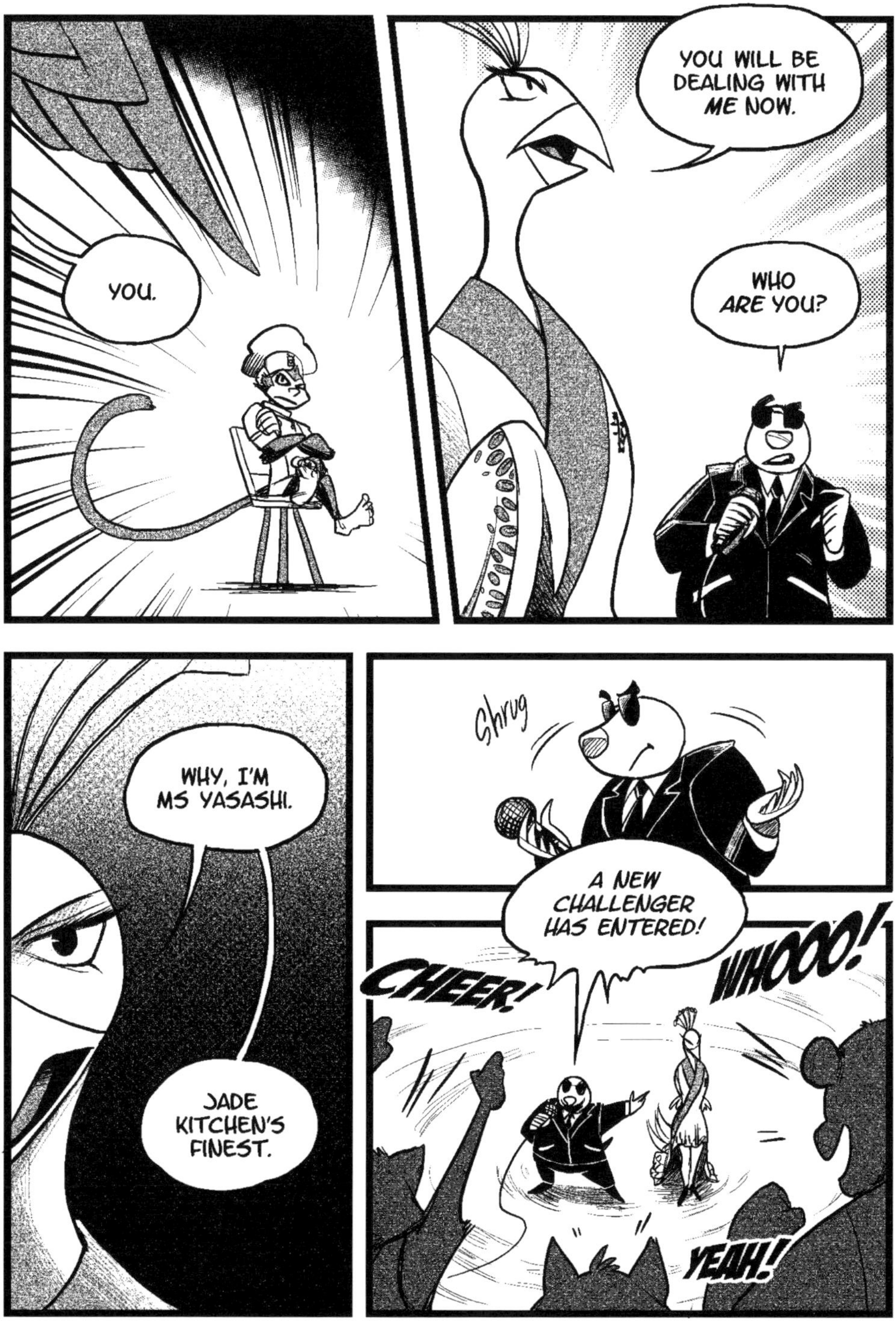
YOU.
YOU WILL BE DEALING WITH ME NOW.
WHO ARE YOU?
WHY, I'M MS YASASHI.
JADE KITCHEN'S FINEST.
Shrug
A NEW CHALLENGER HAS ENTERED!
CHEER!
WHOOO!
YEAH!

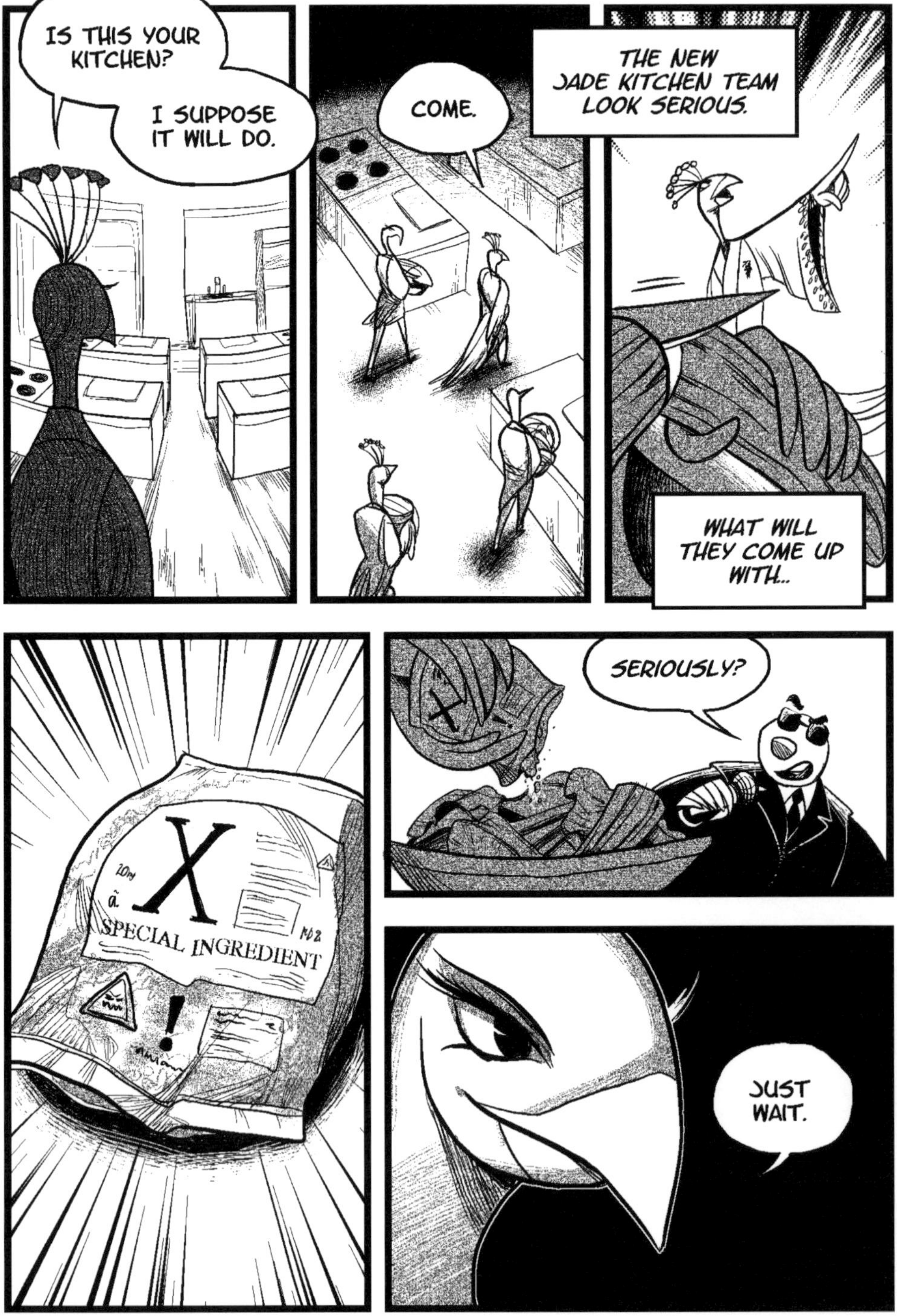
IS THIS YOUR KITCHEN?
I SUPPOSE IT WILL DO.
COME.
THE NEW JADE KITCHEN TEAM LOOK SERIOUS.
WHAT WILL THEY COME UP WITH...
X
SPECIAL INGREDIENT
SERIOUSLY?
JUST WAIT.

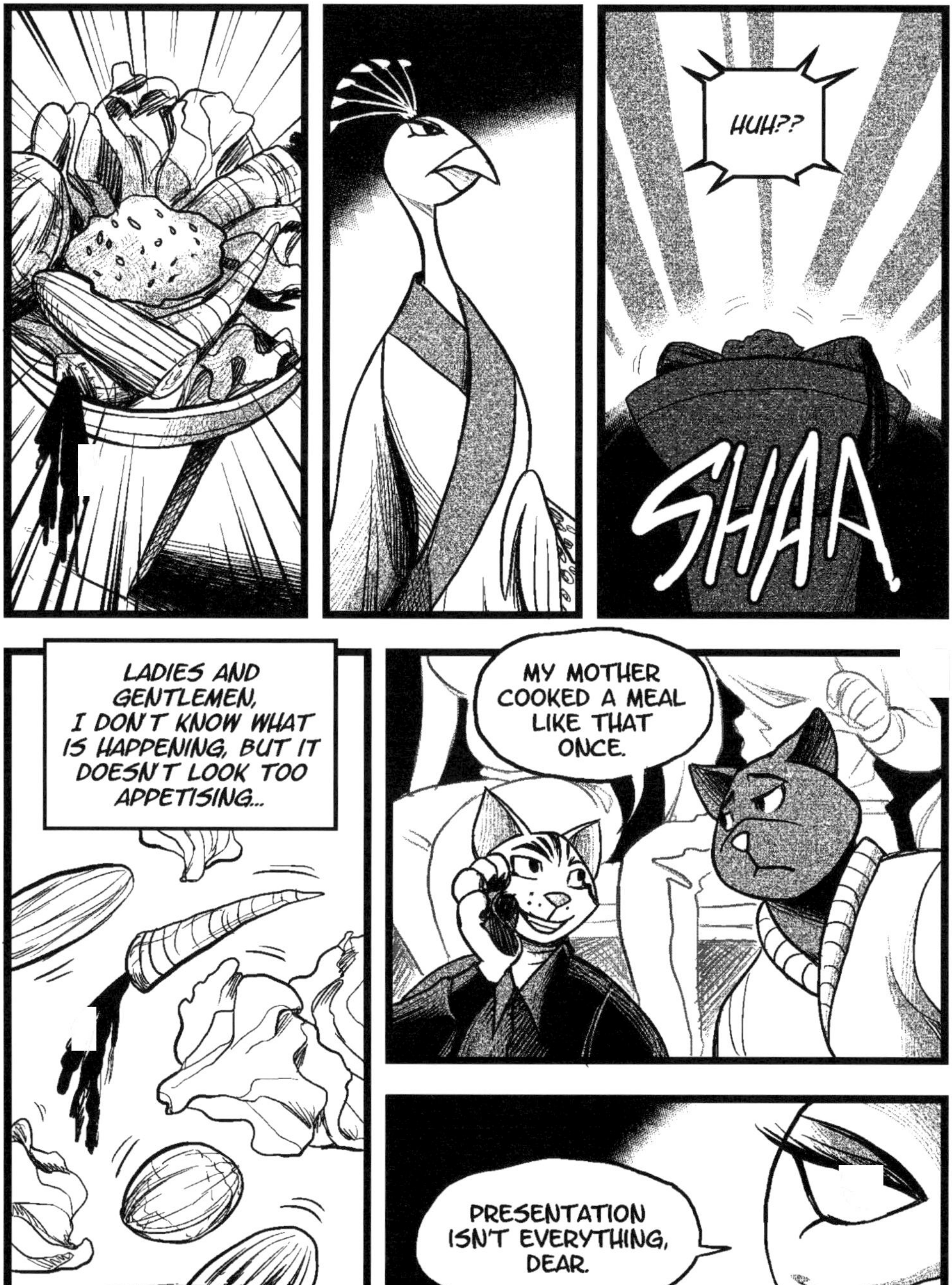
HUH??
SHAA
LADIES AND GENTLEMEN, I DON'T KNOW WHAT IS HAPPENING, BUT IT DOESN'T LOOK TOO APPETISING...
MY MOTHER COOKED A MEAL LIKE THAT ONCE.
PRESENTATION ISN'T EVERYTHING, DEAR.

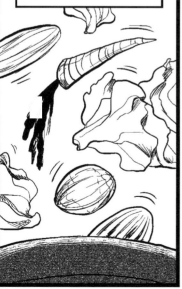

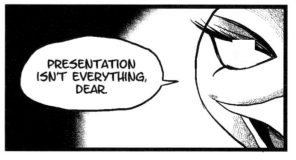

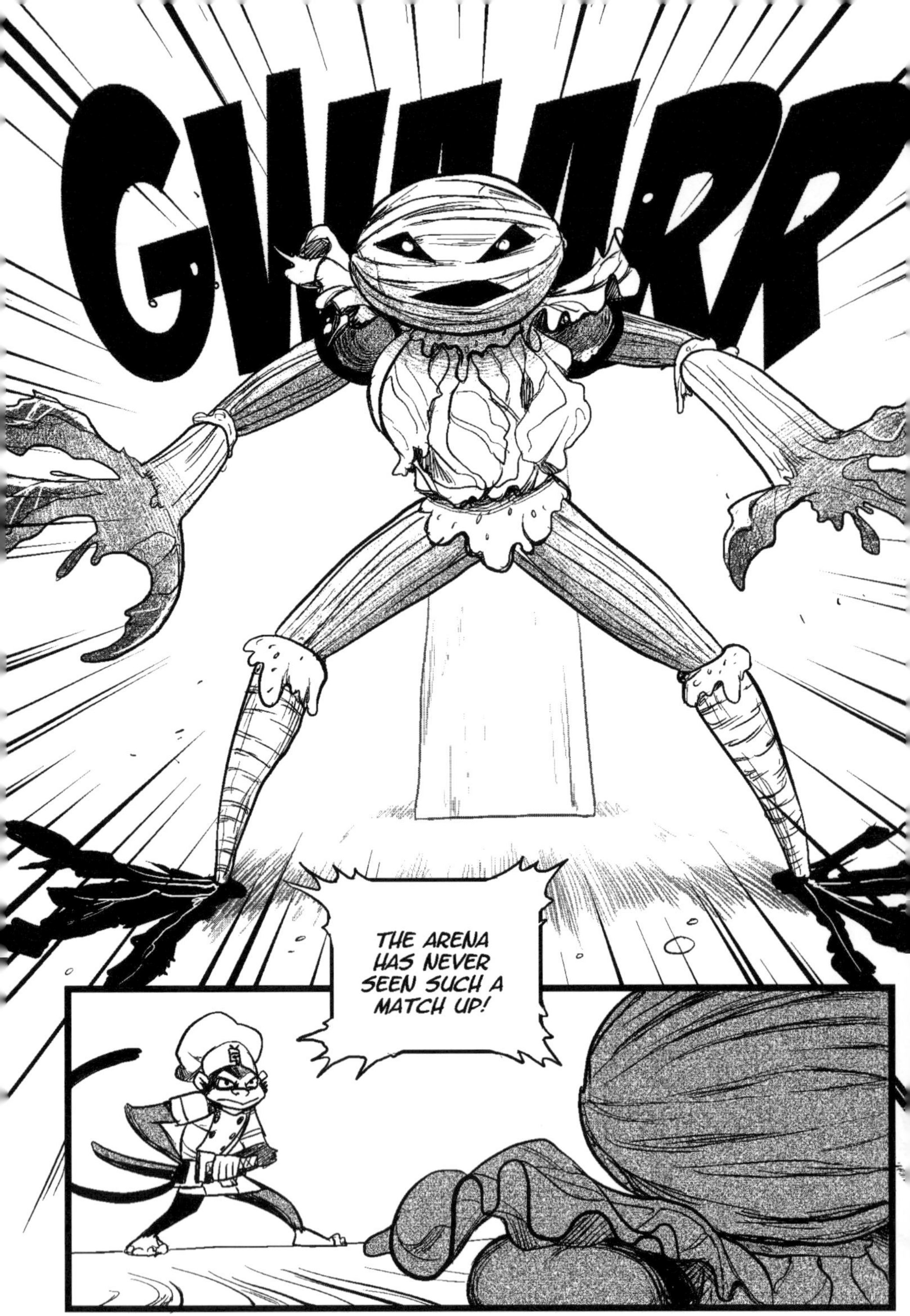
THE ARENA HAS NEVER SEEN SUCH A MATCH UP!

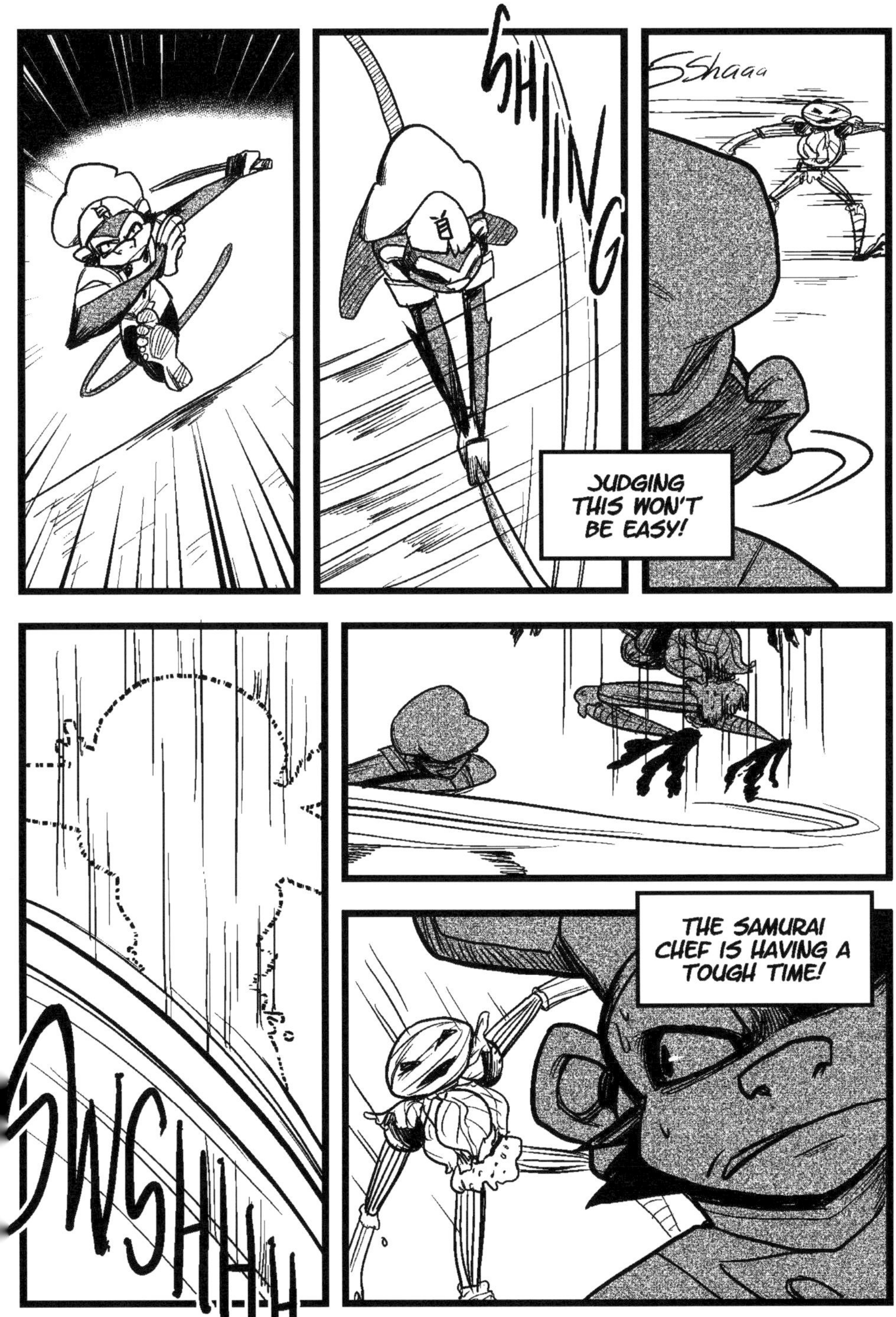
SHING
SShaaa
JUDGING THIS WON'T BE EASY!
SWSHHH
THE SAMURAI CHEF IS HAVING A TOUGH TIME!

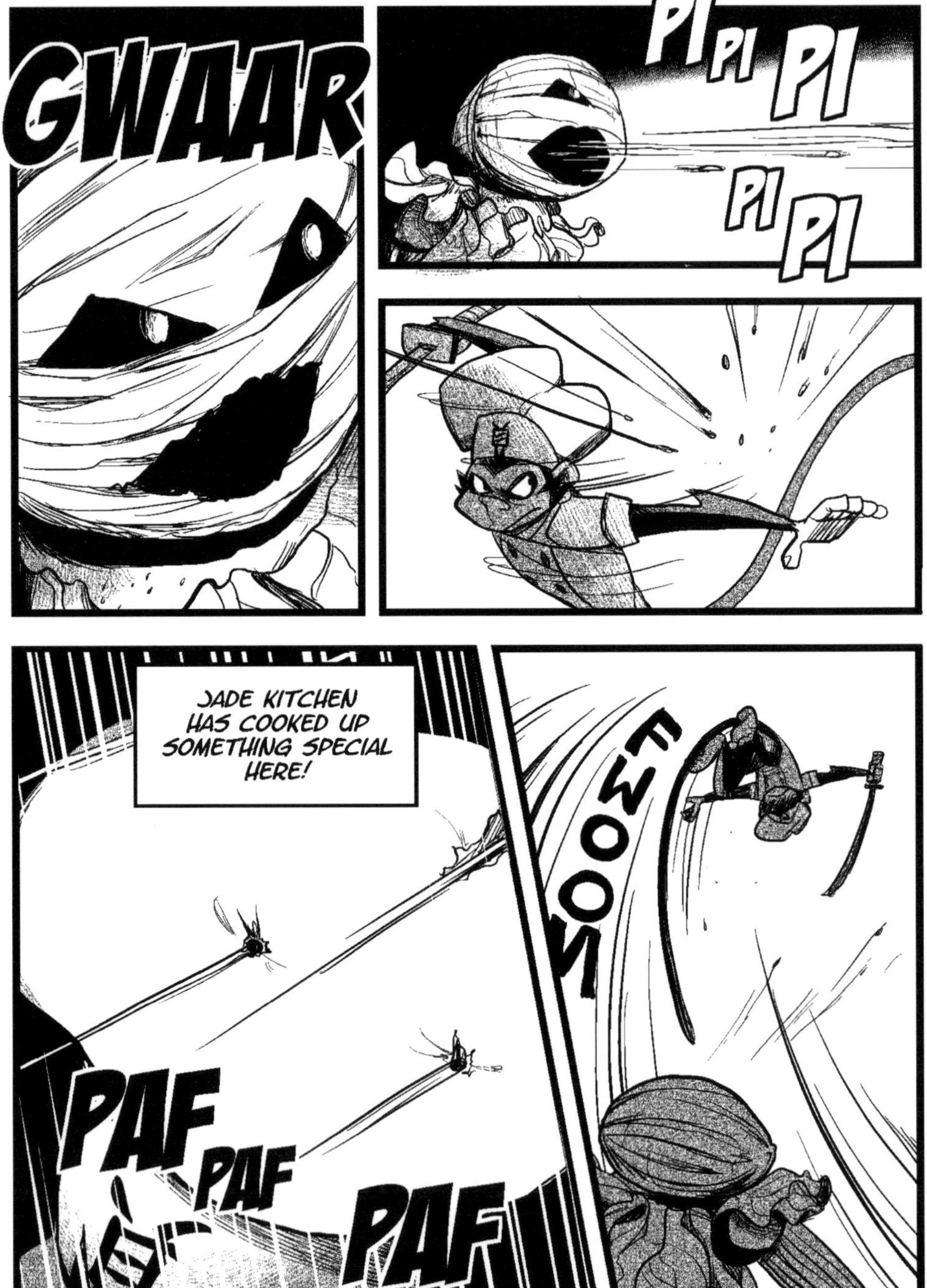
GWAAR
PI PI PI PI
PI PI
JADE KITCHEN HAS COOKED UP SOMETHING SPECIAL HERE!
PAF PAF PAF
FWOOM

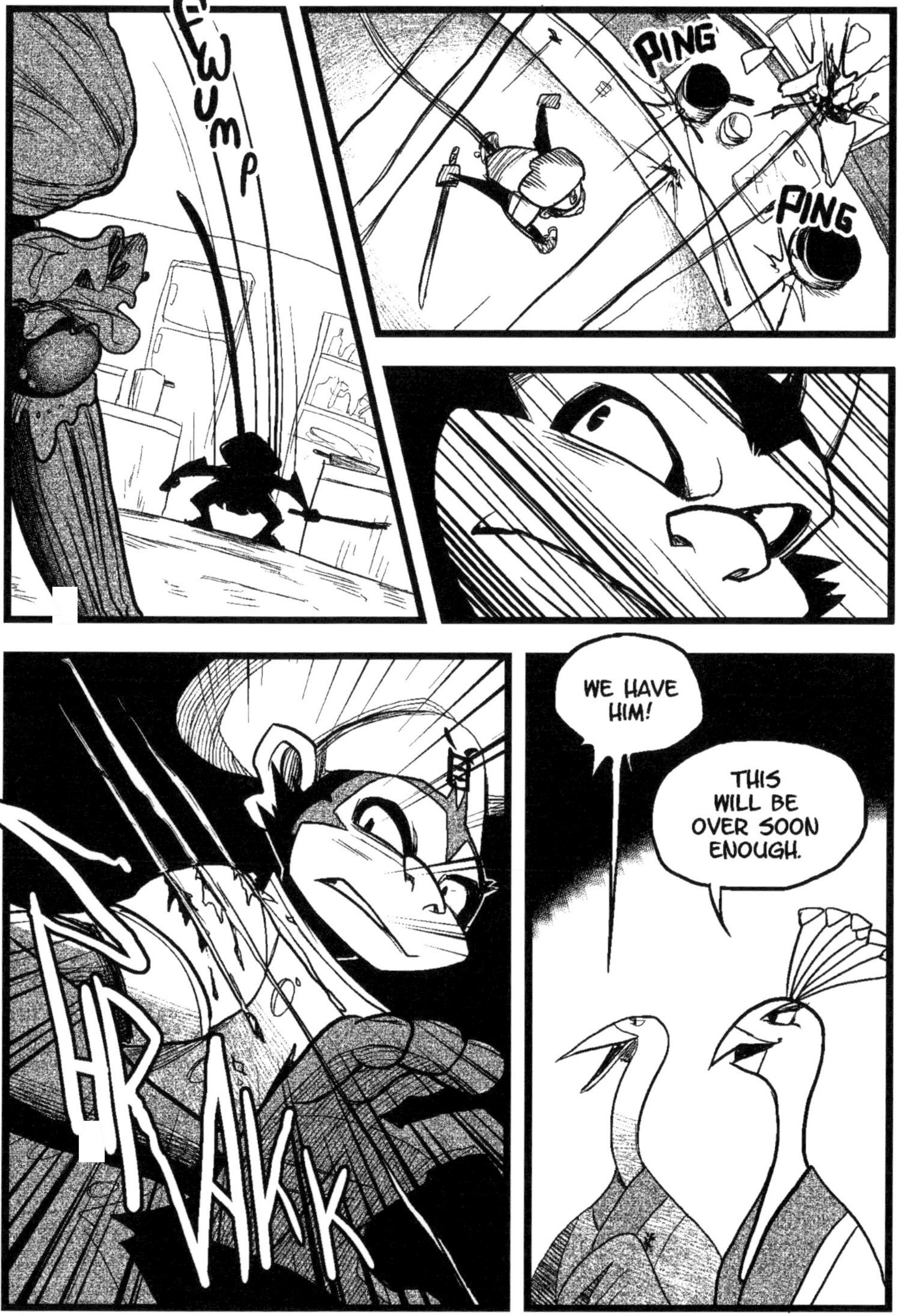
FWUMP
PING
PING
HRAKK
WE HAVE HIM!
THIS WILL BE OVER SOON ENOUGH.

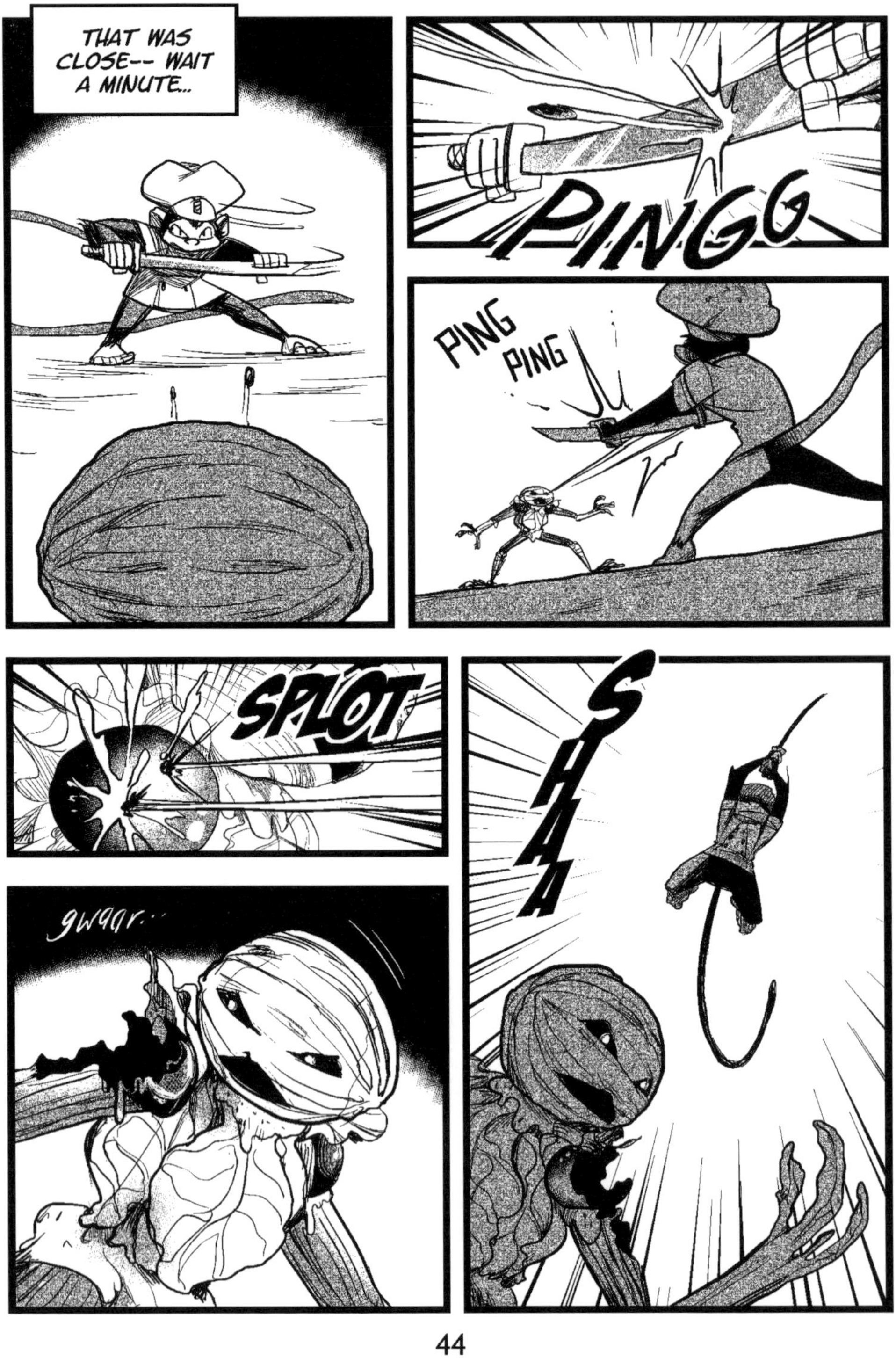
THAT WAS CLOSE-- WAIT A MINUTE...
PINGG
PING
PING
SPLOT
SHAAA
gwaar...

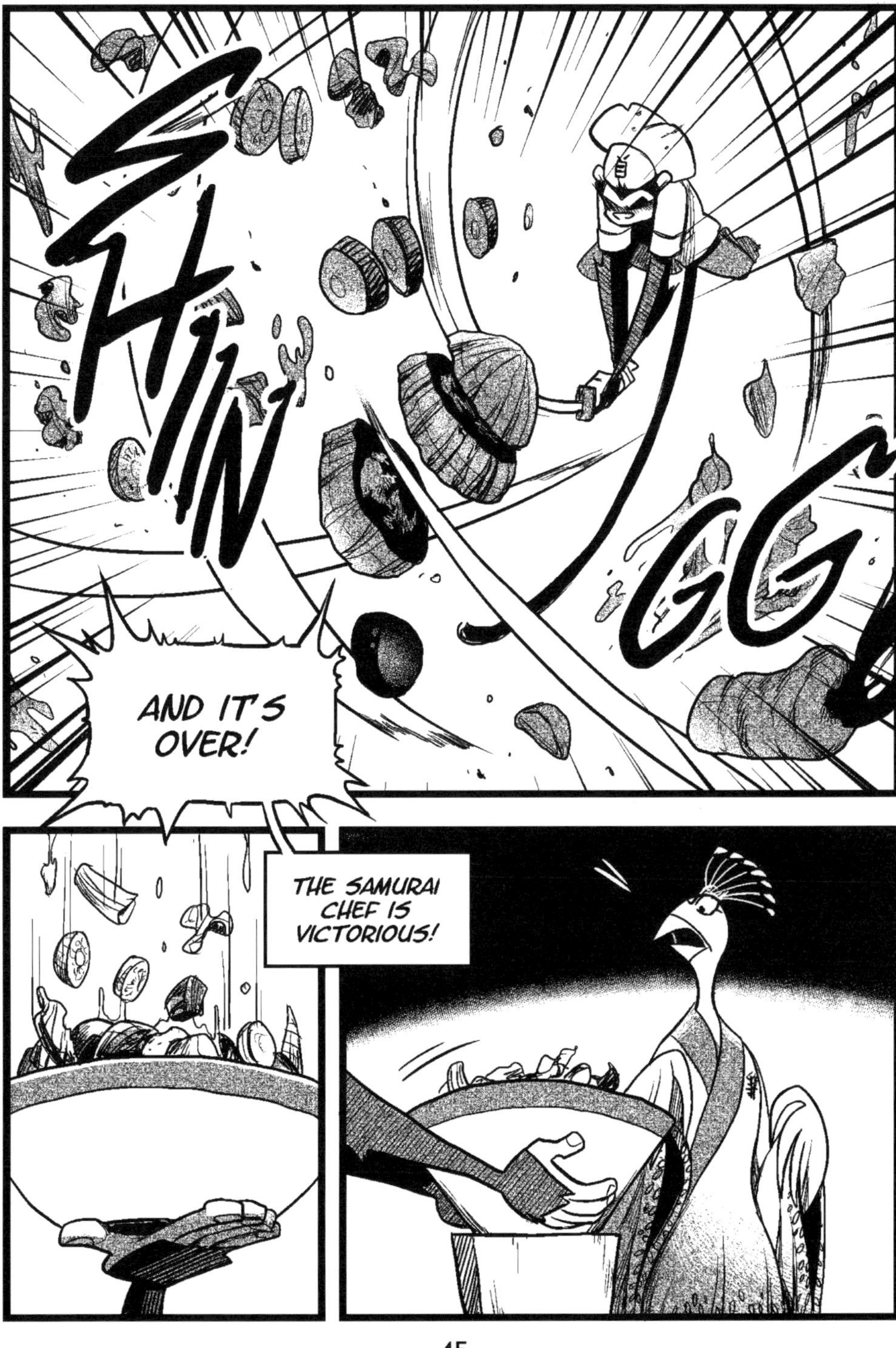
SHHIINNGG
AND IT'S OVER!
THE SAMURAI CHEF IS VICTORIOUS!

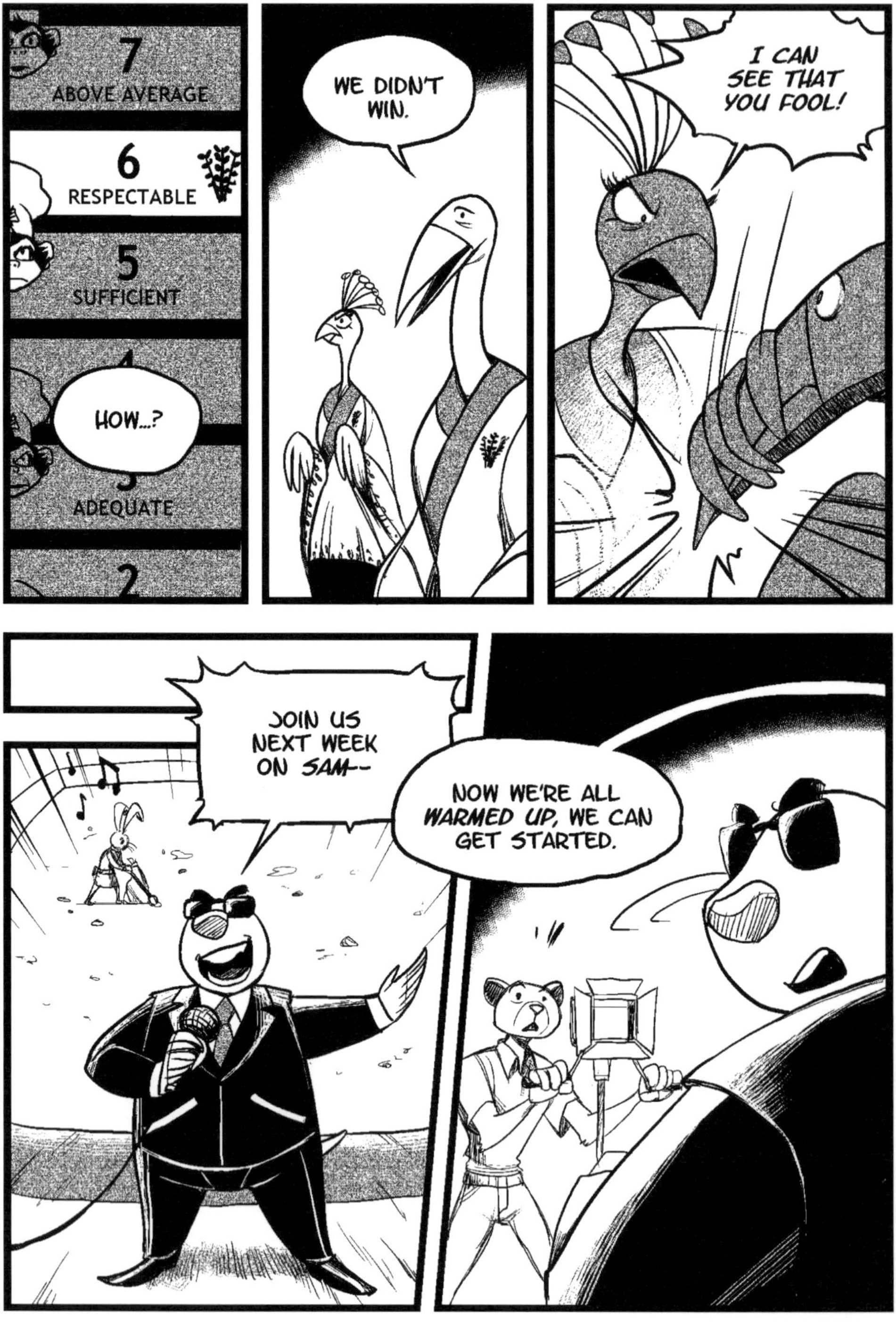
7
ABOVE AVERAGE
6
RESPECTABLE
5
SUFFICIENT
HOW...?
ADEQUATE
2
WE DIDN'T WIN.
I CAN SEE THAT YOU FOOL!
JOIN US NEXT WEEK ON SAM--
NOW WE'RE ALL WARMED UP, WE CAN GET STARTED.

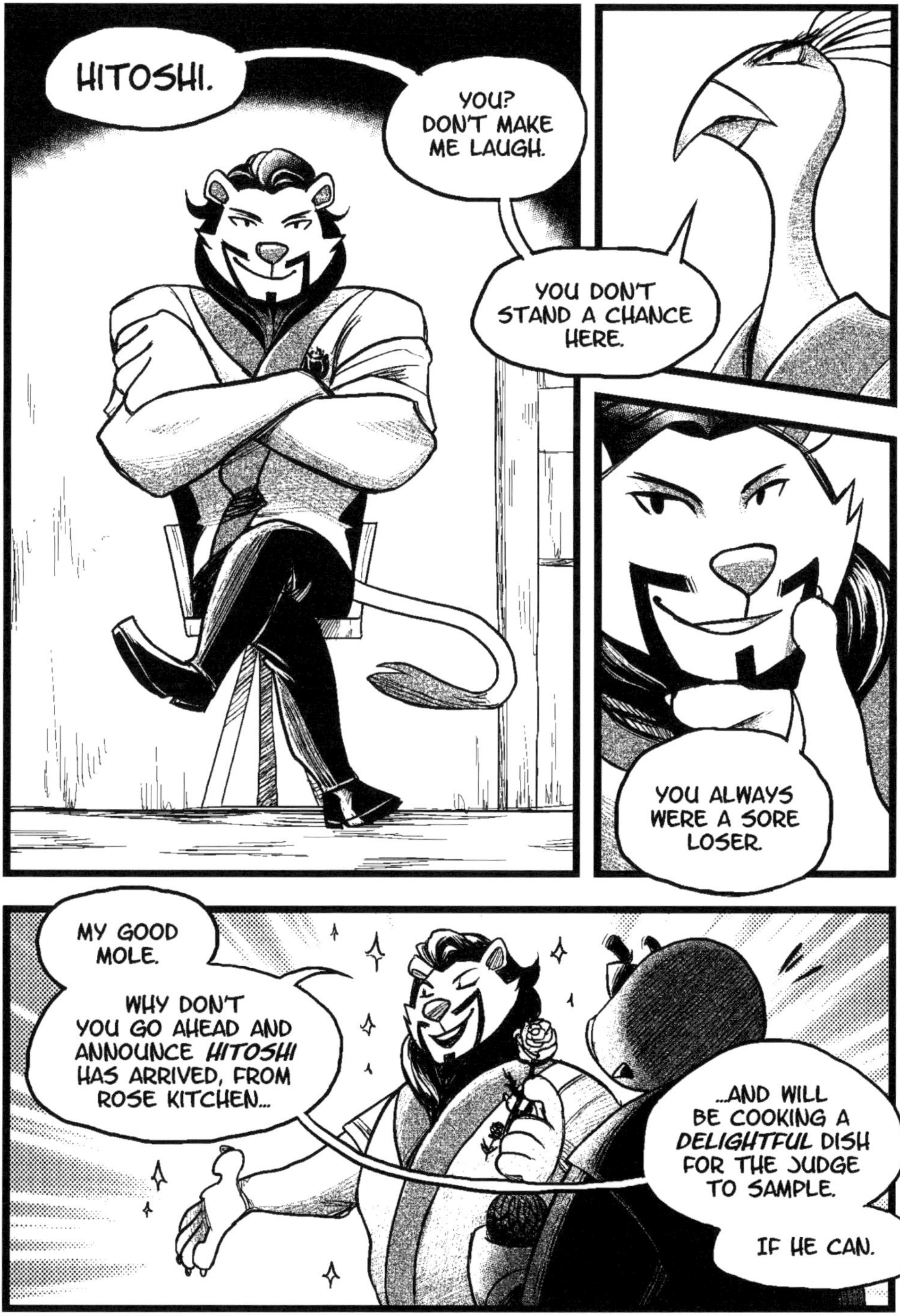
HITOSHI.
YOU? DON'T MAKE ME LAUGH.
YOU DON'T STAND A CHANCE HERE.
YOU ALWAYS WERE A SORE LOSER.
MY GOOD MOLE.
WHY DON'T YOU GO AHEAD AND ANNOUNCE *HITOSHI* HAS ARRIVED, FROM ROSE KITCHEN...
...AND WILL BE COOKING A *DELIGHTFUL* DISH FOR THE JUDGE TO SAMPLE.
IF HE CAN.

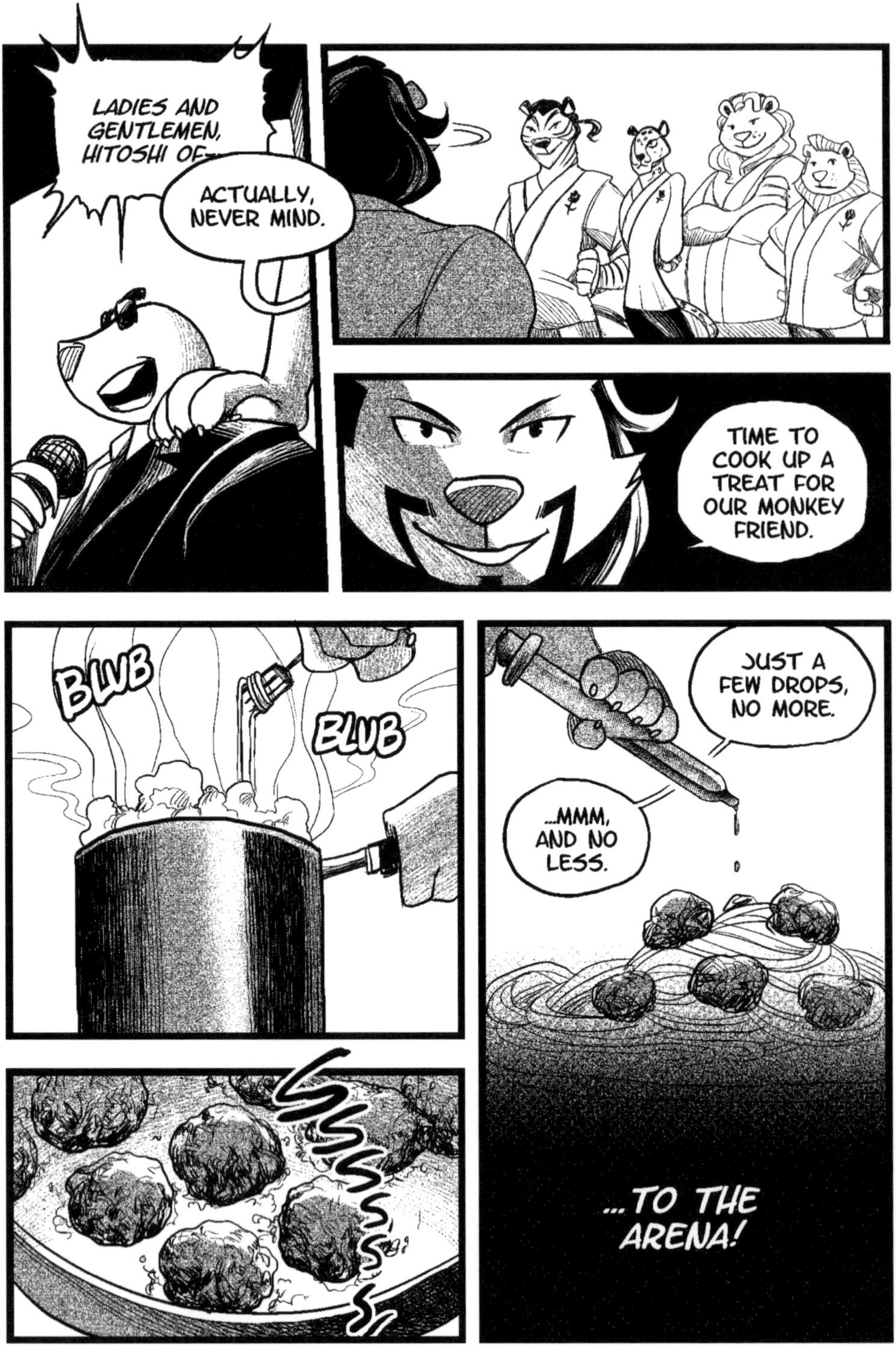
LADIES AND GENTLEMEN, HITOSHI OF--
ACTUALLY, NEVER MIND.
TIME TO COOK UP A TREAT FOR OUR MONKEY FRIEND.
BLUB
BLUB
JUST A FEW DROPS, NO MORE.
...MMM, AND NO LESS.
SSSSSSS
...TO THE ARENA!

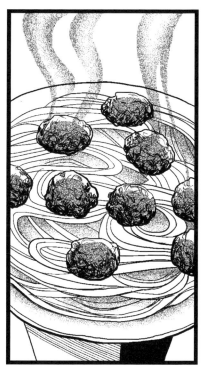

SHALL WE BEGIN?

AND...

AH. RIGHT ON CUE.

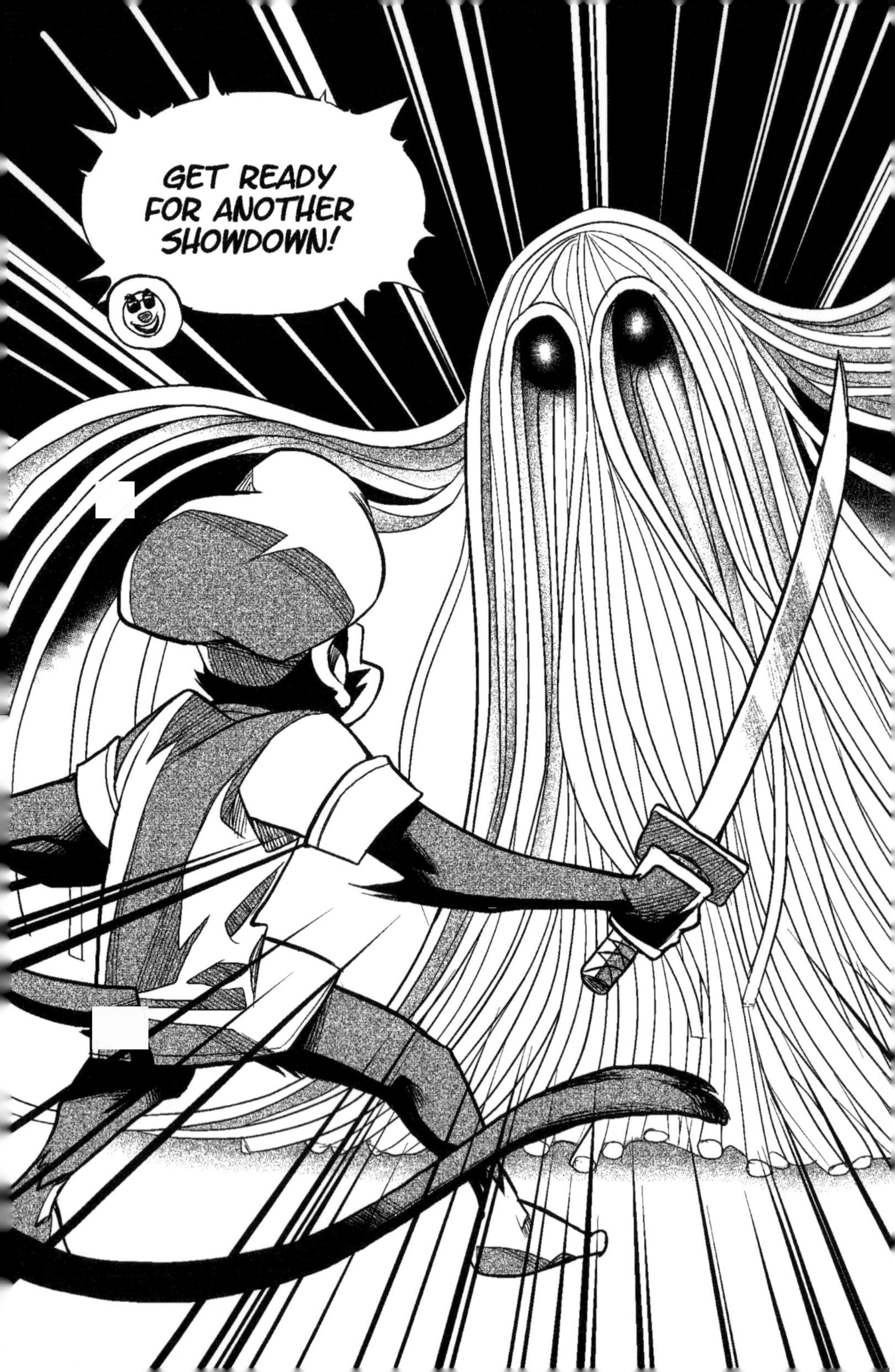
GET READY FOR ANOTHER SHOWDOWN!

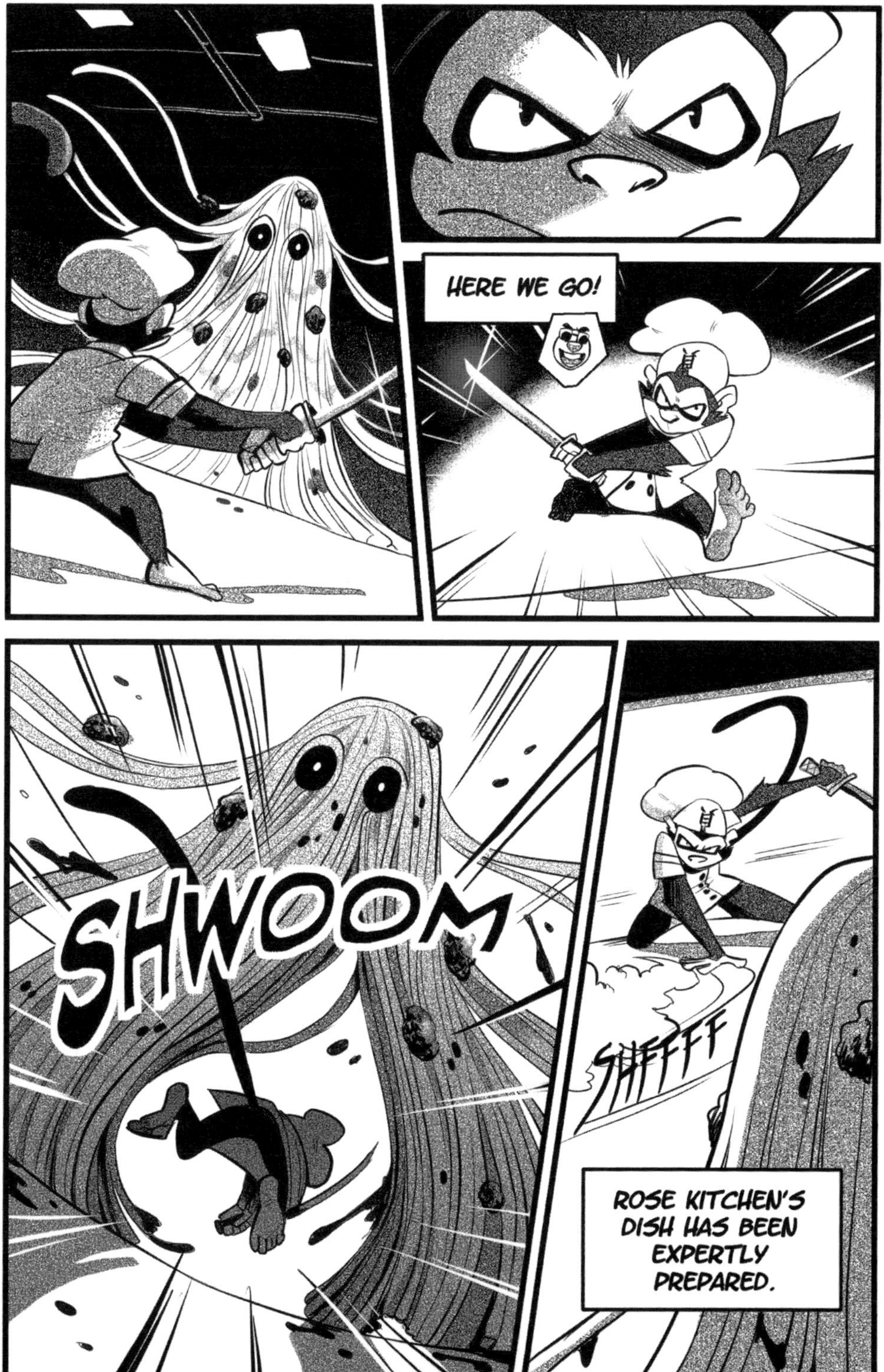
HERE WE GO!
SHWOOM
SHFFFF
ROSE KITCHEN'S DISH HAS BEEN EXPERTLY PREPARED.

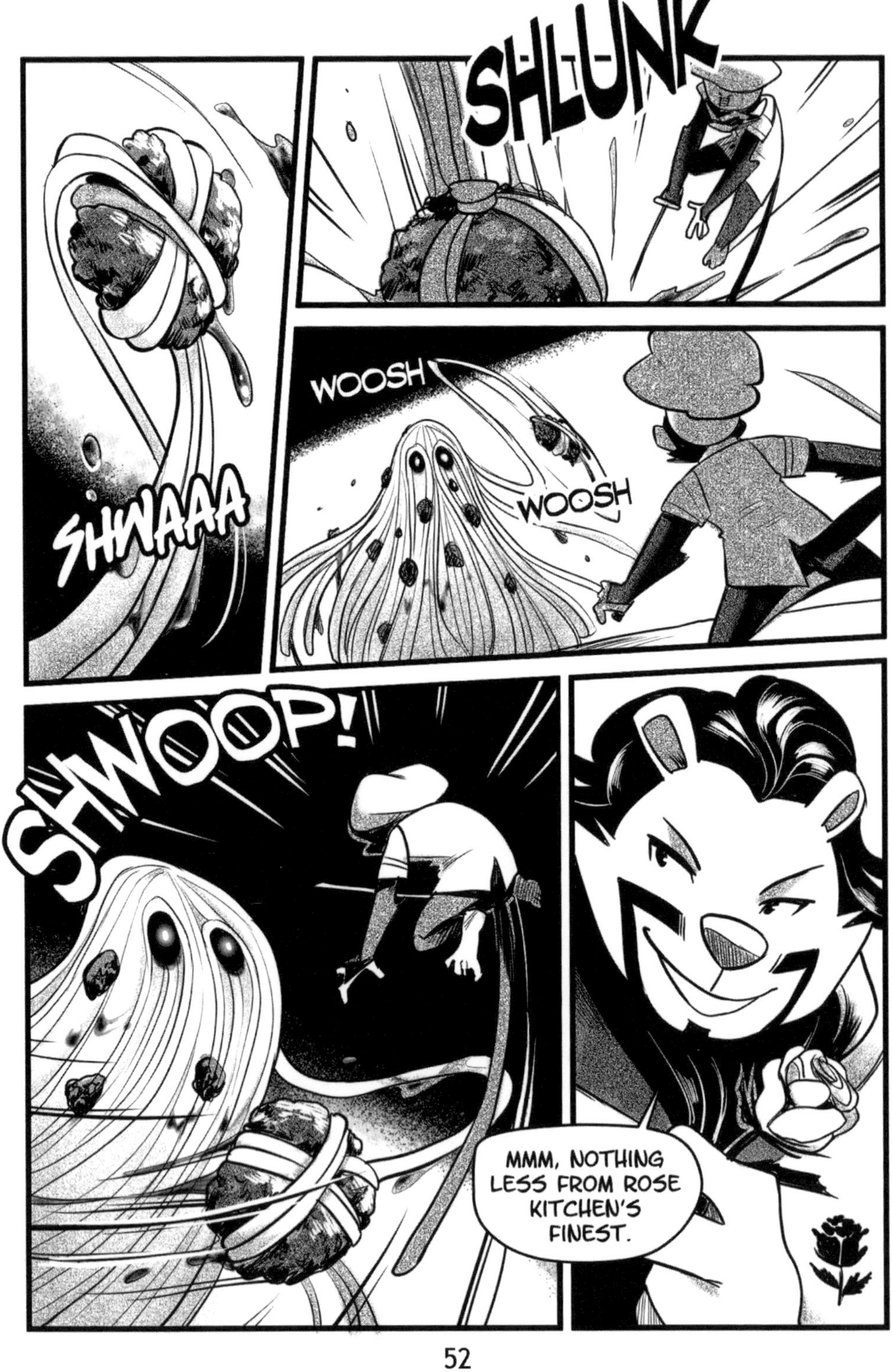
SHWAAA
SHLUNK
WOOSH
WOOSH
SHWOOP!
MMM, NOTHING LESS FROM ROSE KITCHEN'S FINEST.

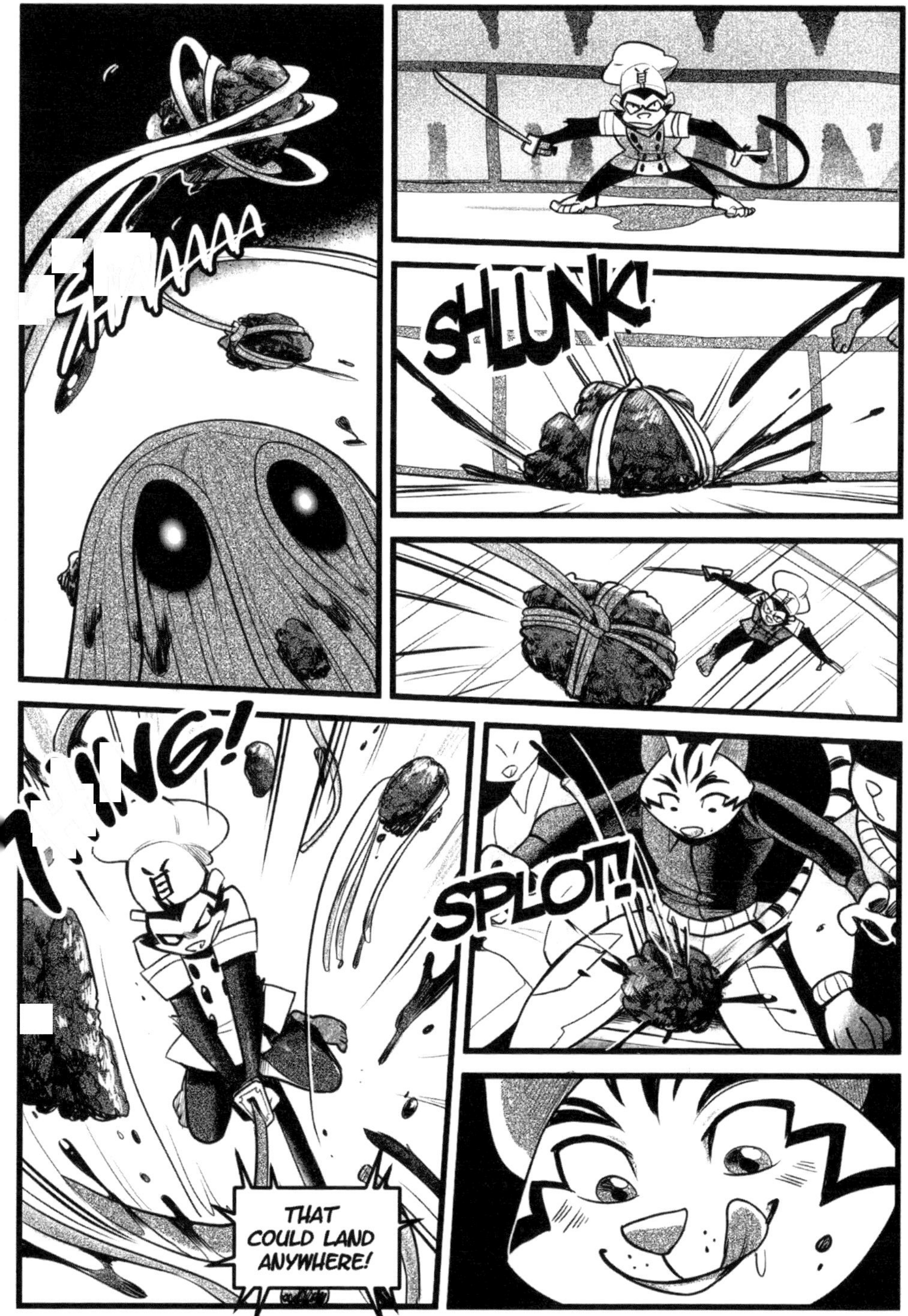
SHLUNK!
SPLOT!
THAT COULD LAND ANYWHERE!

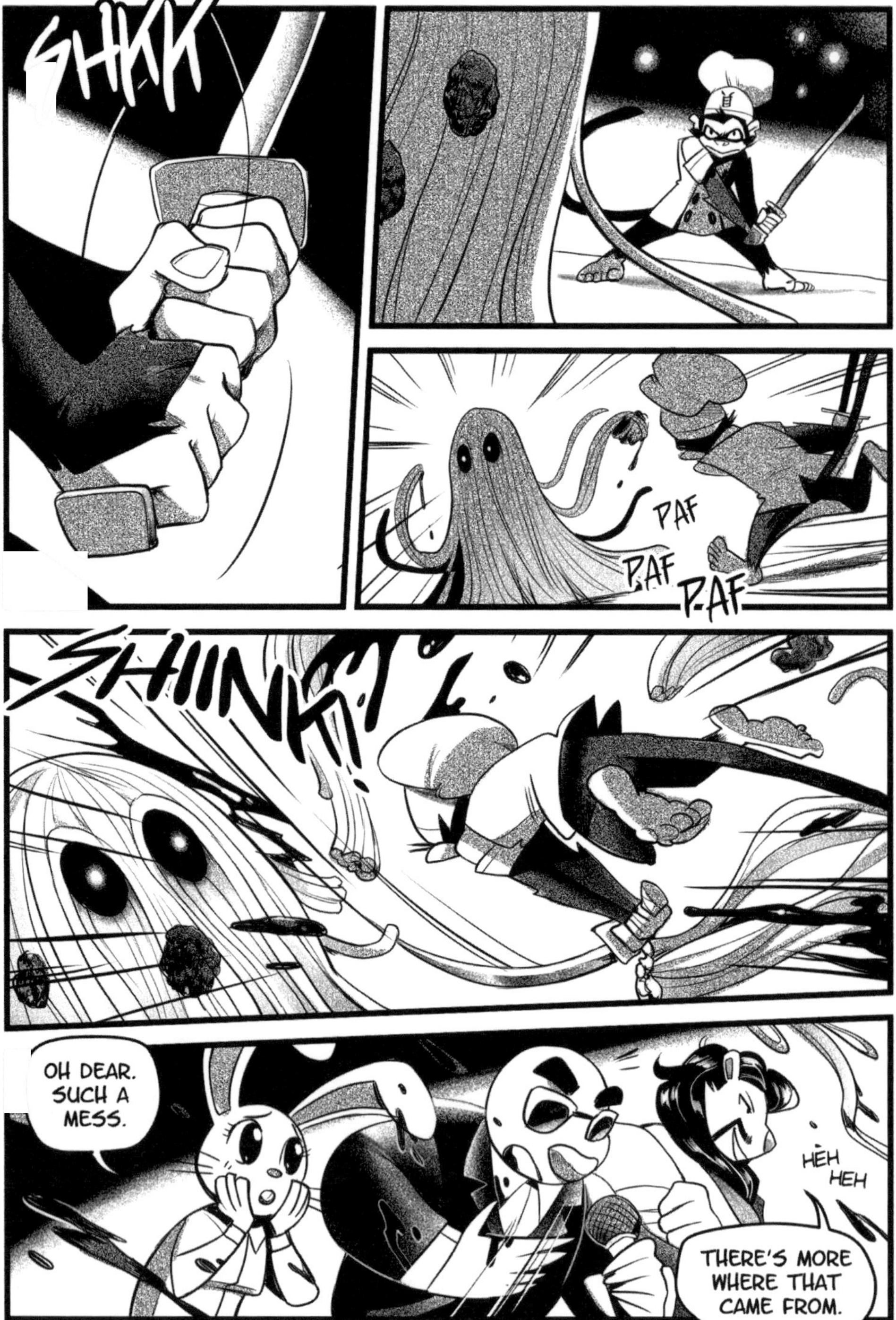
SHKK
PAF
PAF
PAF
SHIINK!!
OH DEAR. SUCH A MESS.
HEH HEH
THERE'S MORE WHERE THAT CAME FROM.

SHAAAÄ

MUNCH

MUNCH

UNLIMITED PASTA!

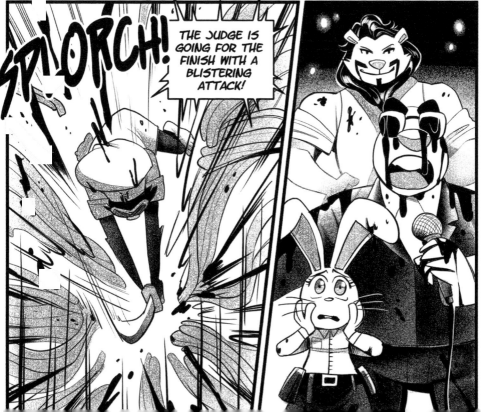

SPLORCH!

THE JUDGE IS GOING FOR THE FINISH WITH A BLISTERING ATTACK!

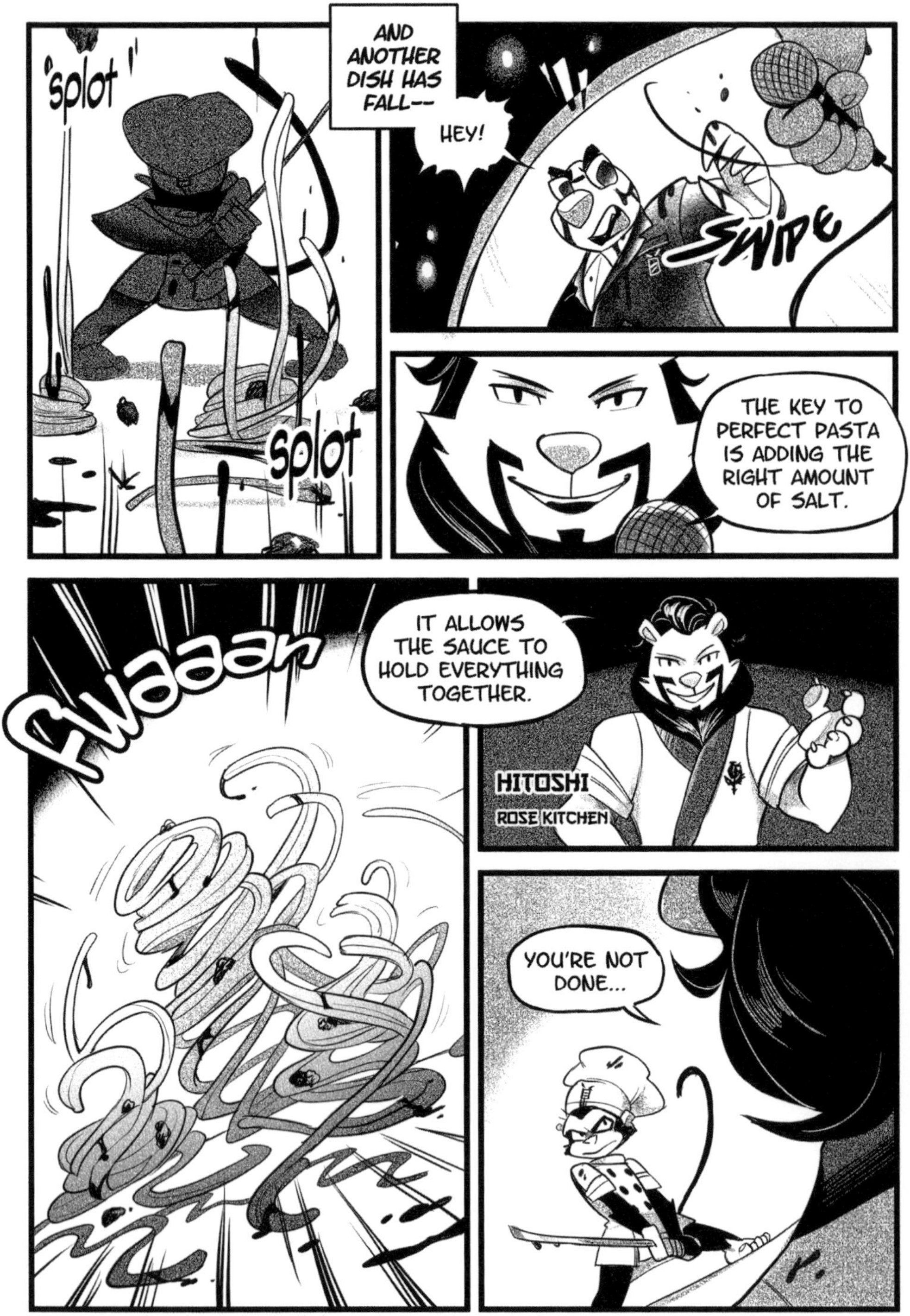
"splot !"
AND ANOTHER DISH HAS FALL--
HEY!
SWIPE
splot
THE KEY TO PERFECT PASTA IS ADDING THE RIGHT AMOUNT OF SALT.
FWAAAAN
IT ALLOWS THE SAUCE TO HOLD EVERYTHING TOGETHER.
HITOSHI
ROSE KITCHEN
YOU'RE NOT DONE...

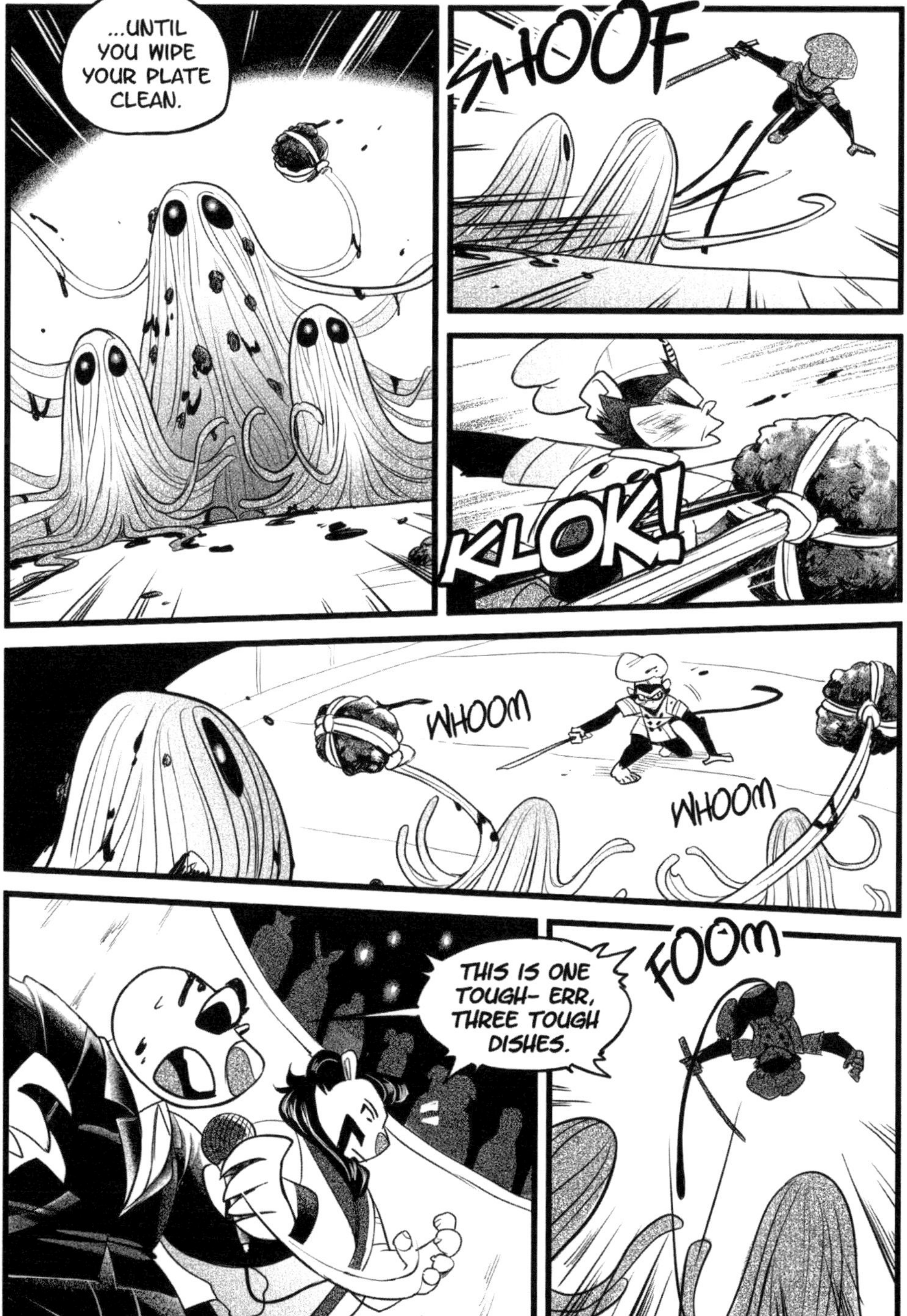
...UNTIL YOU WIPE YOUR PLATE CLEAN.
SHOOF
KLOK!
WHOOM
WHOOM
THIS IS ONE TOUGH- ERR, THREE TOUGH DISHES.
FOOM

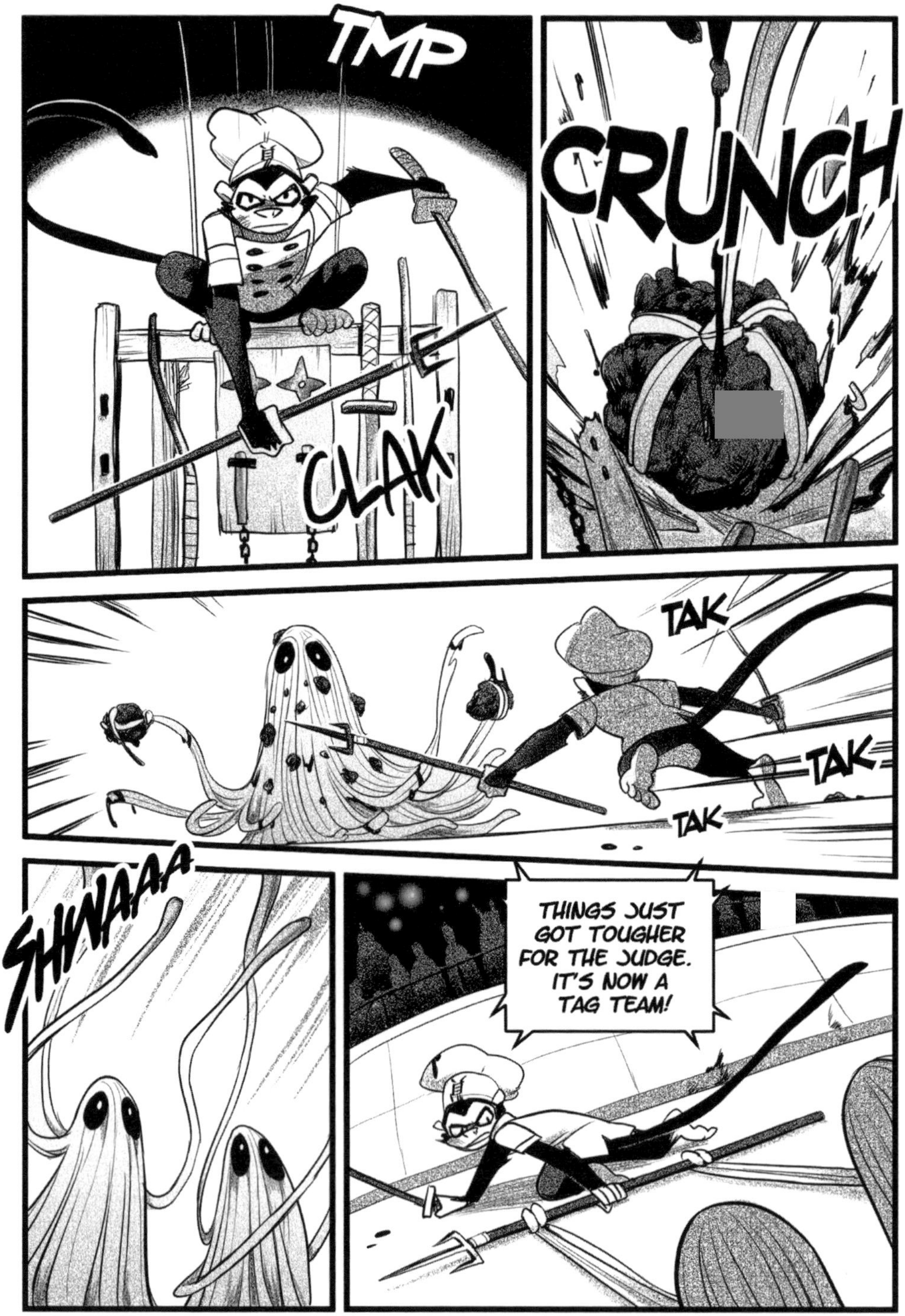
TMP
CLAK
CRUNCH
TAK
TAK
TAK
SHWAAA
THINGS JUST GOT TOUGHER FOR THE JUDGE. IT'S NOW A TAG TEAM!

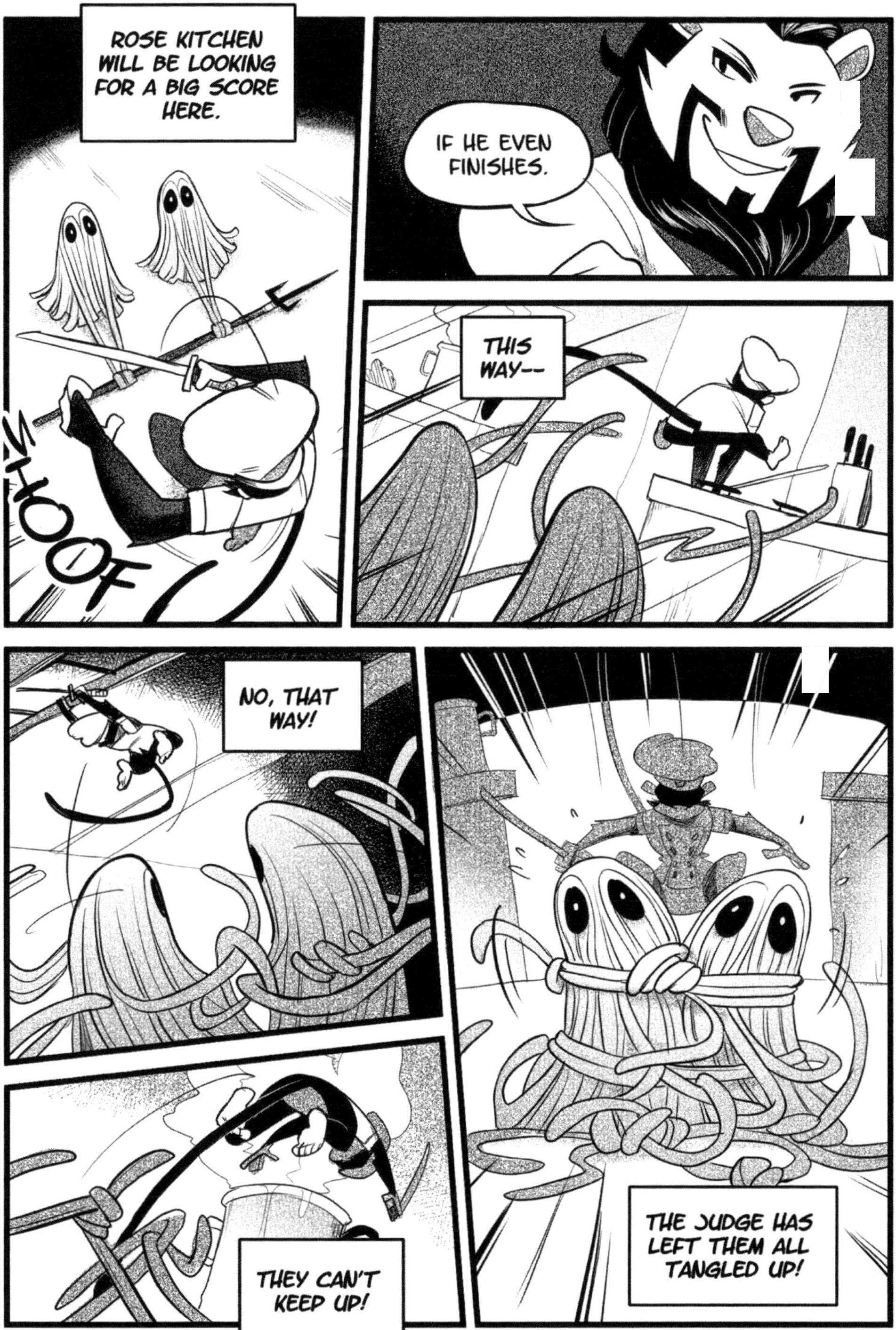
ROSE KITCHEN WILL BE LOOKING FOR A BIG SCORE HERE.
SHOOF
IF HE EVEN FINISHES.
THIS WAY--
NO, THAT WAY!
THEY CAN'T KEEP UP!
THE JUDGE HAS LEFT THEM ALL TANGLED UP!

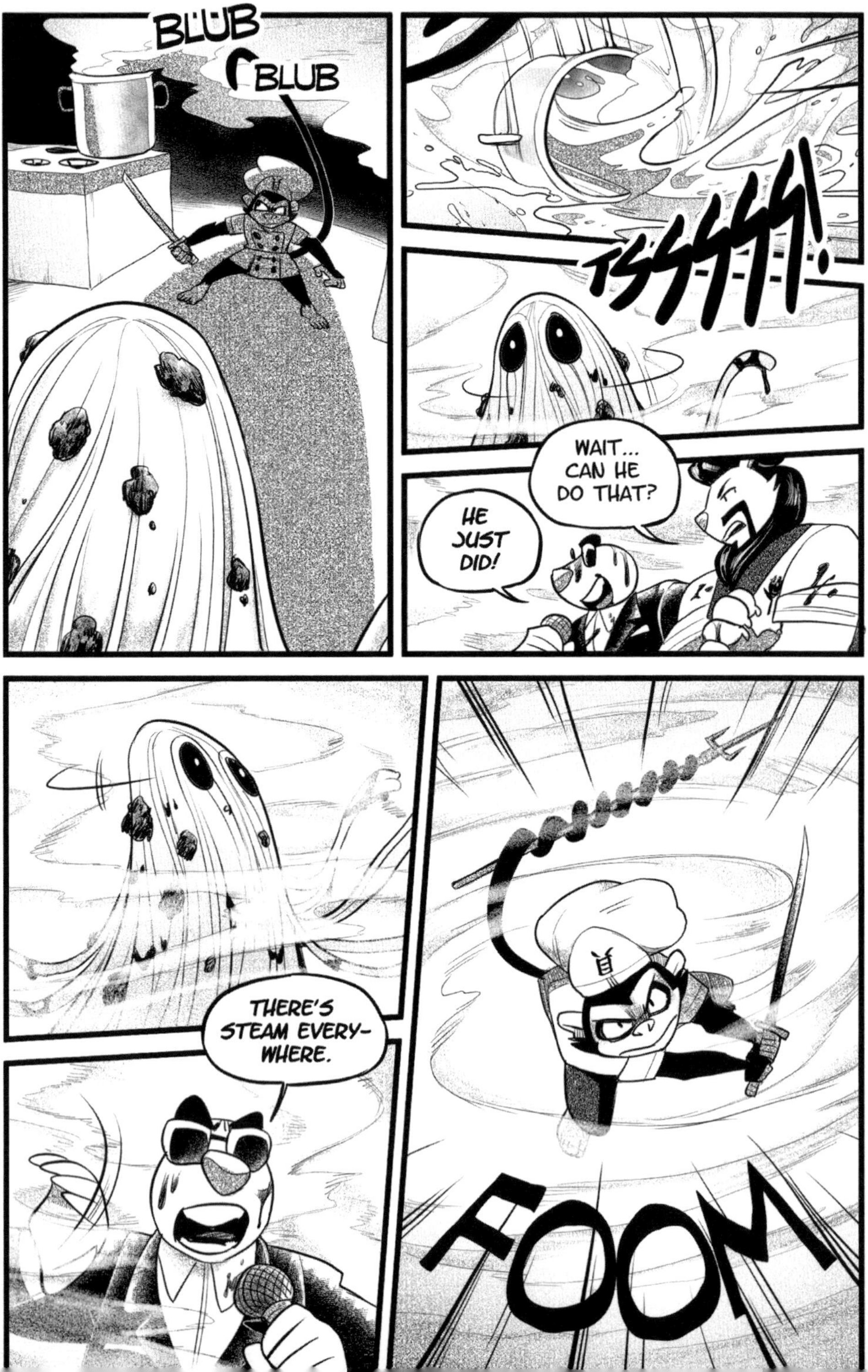
BLUB
BLUB
TSSSSSS!
WAIT... CAN HE DO THAT?
HE JUST DID!
THERE'S STEAM EVERY-WHERE.
FOOM

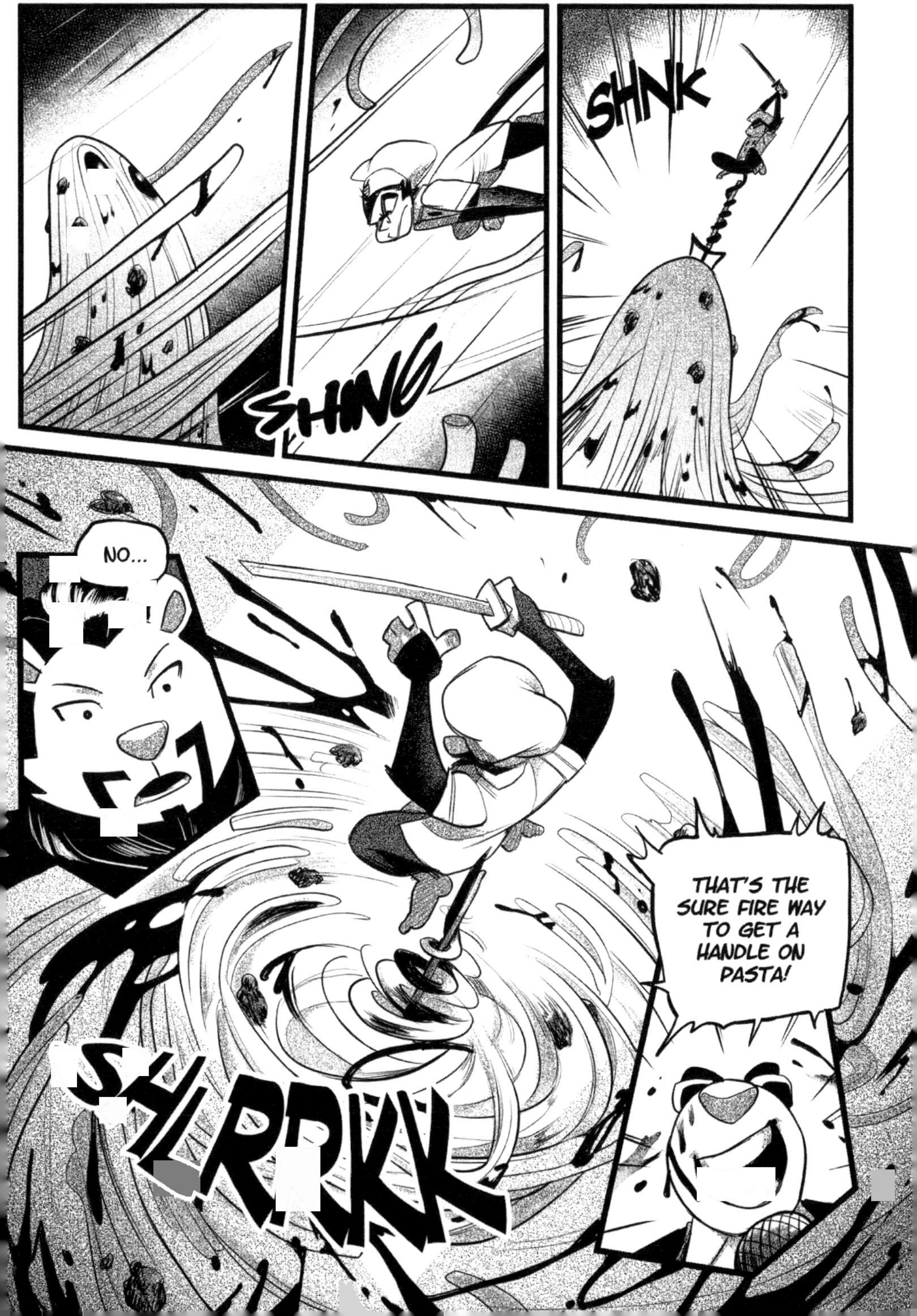
SHING
SHNK
NO...
SHLRRKK
THAT'S THE SURE FIRE WAY TO GET A HANDLE ON PASTA!

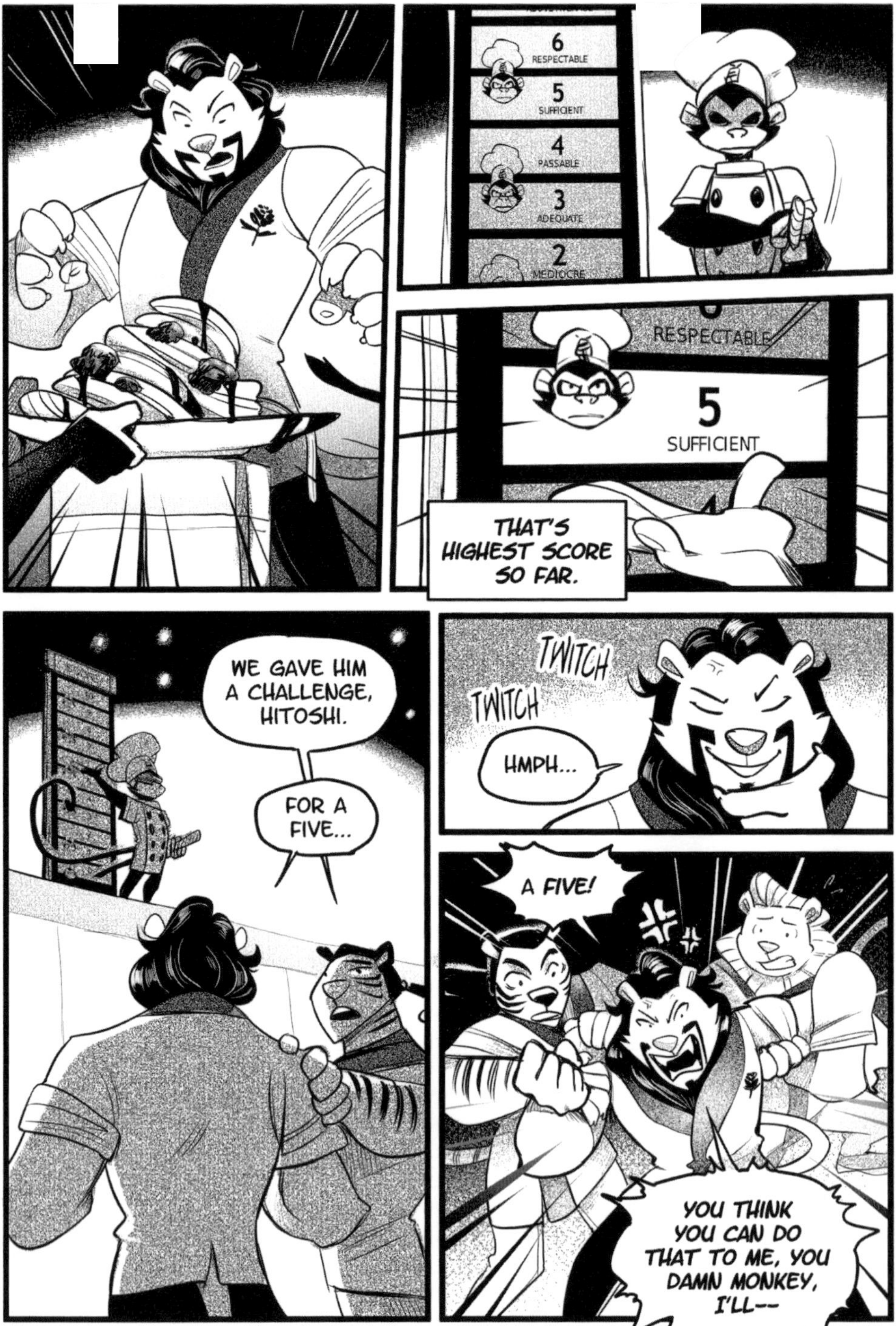
6
RESPECTABLE
5
SUFFICIENT
4
PASSABLE
3
ADEQUATE
2
MEDIOCRE
RESPECTABLE
5
SUFFICIENT
THAT'S HIGHEST SCORE SO FAR.
WE GAVE HIM A CHALLENGE, HITOSHI.
FOR A FIVE...
TWITCH
TWITCH
HMPH...
A FIVE!
YOU THINK YOU CAN DO THAT TO ME, YOU DAMN MONKEY, I'LL--

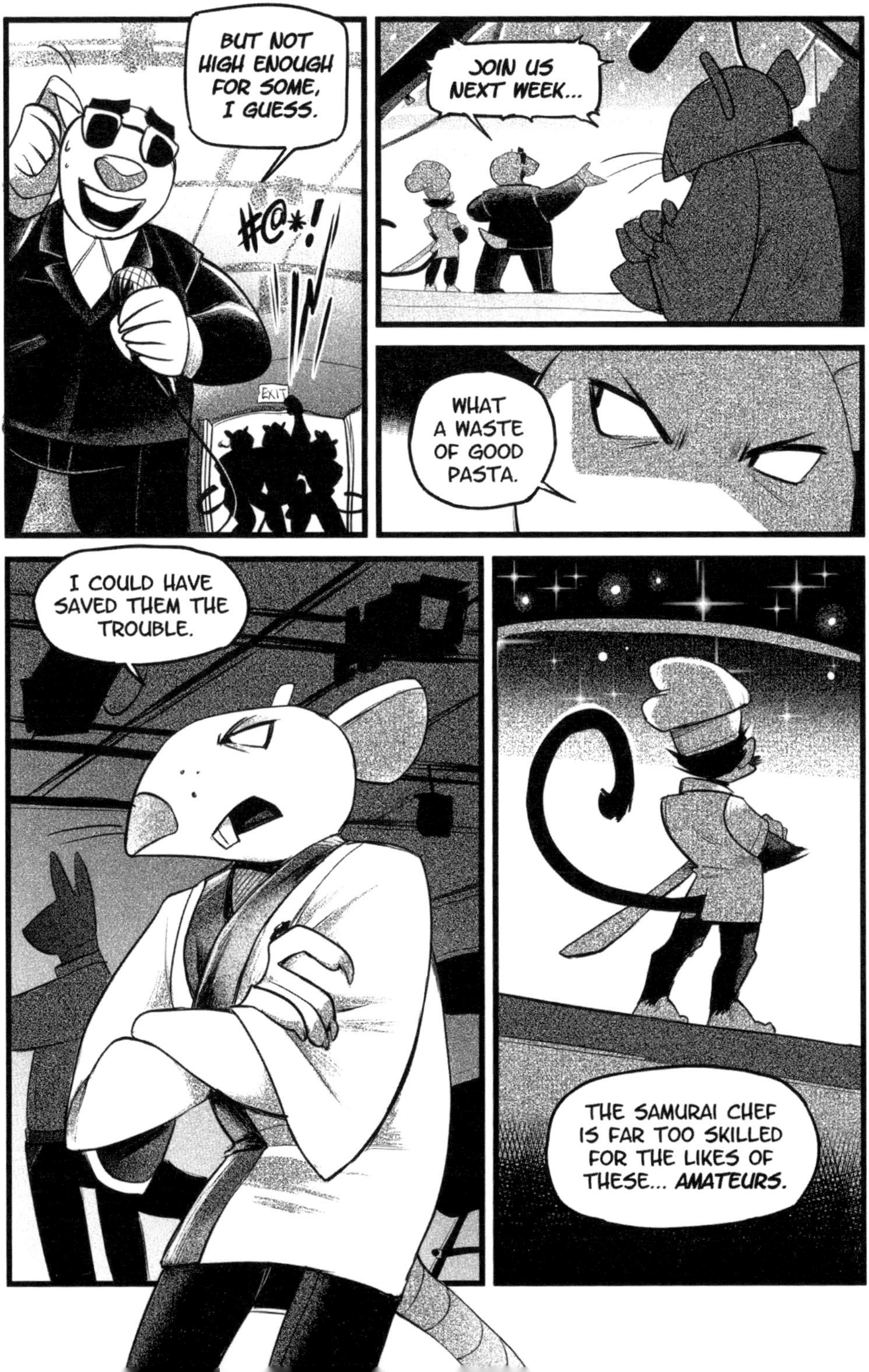
BUT NOT HIGH ENOUGH FOR SOME, I GUESS.
#@*!
EXIT
JOIN US NEXT WEEK...
WHAT A WASTE OF GOOD PASTA.
I COULD HAVE SAVED THEM THE TROUBLE.
THE SAMURAI CHEF IS FAR TOO SKILLED FOR THE LIKES OF THESE... *AMATEURS.*

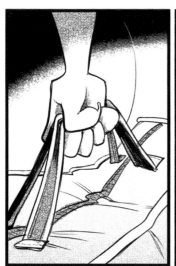

MOVE!

SHOOF

I'LL SEE HE GETS WHAT IS COMING TO HIM...

EXIT

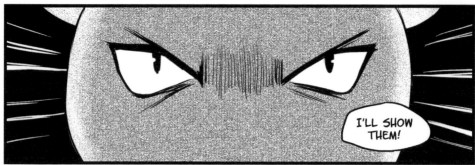

I'LL SHOW THEM!

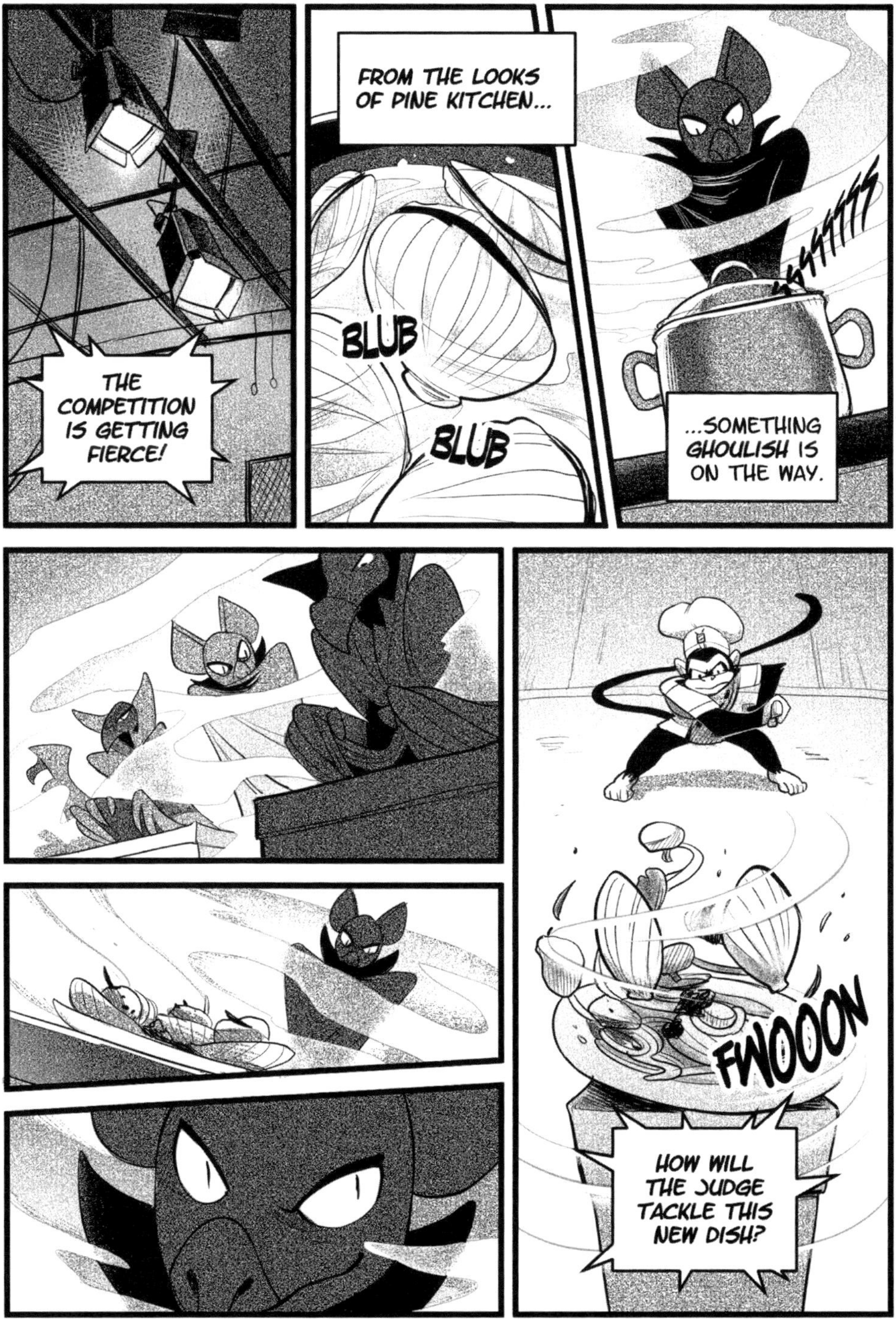
THE COMPETITION IS GETTING FIERCE!
FROM THE LOOKS OF PINE KITCHEN...
BLUB
BLUB
...SOMETHING GHOULISH IS ON THE WAY.
FWOOON
HOW WILL THE JUDGE TACKLE THIS NEW DISH?

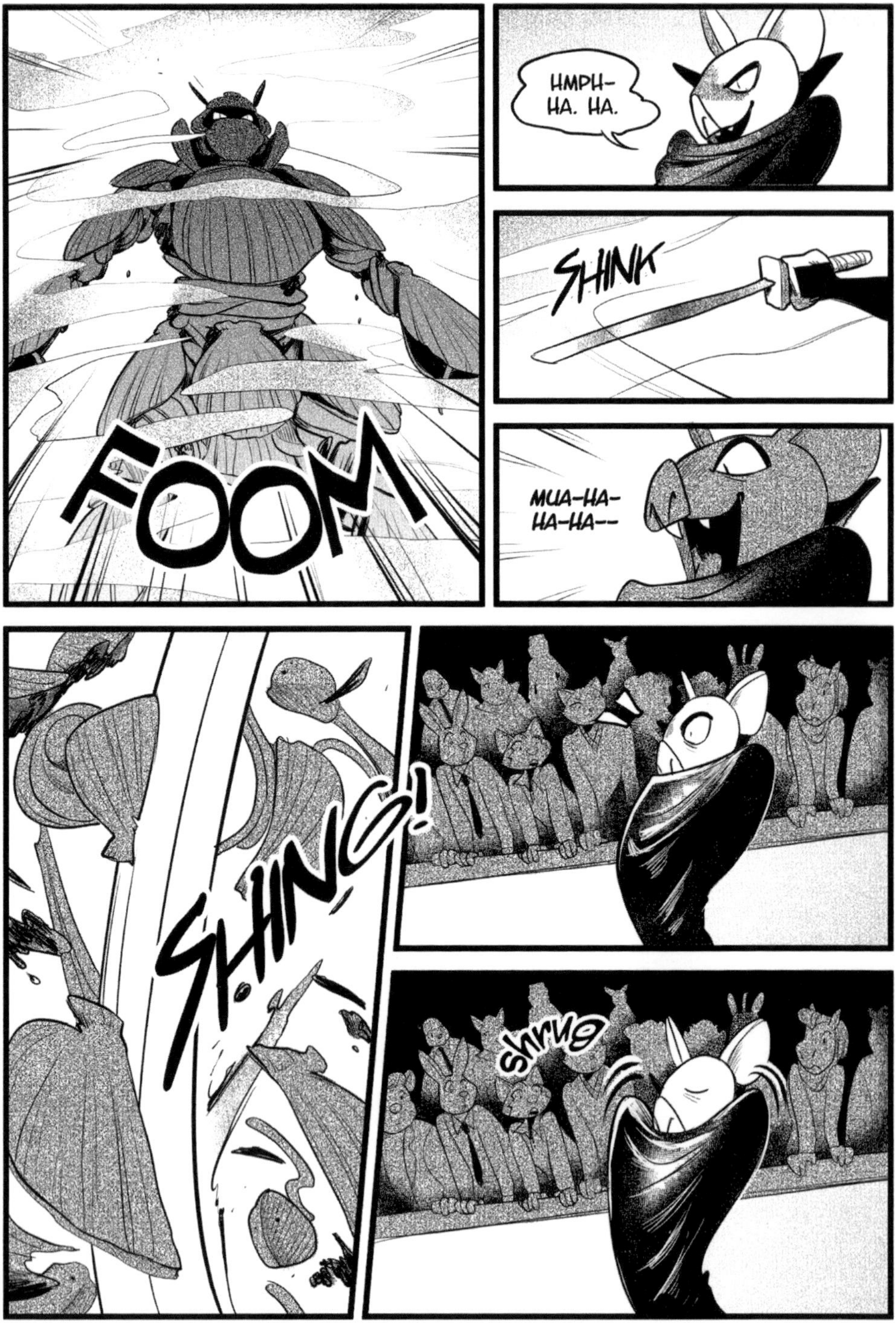
FOOM
HMPH-
HA. HA.
SHINK
MUA-HA-
HA-HA--
SHING!
shrug

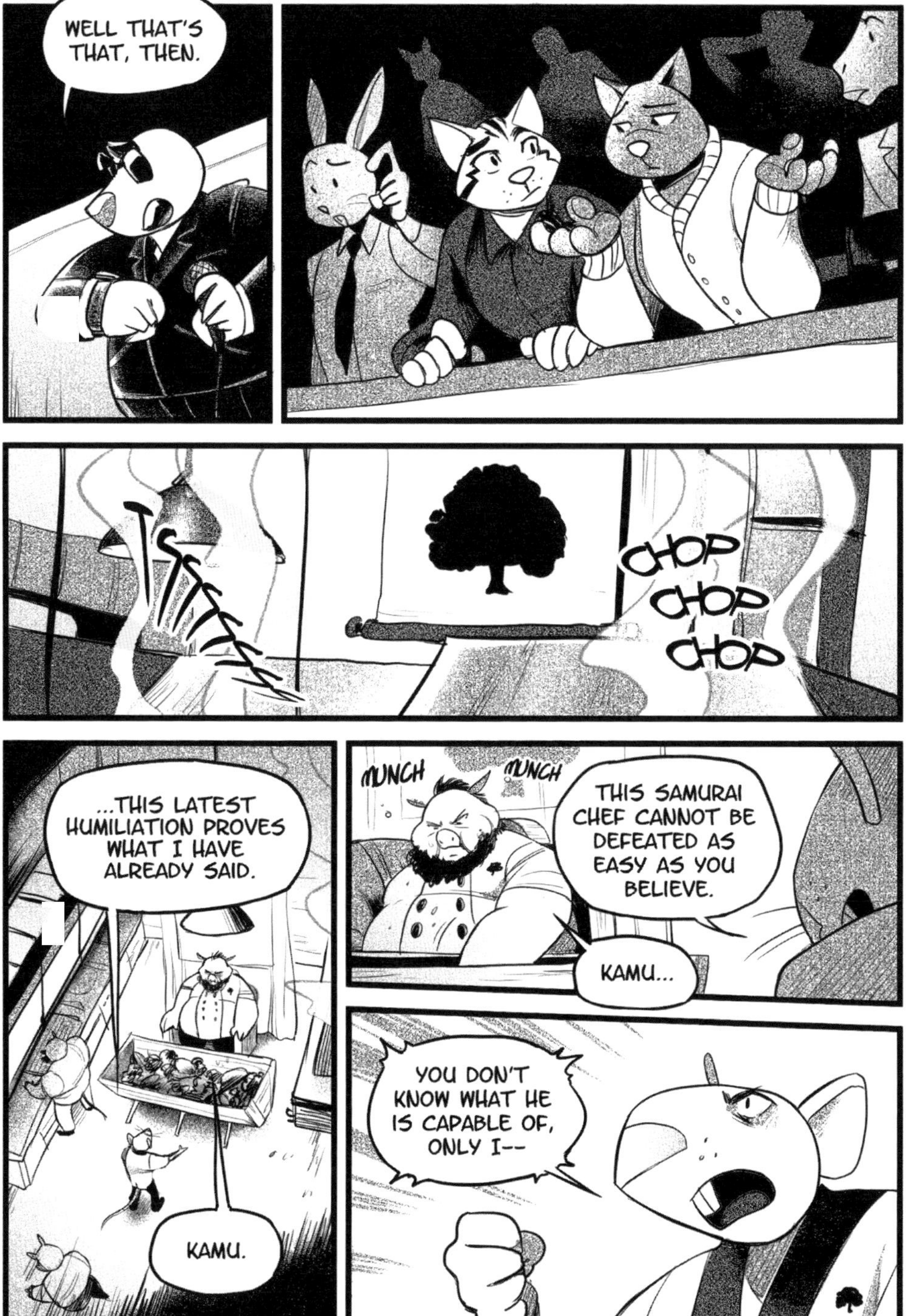
WELL THAT'S THAT, THEN.
TSSSSSSHHH
CHOP CHOP CHOP
...THIS LATEST HUMILIATION PROVES WHAT I HAVE ALREADY SAID.
KAMU.
MUNCH MUNCH
THIS SAMURAI CHEF CANNOT BE DEFEATED AS EASY AS YOU BELIEVE.
KAMU...
YOU DON'T KNOW WHAT HE IS CAPABLE OF, ONLY I--

KAMU! ENOUGH!

YOU HAVE SAID YOUR PIECE.

NOMF NOMF

HE HAS TRAINED WITH THE BEST AND HAS EXPERIENCE IN THE UNDERGROUND TOURNAMENTS.

I'M THE ONLY ONE IN OAK KITCHEN WITH THE NECESSARY EXPERIENCE.

mm!

NUMF

I SHOULD LEAD THE NEXT TEAM.

POP

THAT WON'T BE NECESSARY.

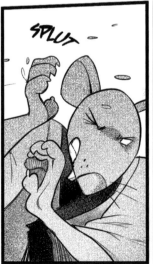

SPLUT

WE HAVE SENT FOR *CHOP-CHOP* AND HIS CHEFS.

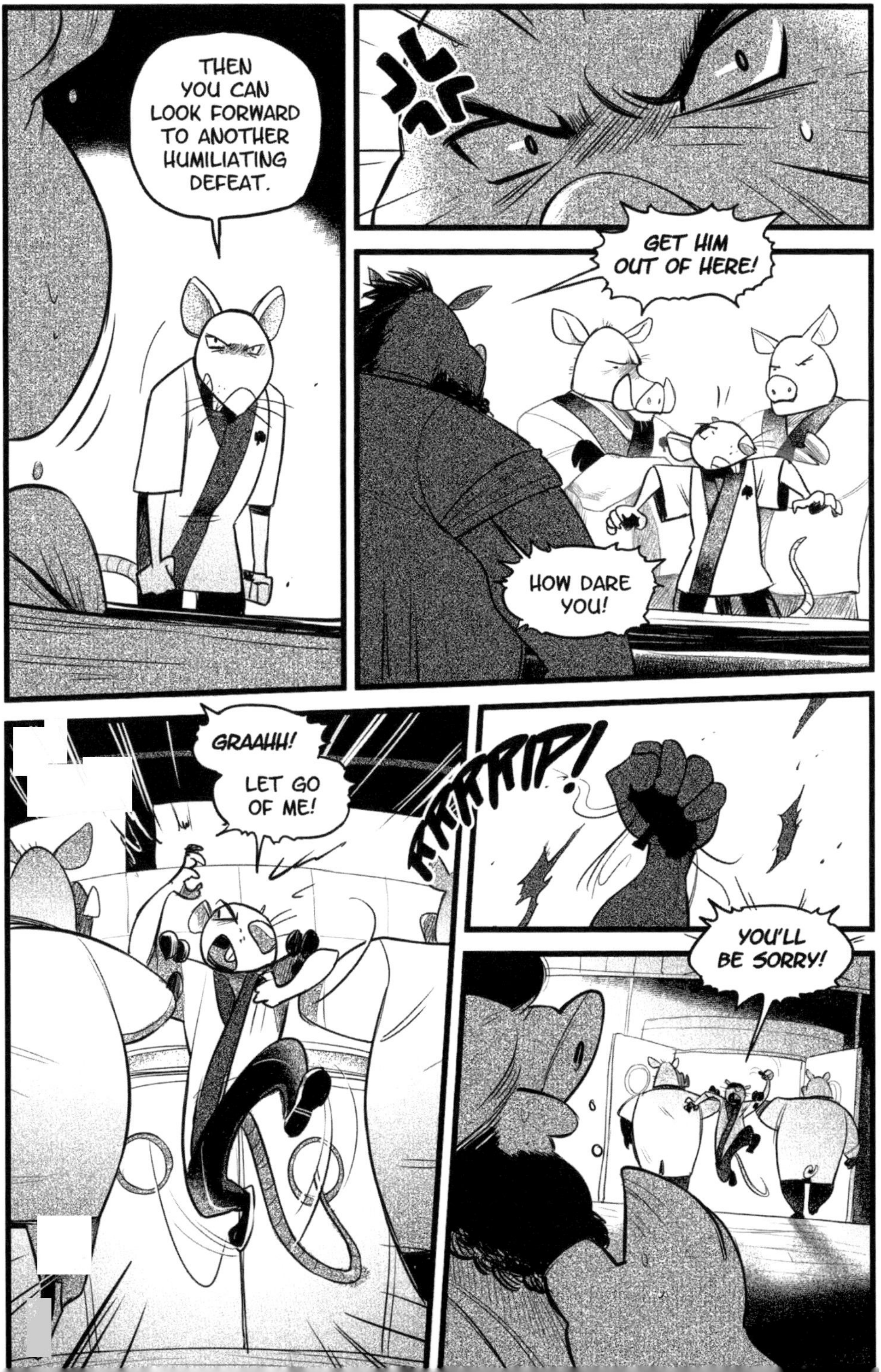
THEN YOU CAN LOOK FORWARD TO ANOTHER HUMILIATING DEFEAT.
GET HIM OUT OF HERE!
HOW DARE YOU!
GRAAHH!
LET GO OF ME!
RRRRIP!
YOU'LL BE SORRY!

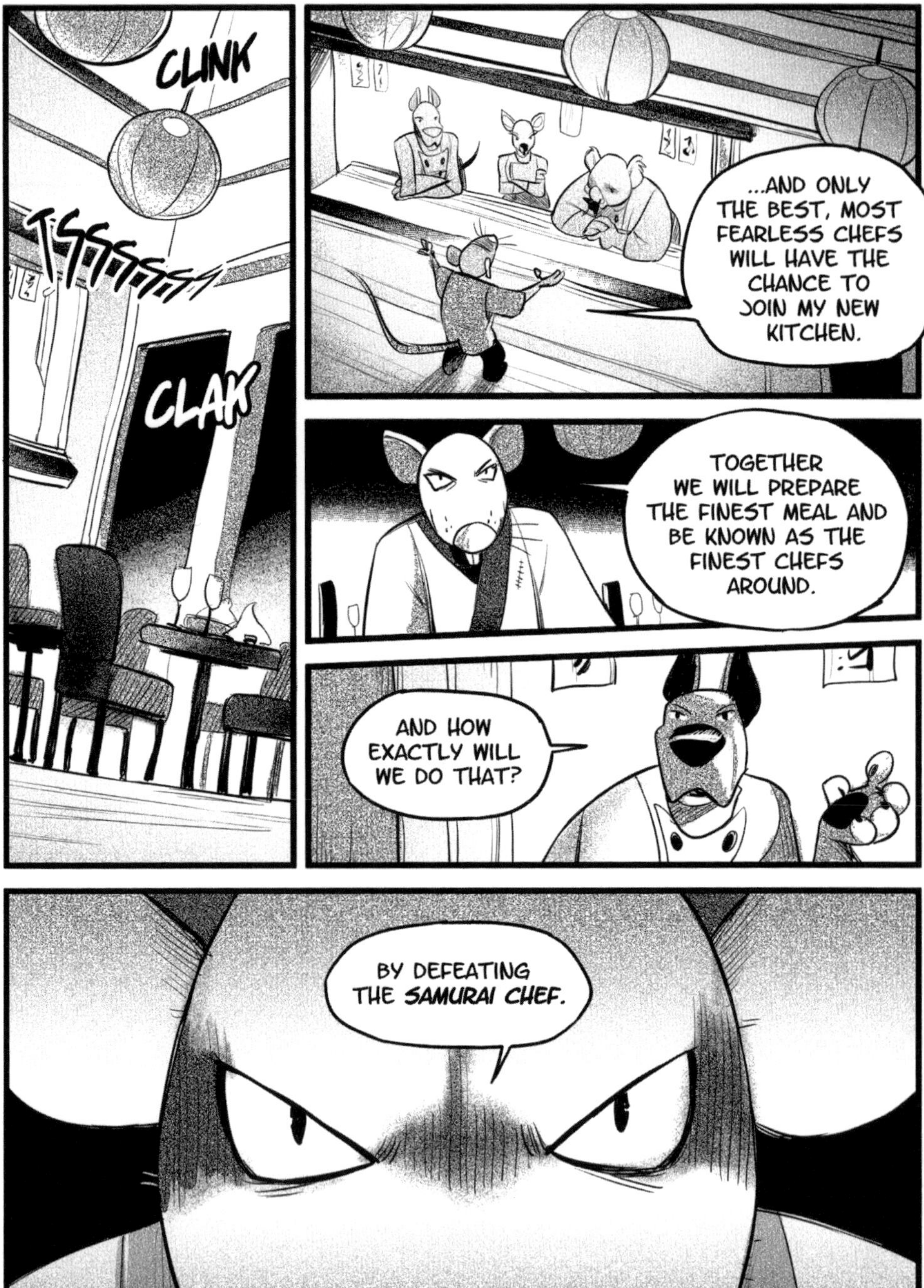
CLINK
TSSSSSSS
CLAK
...AND ONLY THE BEST, MOST FEARLESS CHEFS WILL HAVE THE CHANCE TO JOIN MY NEW KITCHEN.
TOGETHER WE WILL PREPARE THE FINEST MEAL AND BE KNOWN AS THE FINEST CHEFS AROUND.
AND HOW EXACTLY WILL WE DO THAT?
BY DEFEATING THE *SAMURAI CHEF*.

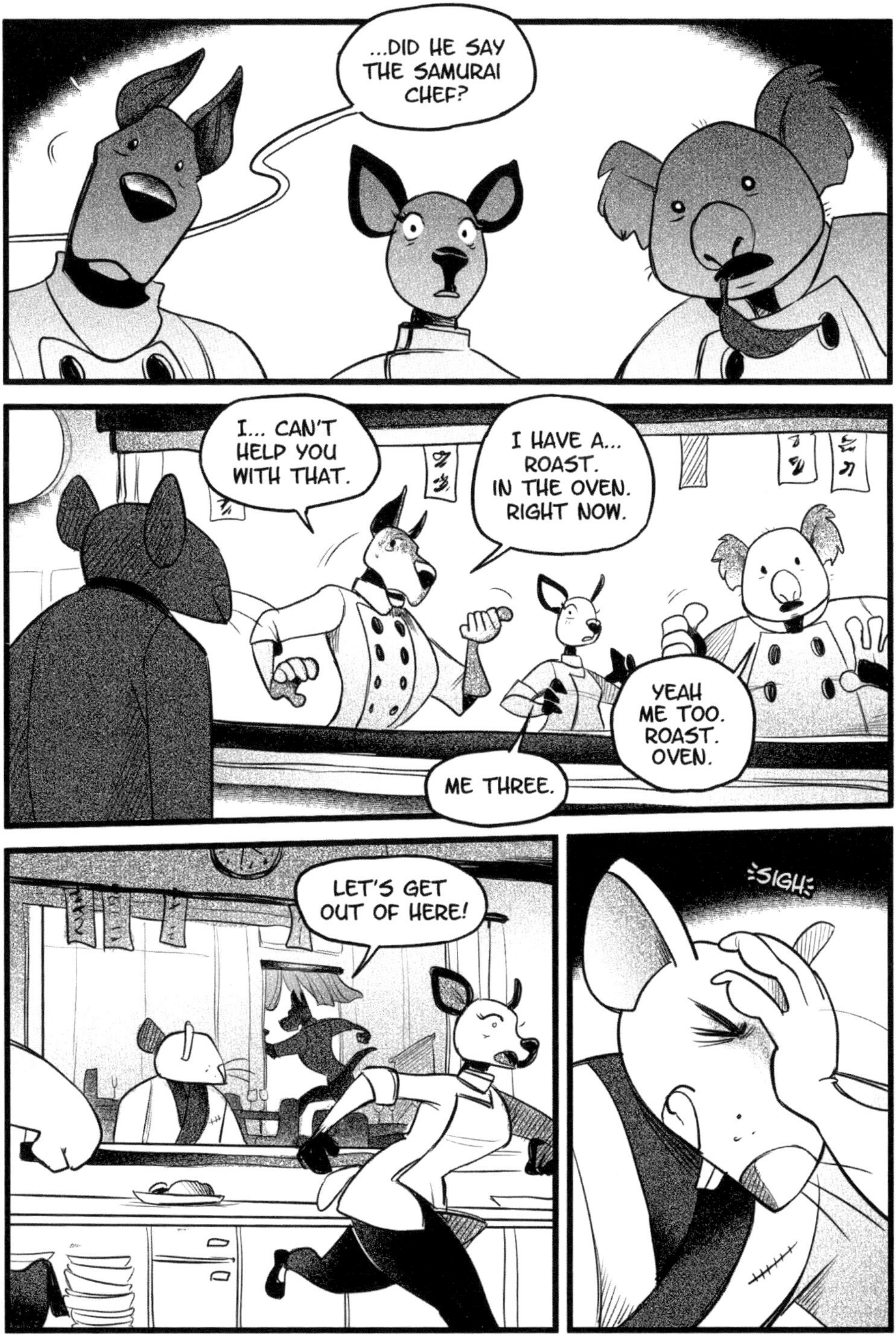
...DID HE SAY THE SAMURAI CHEF?
I... CAN'T HELP YOU WITH THAT.
I HAVE A... ROAST. IN THE OVEN. RIGHT NOW.
YEAH ME TOO. ROAST. OVEN.
ME THREE.
LET'S GET OUT OF HERE!
SIGH

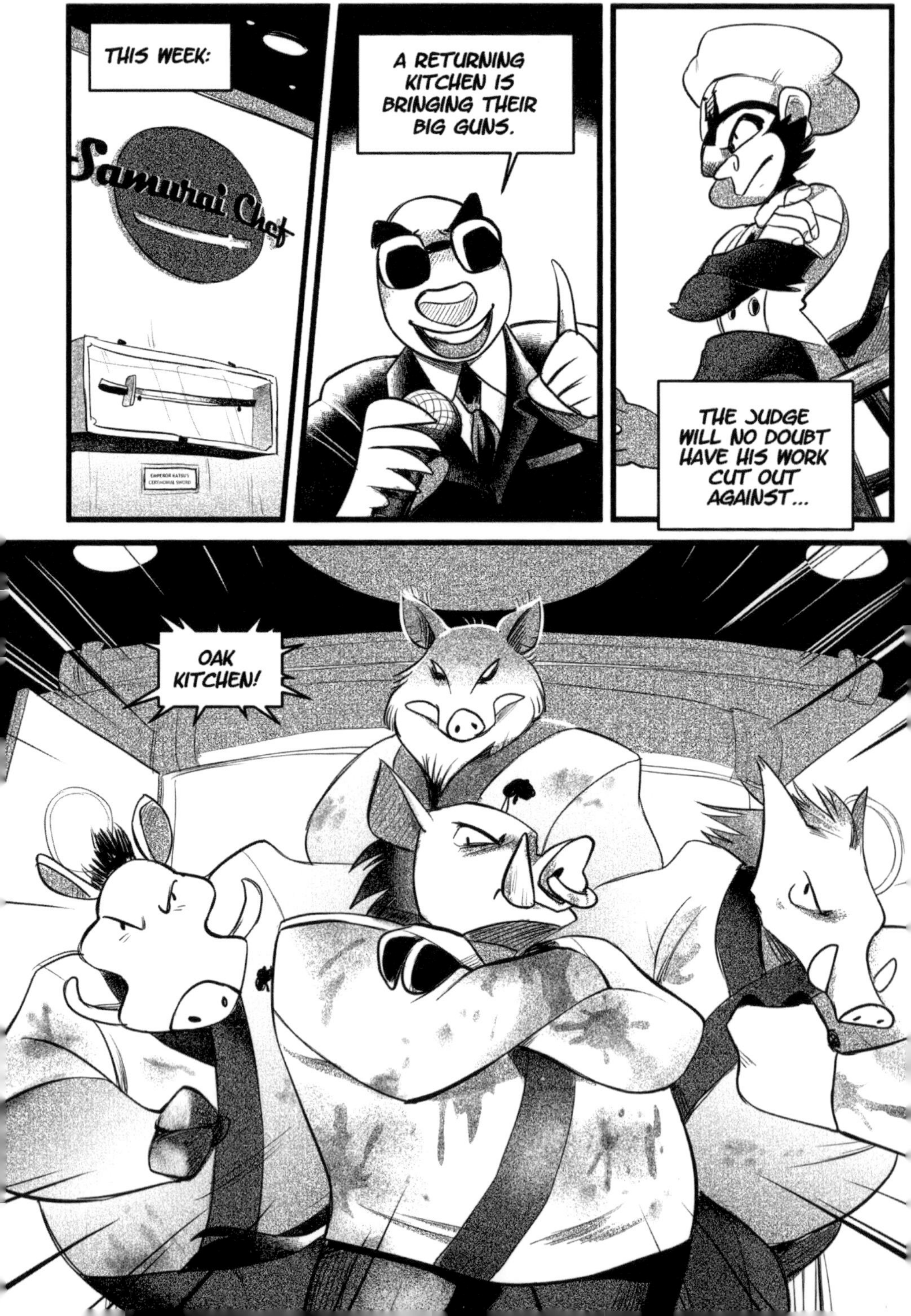
THIS WEEK:
Samurai Chef
EMPEROR KATSU'S CEREMONIAL SWORD
A RETURNING KITCHEN IS BRINGING THEIR BIG GUNS.
THE JUDGE WILL NO DOUBT HAVE HIS WORK CUT OUT AGAINST...
OAK KITCHEN!

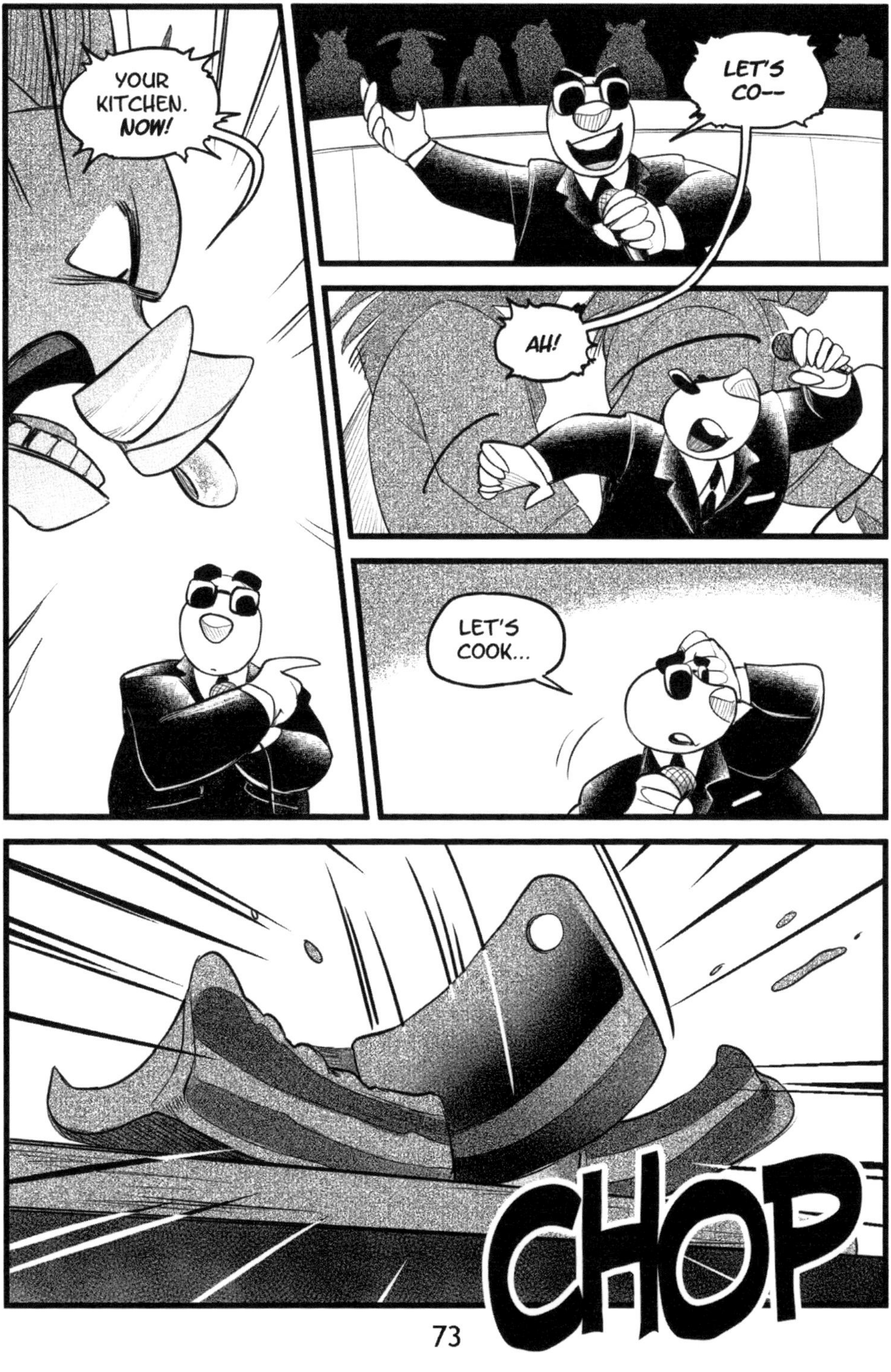
YOUR KITCHEN. NOW!
LET'S CO--
AH!
LET'S COOK...
CHOP

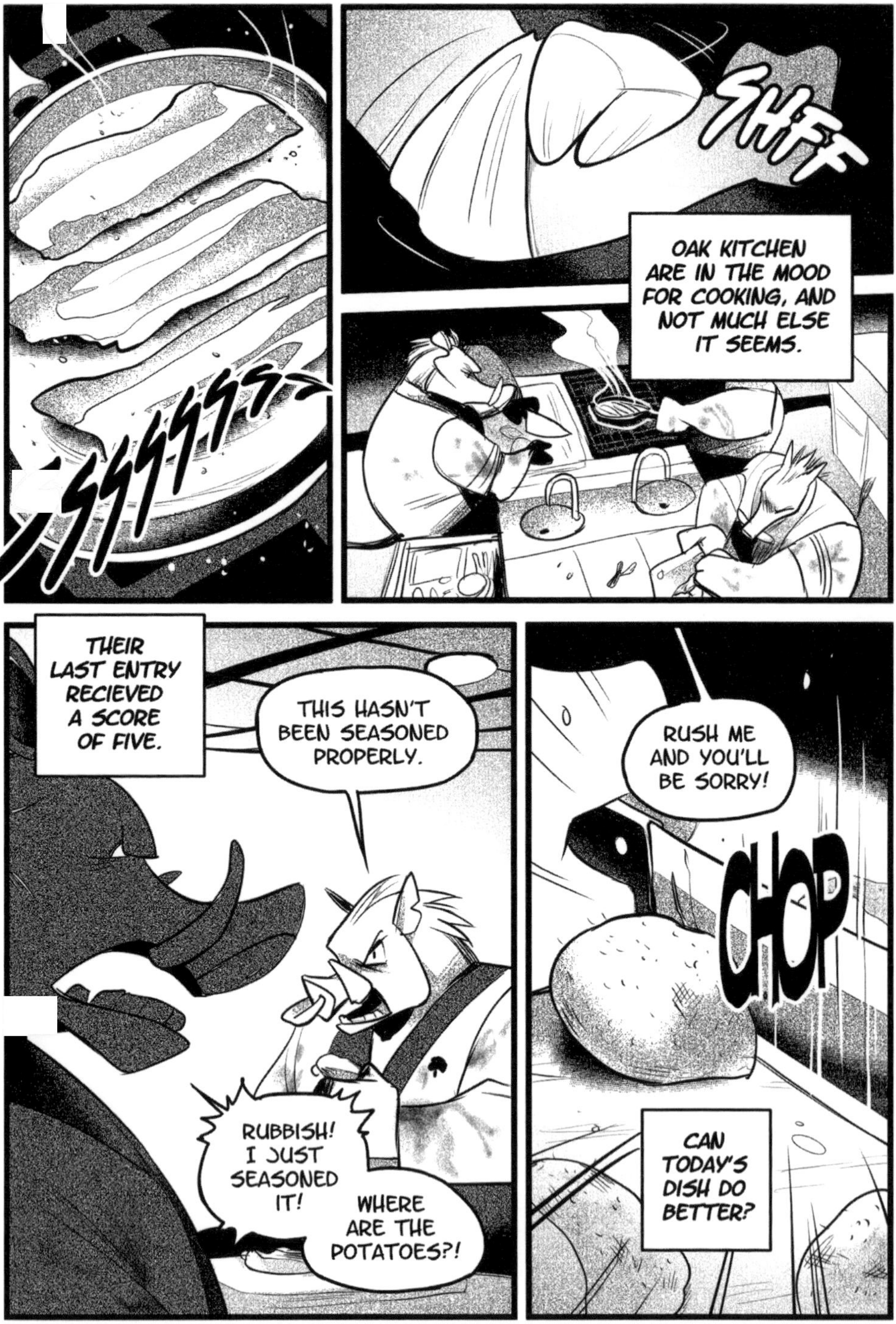
SSSSSSSS
SHFF
OAK KITCHEN ARE IN THE MOOD FOR COOKING, AND NOT MUCH ELSE IT SEEMS.
THEIR LAST ENTRY RECIEVED A SCORE OF FIVE.
THIS HASN'T BEEN SEASONED PROPERLY.
RUBBISH! I JUST SEASONED IT!
WHERE ARE THE POTATOES?!
RUSH ME AND YOU'LL BE SORRY!
CHOP
CAN TODAY'S DISH DO BETTER?

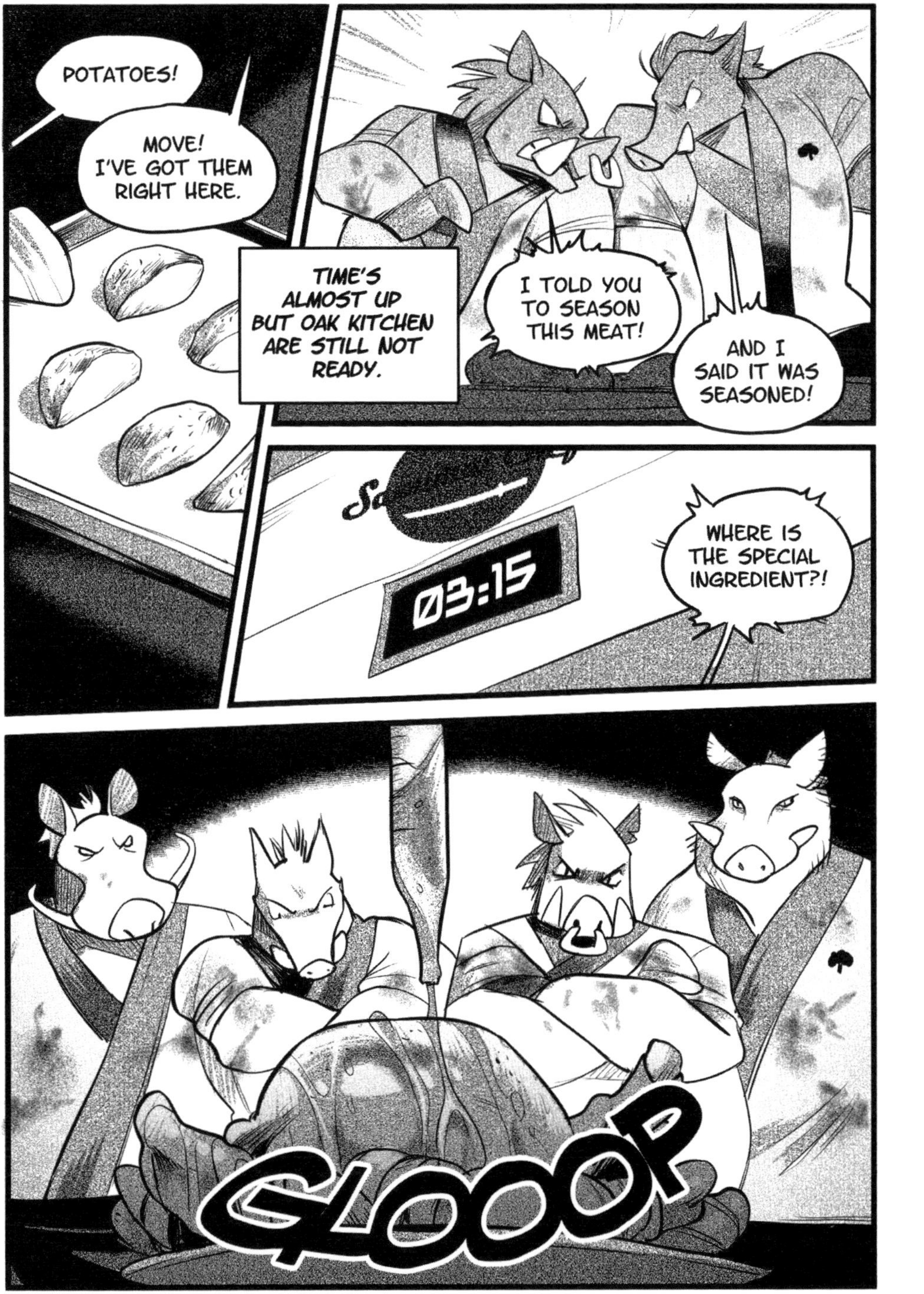
POTATOES!
MOVE! I'VE GOT THEM RIGHT HERE.
TIME'S ALMOST UP BUT OAK KITCHEN ARE STILL NOT READY.
I TOLD YOU TO SEASON THIS MEAT!
AND I SAID IT WAS SEASONED!
03:15
WHERE IS THE SPECIAL INGREDIENT?!
GLOOOP

FWOOON

OAK KITCHEN'S DISH IS READY FOR JUDGING. IT'S...

...ENORMOUS.

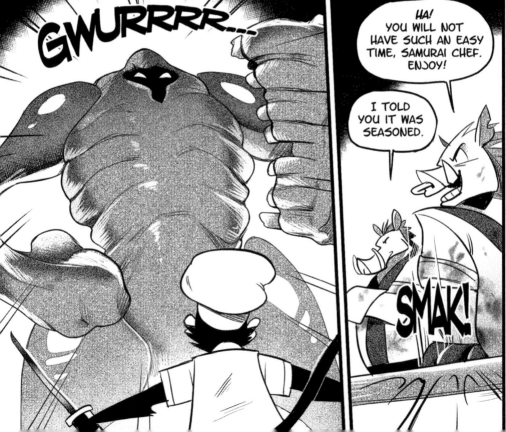

GWURRRR...

HA! YOU WILL NOT HAVE SUCH AN EASY TIME, SAMURAI CHEF. ENJOY!

I TOLD YOU IT WAS SEASONED.

SMAK!

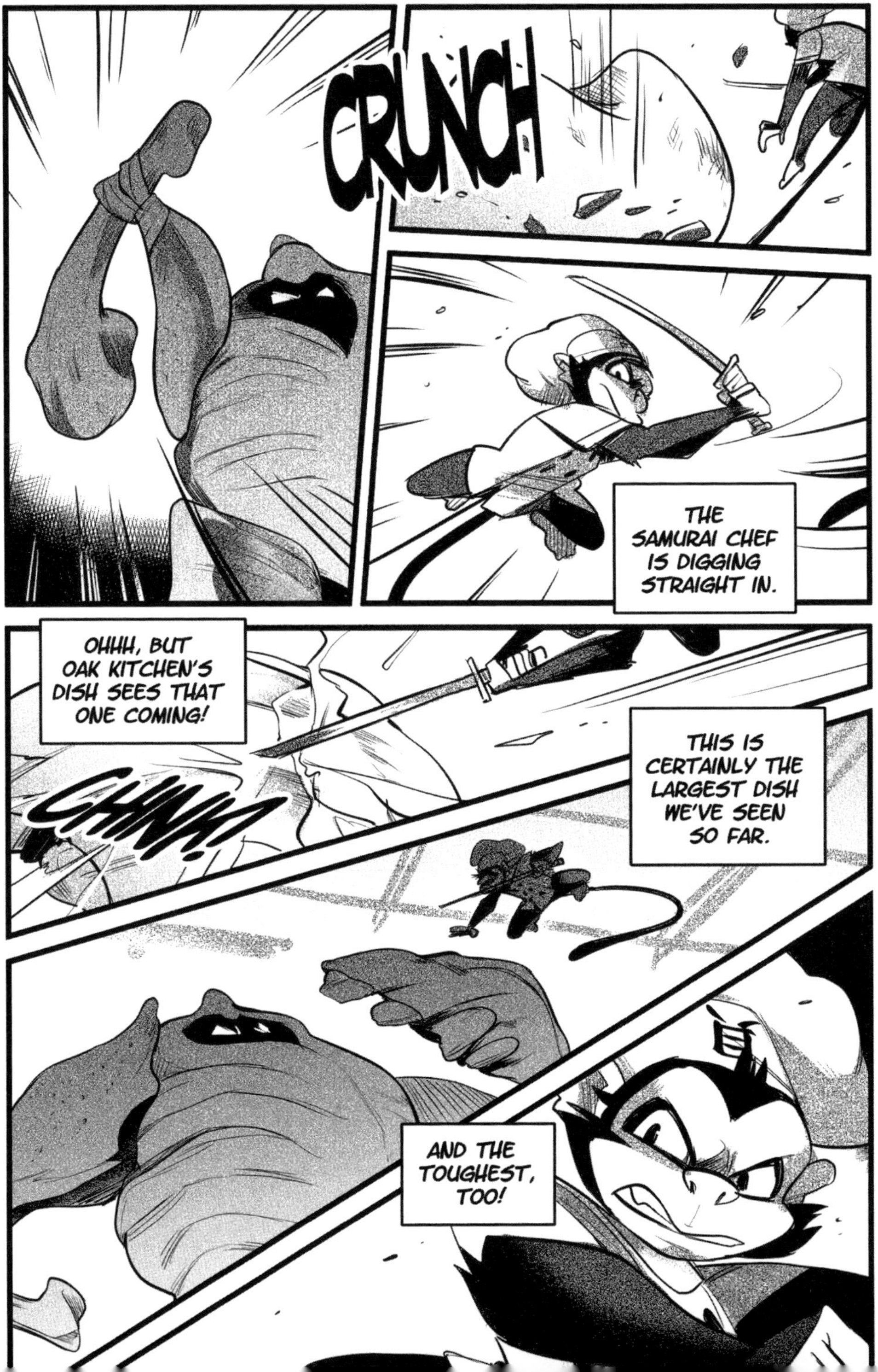
CRUNCH
THE SAMURAI CHEF IS DIGGING STRAIGHT IN.
OHHH, BUT OAK KITCHEN'S DISH SEES THAT ONE COMING!
CHNK!
THIS IS CERTAINLY THE LARGEST DISH WE'VE SEEN SO FAR.
AND THE TOUGHEST, TOO!

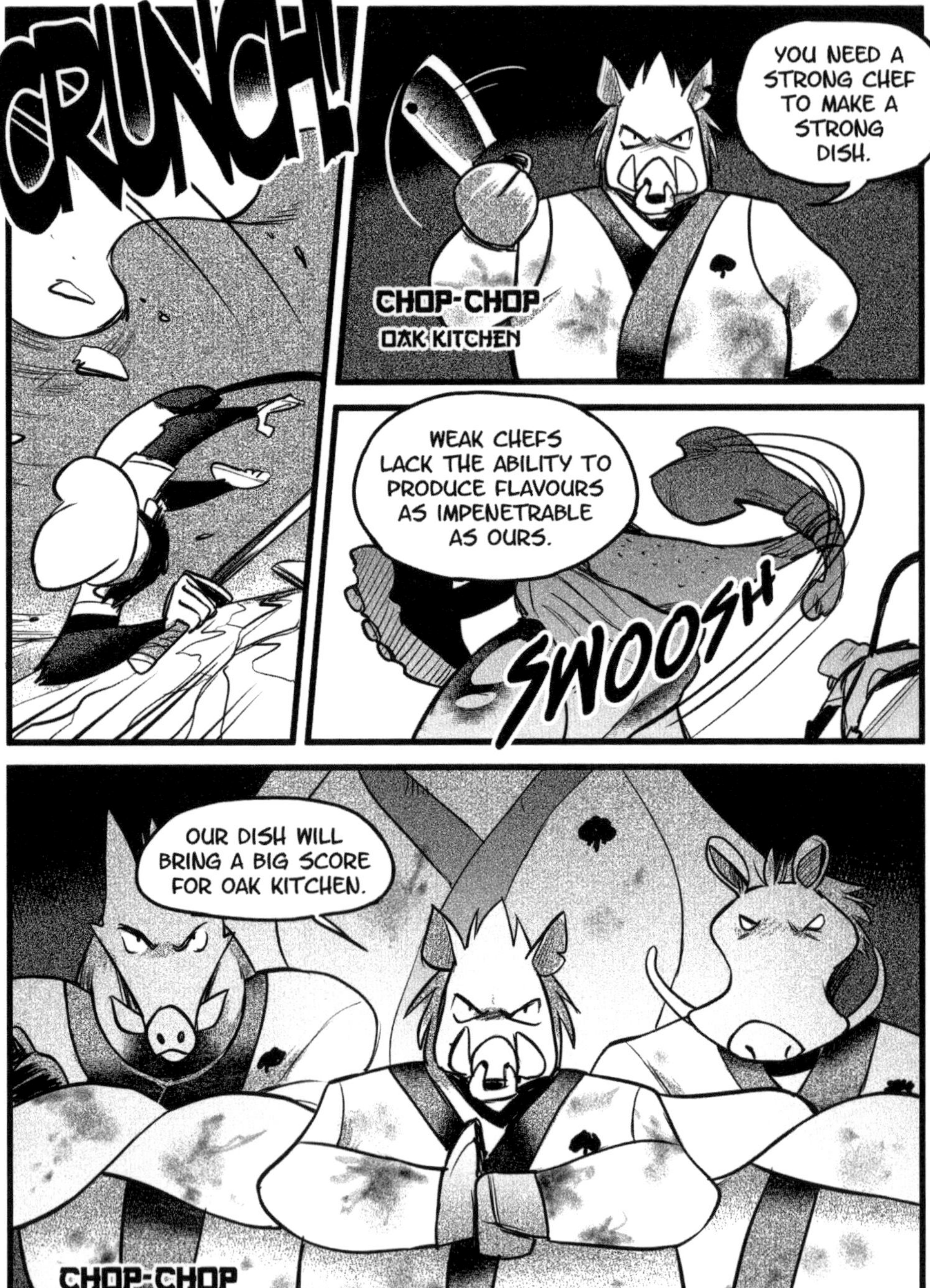
CRUNCH!!
YOU NEED A STRONG CHEF TO MAKE A STRONG DISH.
CHOP-CHOP
OAK KITCHEN
WEAK CHEFS LACK THE ABILITY TO PRODUCE FLAVOURS AS IMPENETRABLE AS OURS.
SWOOSH
OUR DISH WILL BRING A BIG SCORE FOR OAK KITCHEN.
CHOP-CHOP
OAK KITCHEN

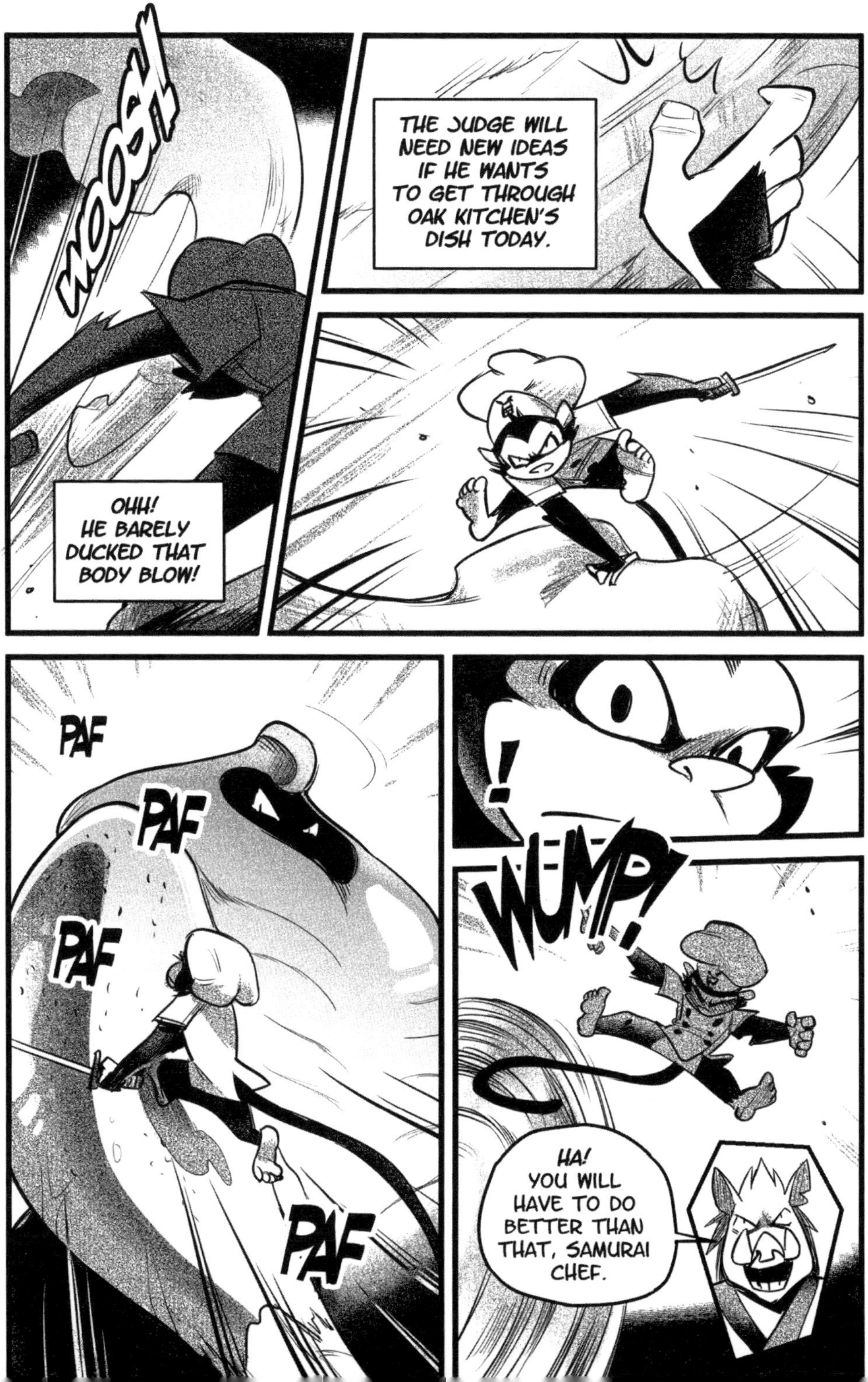
WOOSH!
OHH! HE BARELY DUCKED THAT BODY BLOW!
THE JUDGE WILL NEED NEW IDEAS IF HE WANTS TO GET THROUGH OAK KITCHEN'S DISH TODAY.
PAF
PAF
PAF
PAF
!
WUMP!
HA! YOU WILL HAVE TO DO BETTER THAN THAT, SAMURAI CHEF.

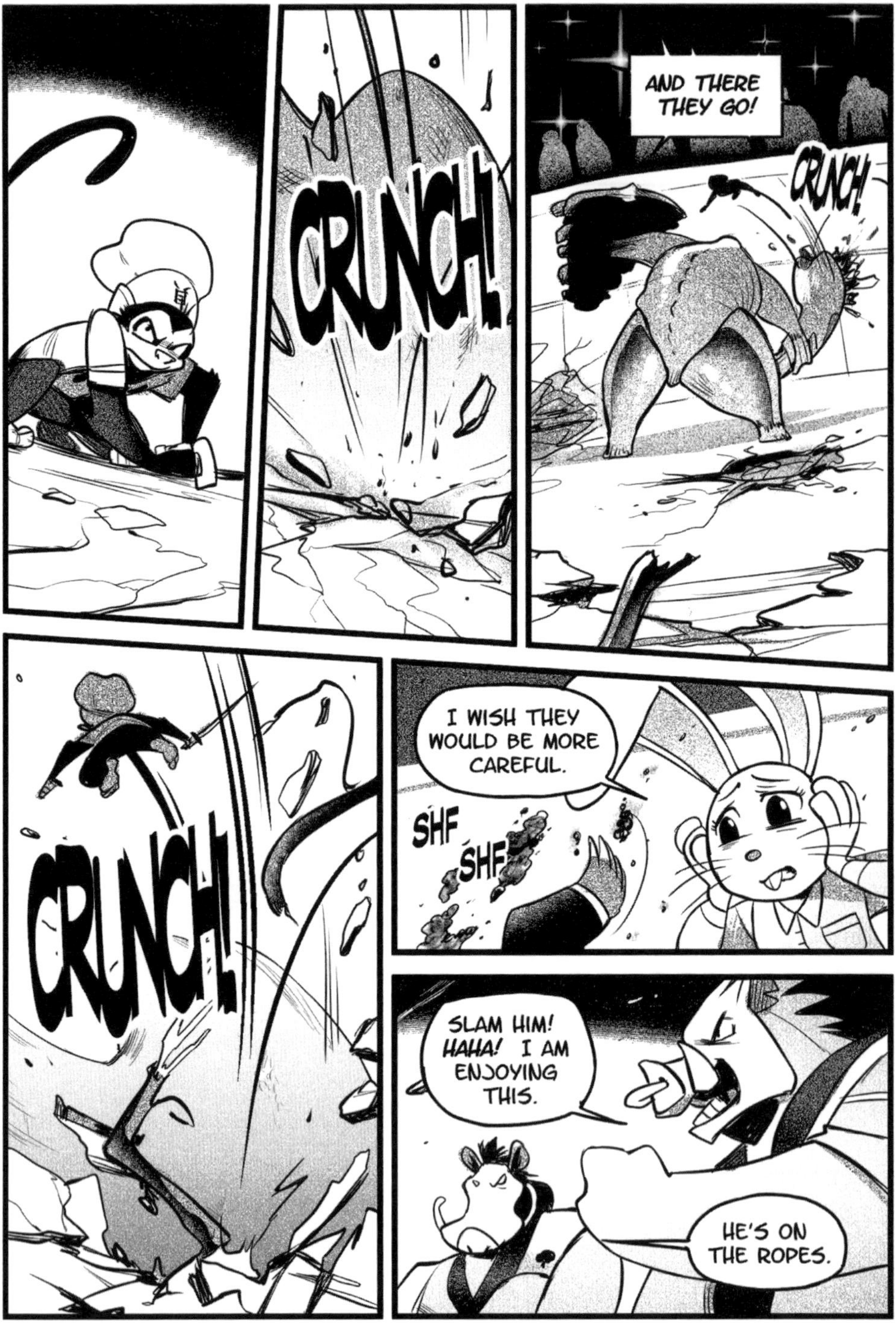
CRUNCH!
AND THERE THEY GO!
CRUNCH!
CRUNCH!
I WISH THEY WOULD BE MORE CAREFUL.
SHF SHF
SLAM HIM! HAHA! I AM ENJOYING THIS.
HE'S ON THE ROPES.

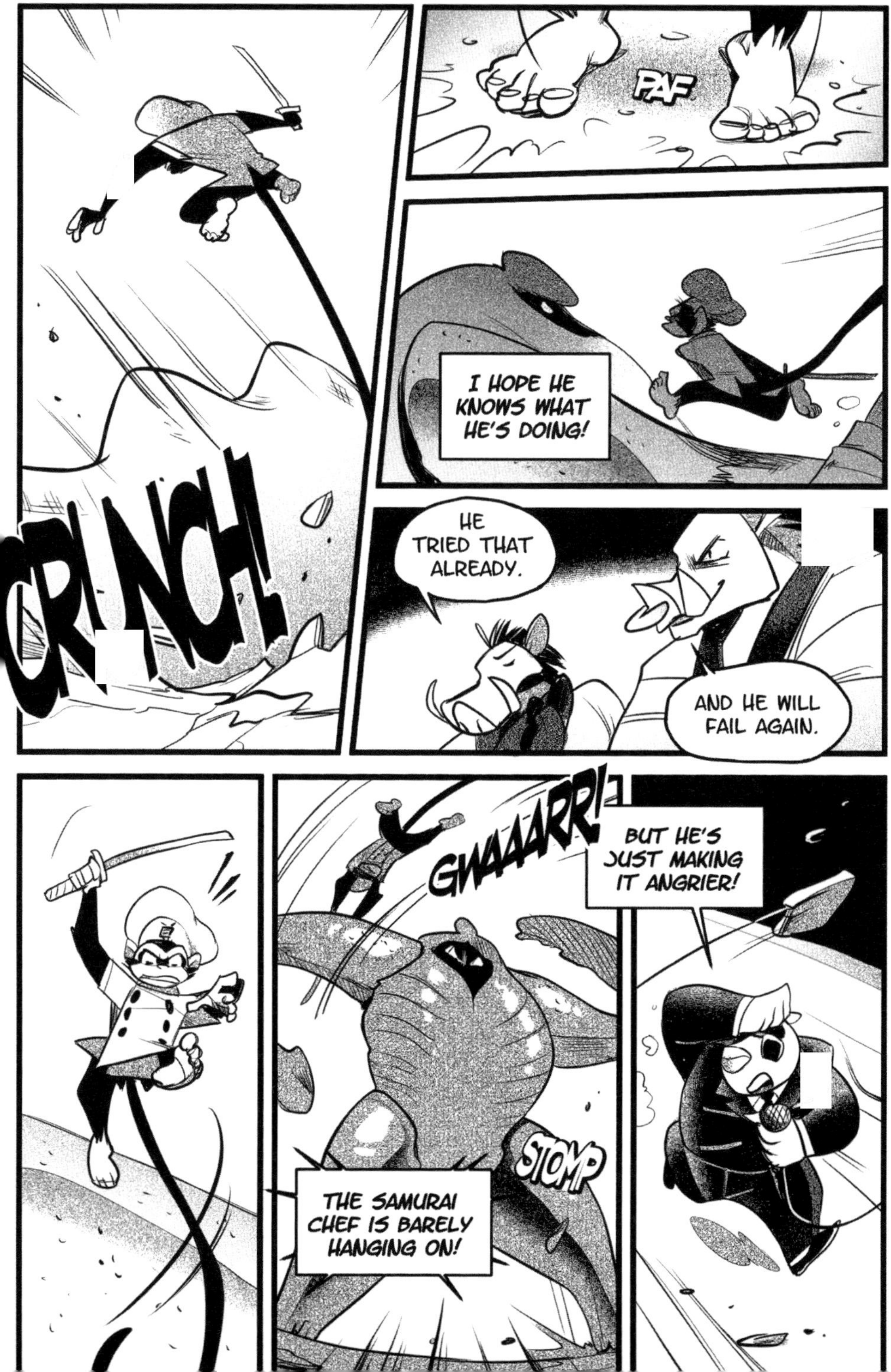
CRUNCH!
PAF
I HOPE HE KNOWS WHAT HE'S DOING!
HE TRIED THAT ALREADY.
AND HE WILL FAIL AGAIN.
GWAAARR!
STOMP
THE SAMURAI CHEF IS BARELY HANGING ON!
BUT HE'S JUST MAKING IT ANGRIER!

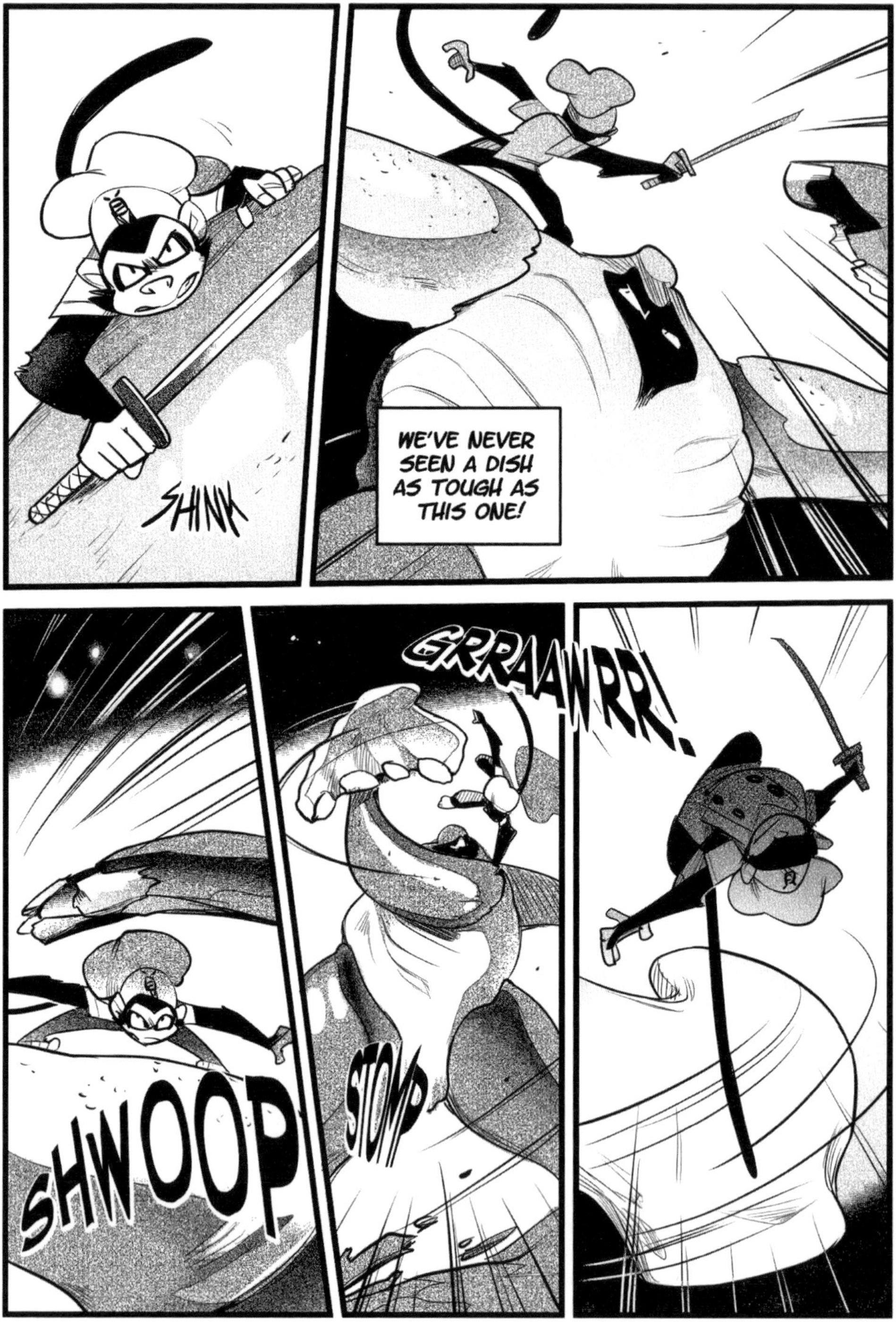
SHINK
WE'VE NEVER SEEN A DISH AS TOUGH AS THIS ONE!
SHWOOP
GRRAAWRR!
STOMP

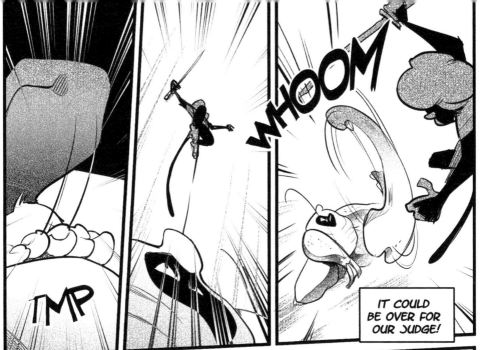

IT COULD BE OVER FOR OUR JUDGE!

HERE COMES THE FINISH.

WAIT A MINUTE...

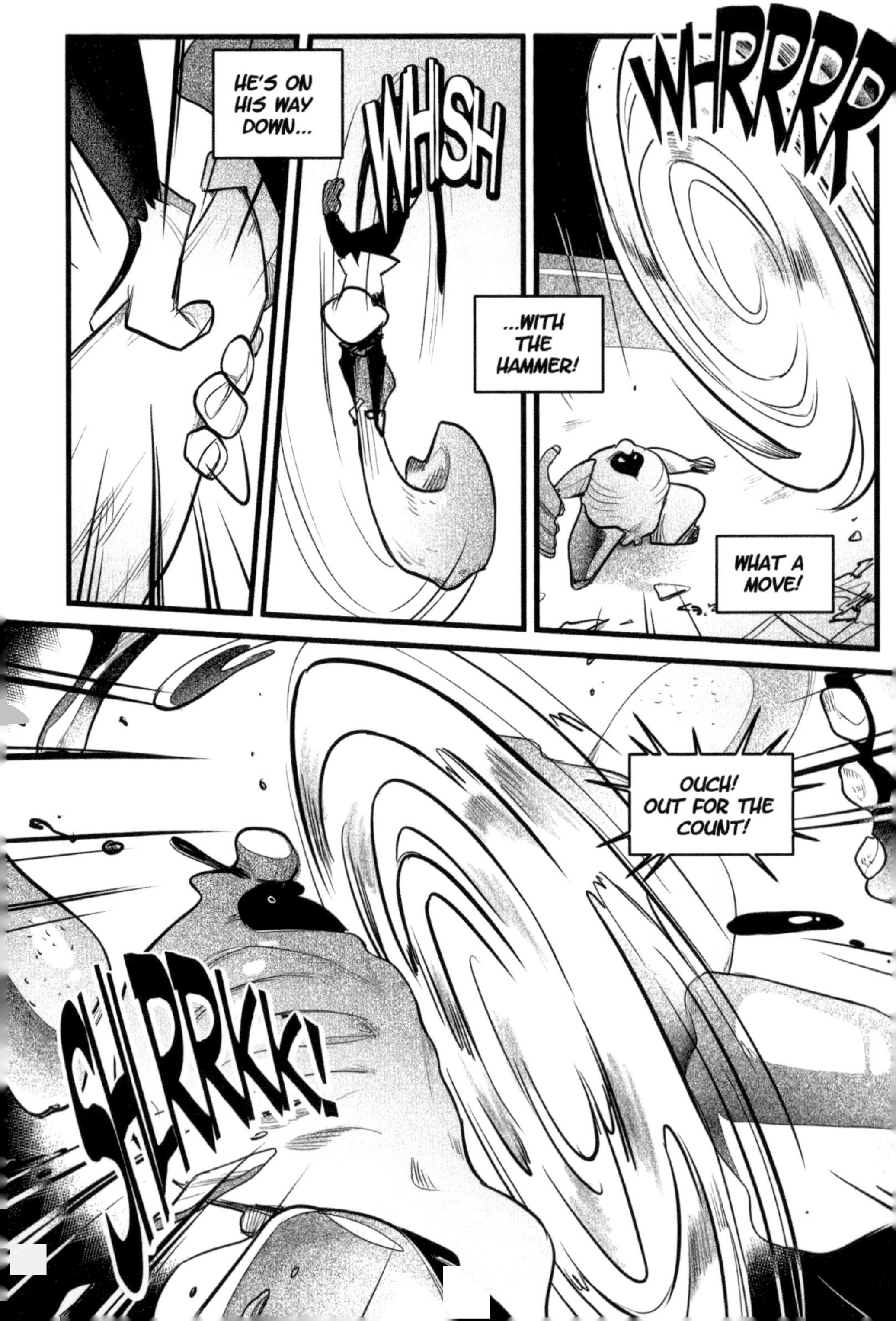
HE'S ON HIS WAY DOWN...
WHISH
WHRRRRR
...WITH THE HAMMER!
WHAT A MOVE!
OUCH! OUT FOR THE COUNT!
SHRRKK!

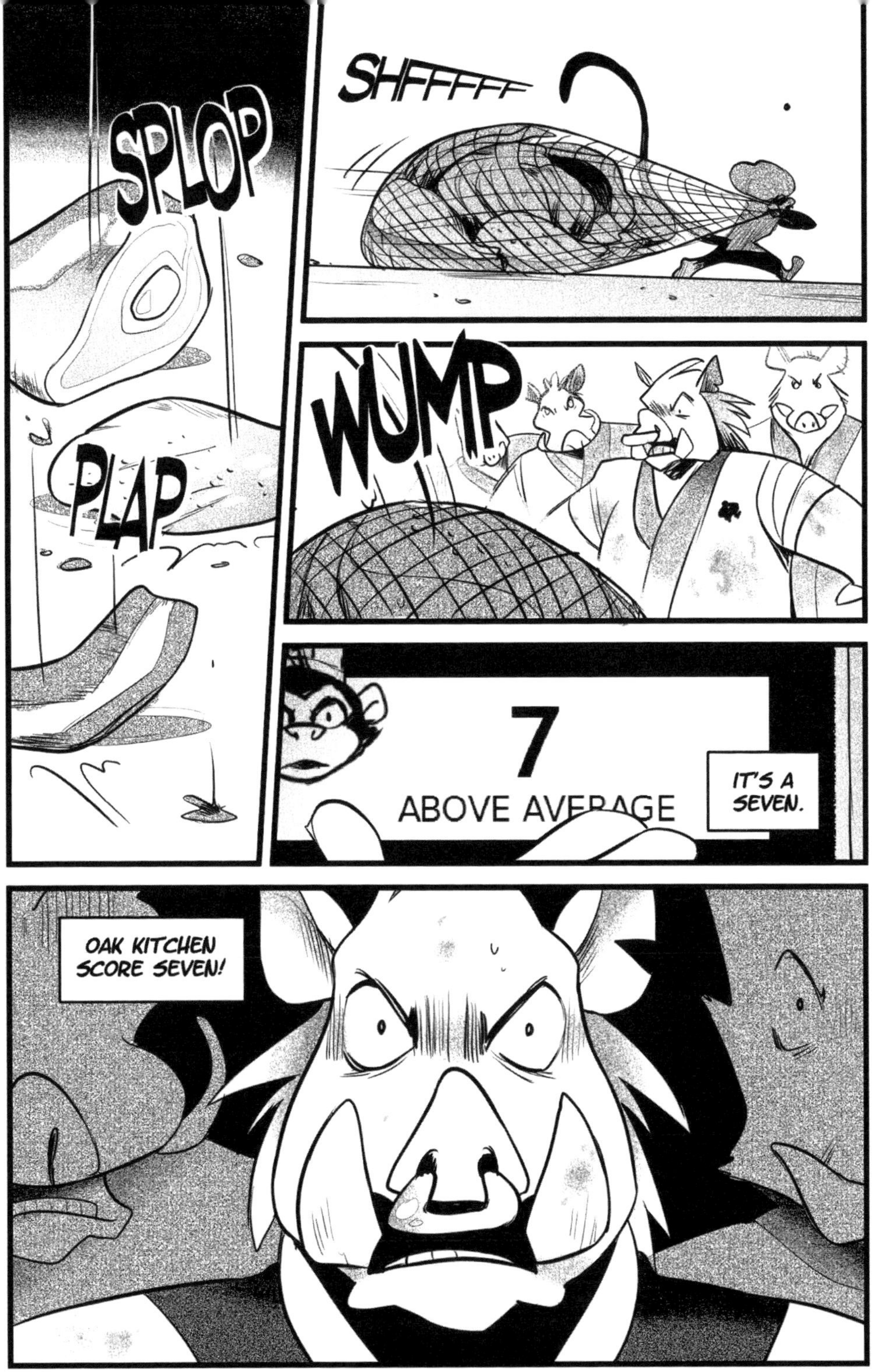
SPLOP
PLAP
SHFFFFFF
WUMP
7
ABOVE AVERAGE
IT'S A SEVEN.
OAK KITCHEN SCORE SEVEN!

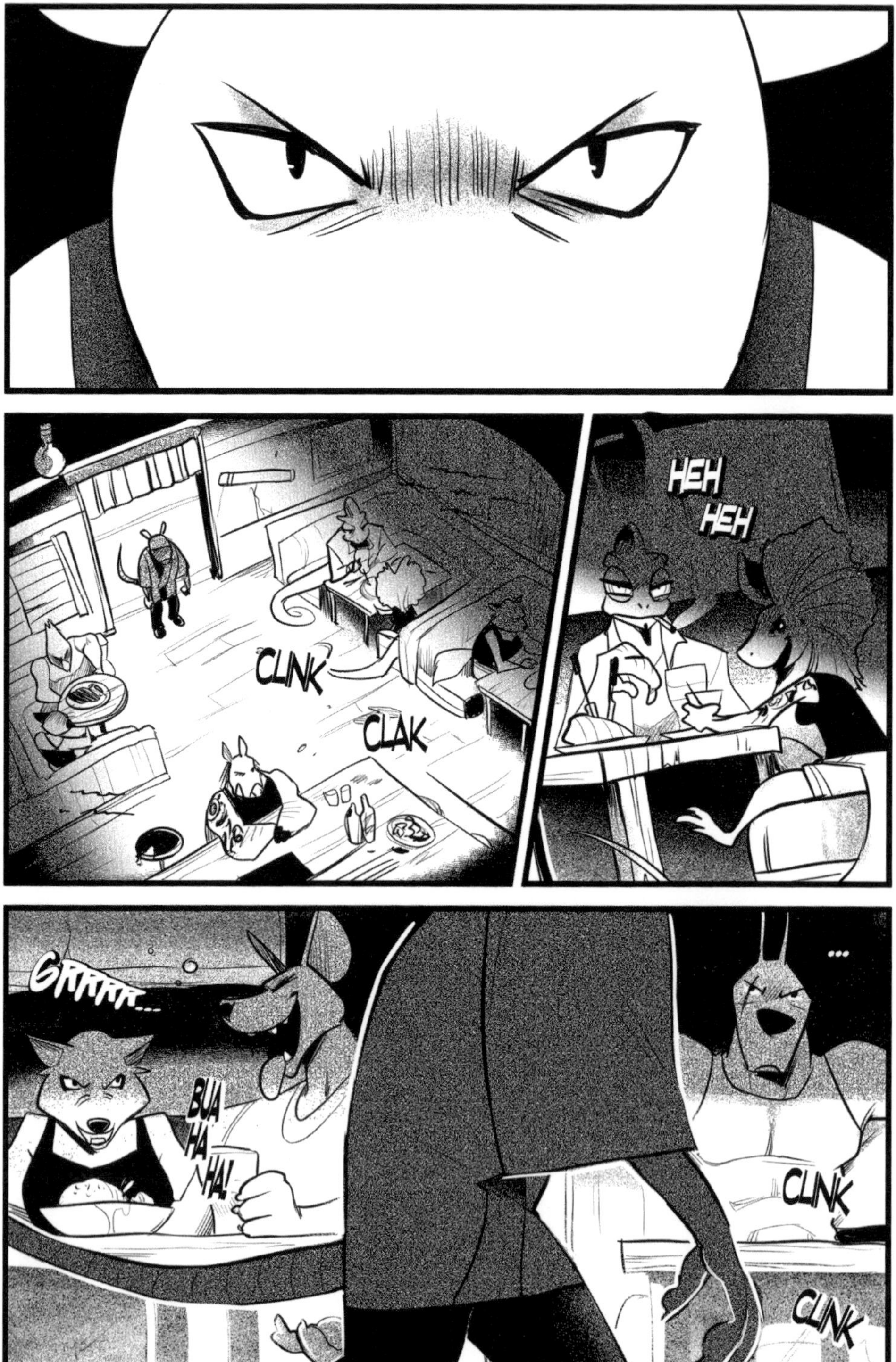
CLINK
CLAK
HEH
HEH
GRRRR...
BUA HA HA!
...
CLINK
CLINK

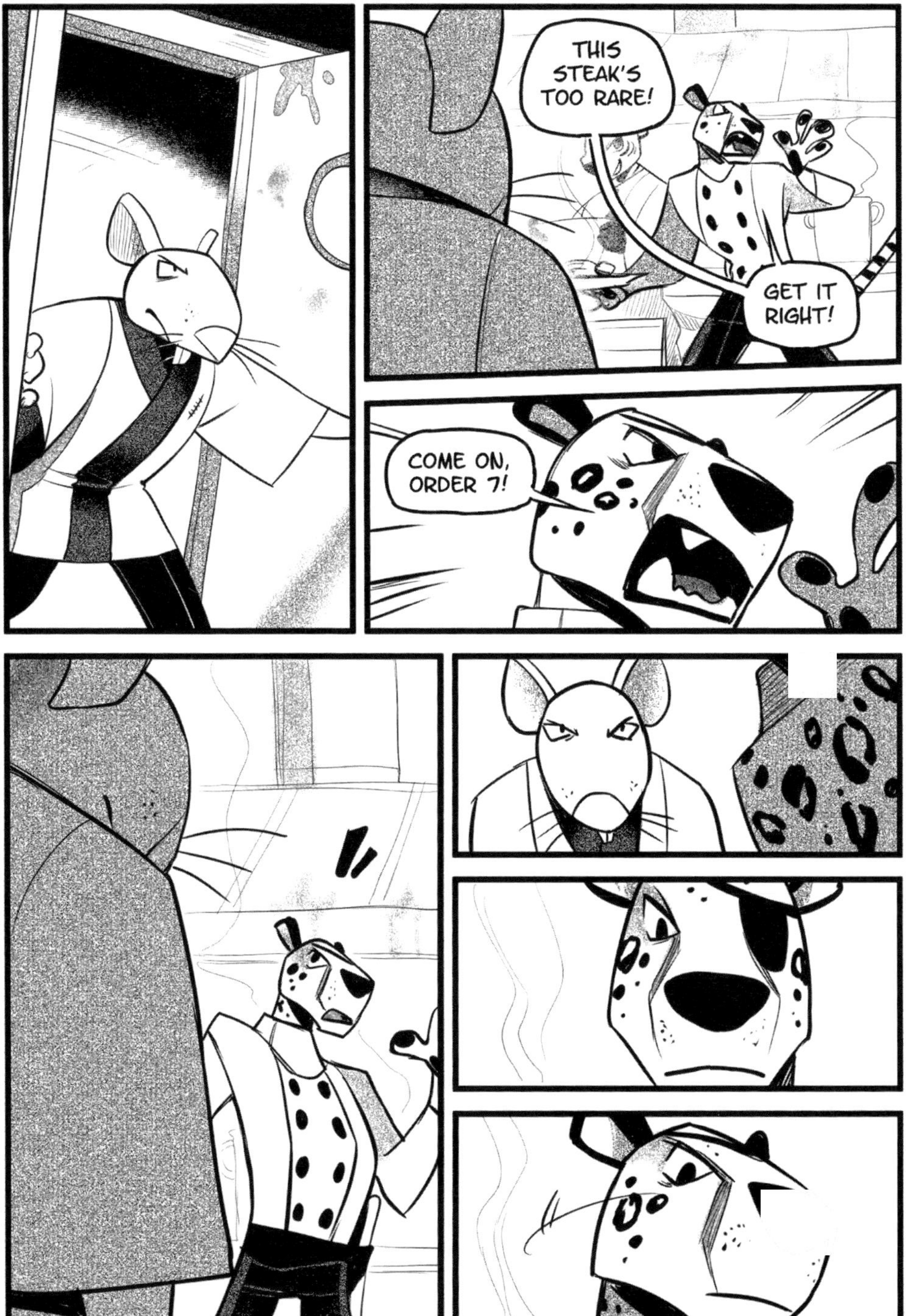
THIS STEAK'S TOO RARE!
GET IT RIGHT!
COME ON, ORDER 7!

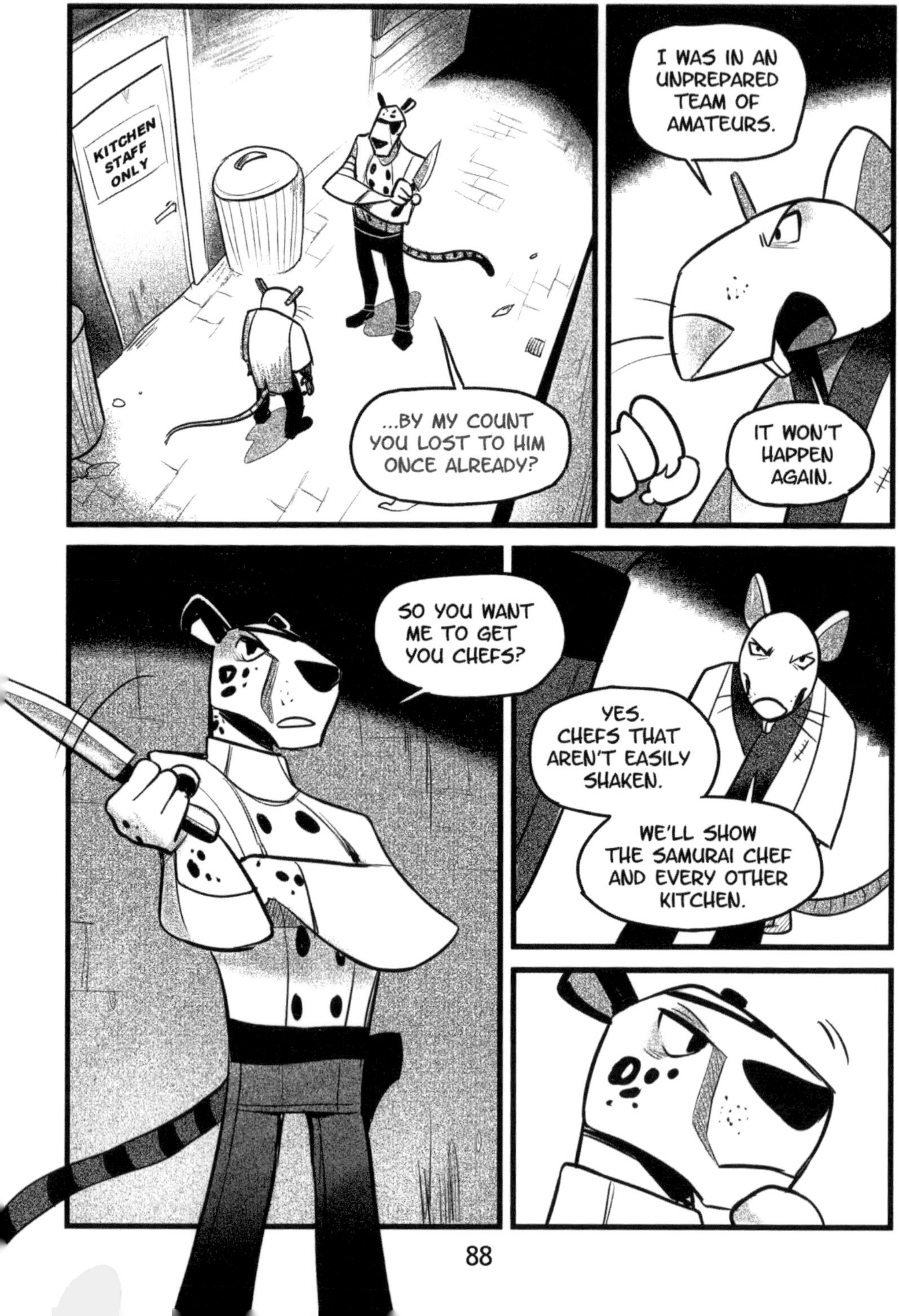
KITCHEN STAFF ONLY
...BY MY COUNT YOU LOST TO HIM ONCE ALREADY?
I WAS IN AN UNPREPARED TEAM OF AMATEURS.
IT WON'T HAPPEN AGAIN.
SO YOU WANT ME TO GET YOU CHEFS?
YES. CHEFS THAT AREN'T EASILY SHAKEN.
WE'LL SHOW THE SAMURAI CHEF AND EVERY OTHER KITCHEN.

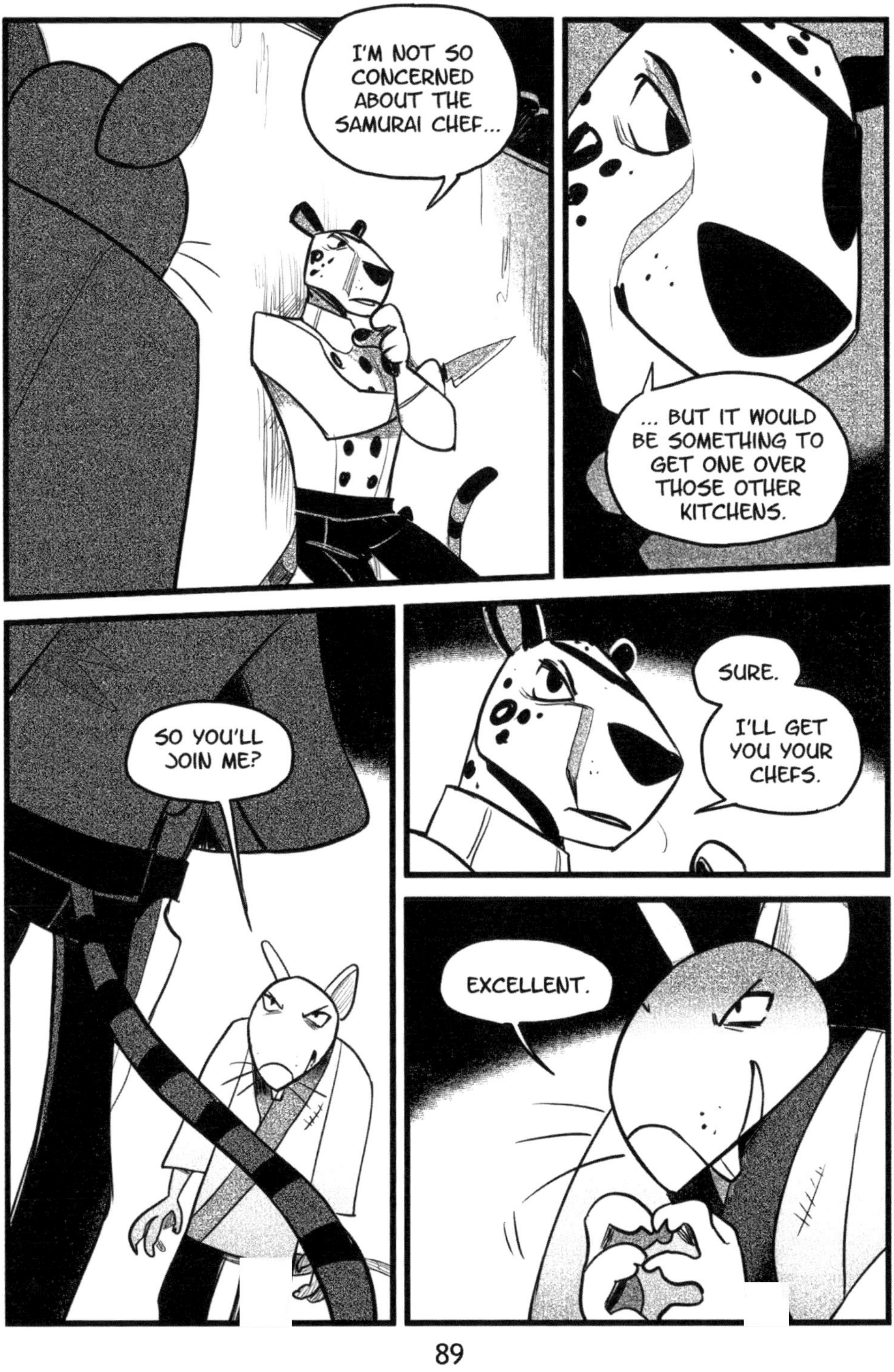
I'M NOT SO CONCERNED ABOUT THE SAMURAI CHEF...
... BUT IT WOULD BE SOMETHING TO GET ONE OVER THOSE OTHER KITCHENS.
SO YOU'LL JOIN ME?
SURE.
I'LL GET YOU YOUR CHEFS.
EXCELLENT.

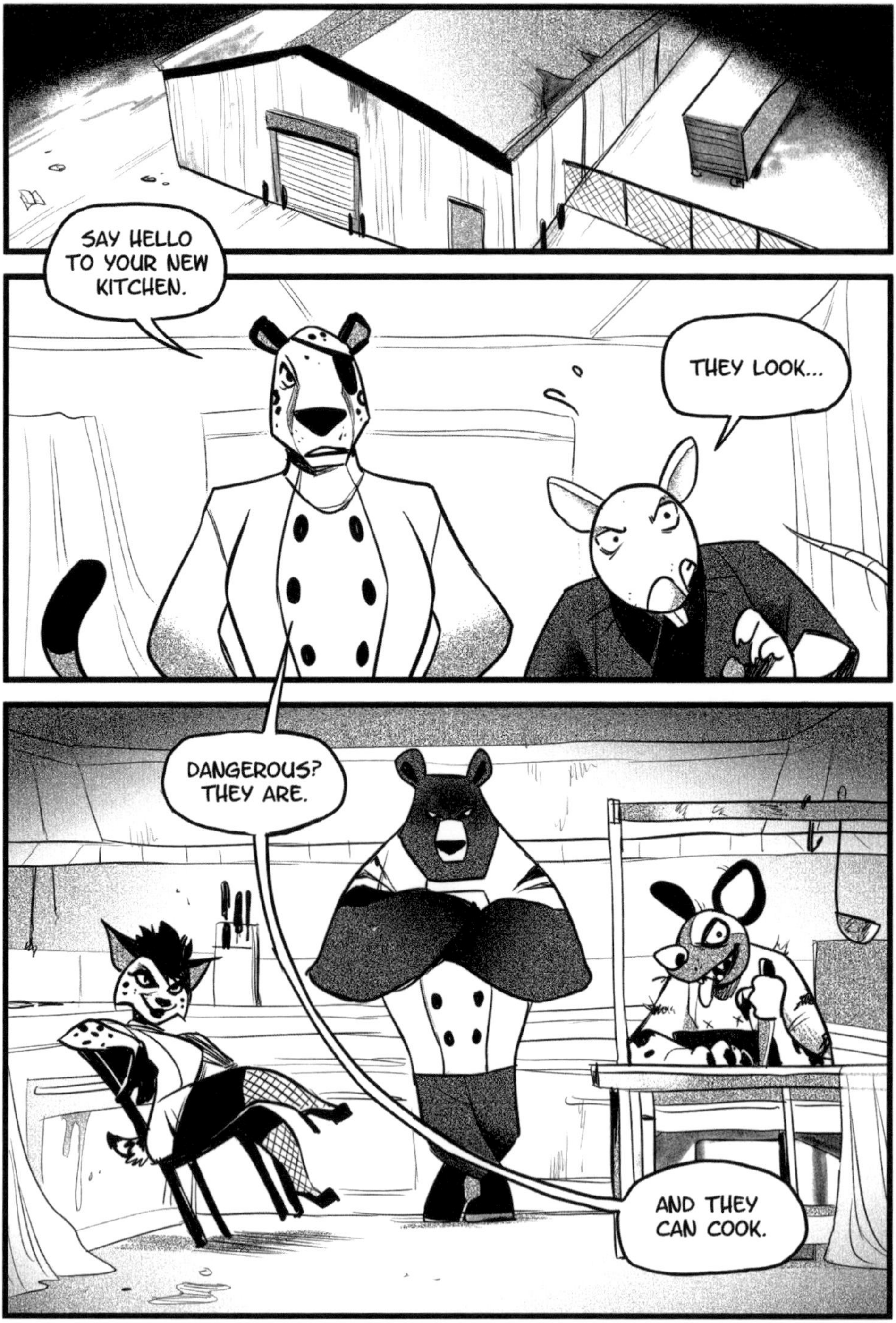
SAY HELLO TO YOUR NEW KITCHEN.
THEY LOOK...
DANGEROUS? THEY ARE.
AND THEY CAN COOK.

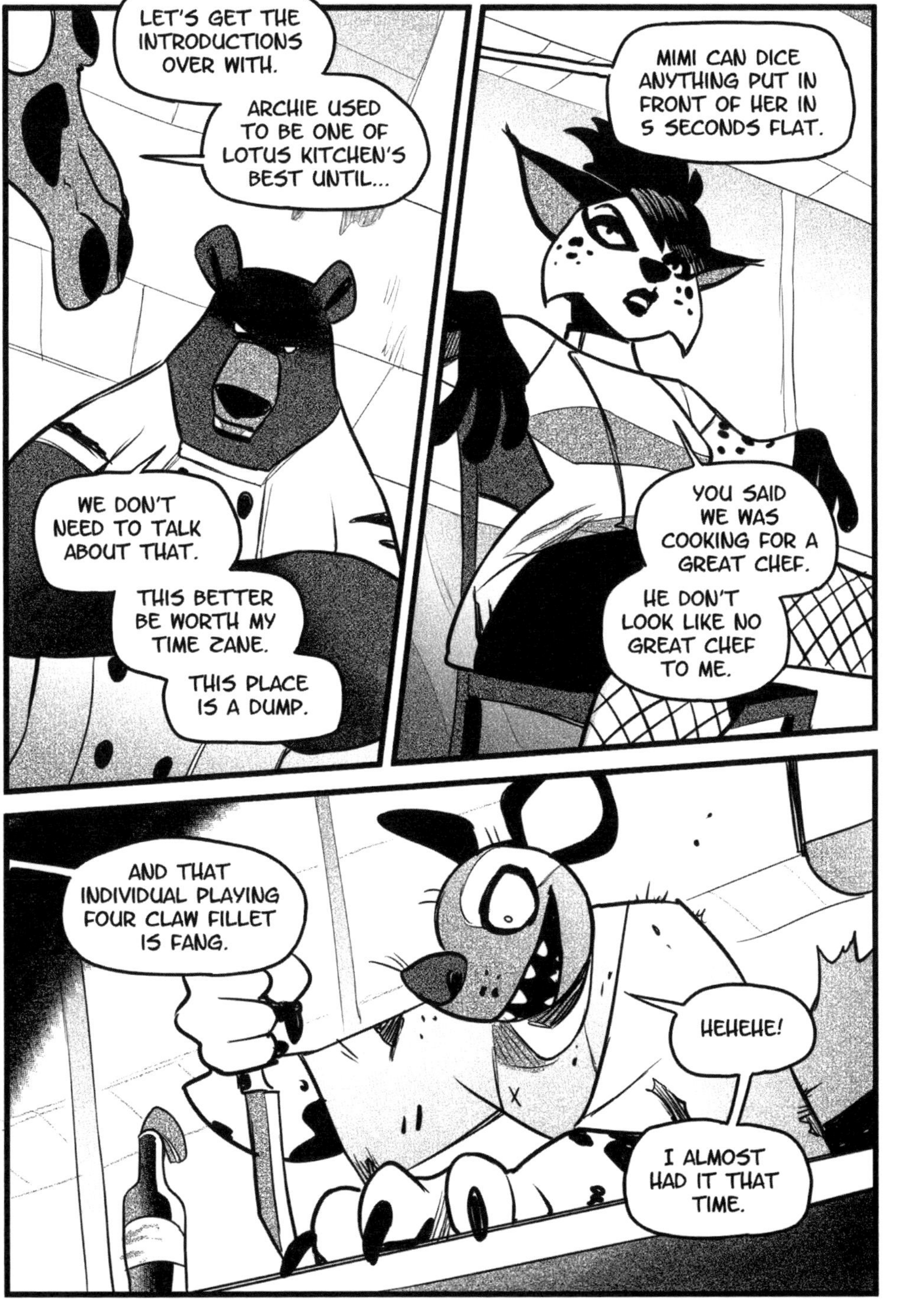
LET'S GET THE INTRODUCTIONS OVER WITH.
ARCHIE USED TO BE ONE OF LOTUS KITCHEN'S BEST UNTIL...
WE DON'T NEED TO TALK ABOUT THAT.
THIS BETTER BE WORTH MY TIME ZANE.
THIS PLACE IS A DUMP.
MIMI CAN DICE ANYTHING PUT IN FRONT OF HER IN 5 SECONDS FLAT.
YOU SAID WE WAS COOKING FOR A GREAT CHEF.
HE DON'T LOOK LIKE NO GREAT CHEF TO ME.
AND THAT INDIVIDUAL PLAYING FOUR CLAW FILLET IS FANG.
HEHEHE!
I ALMOST HAD IT THAT TIME.

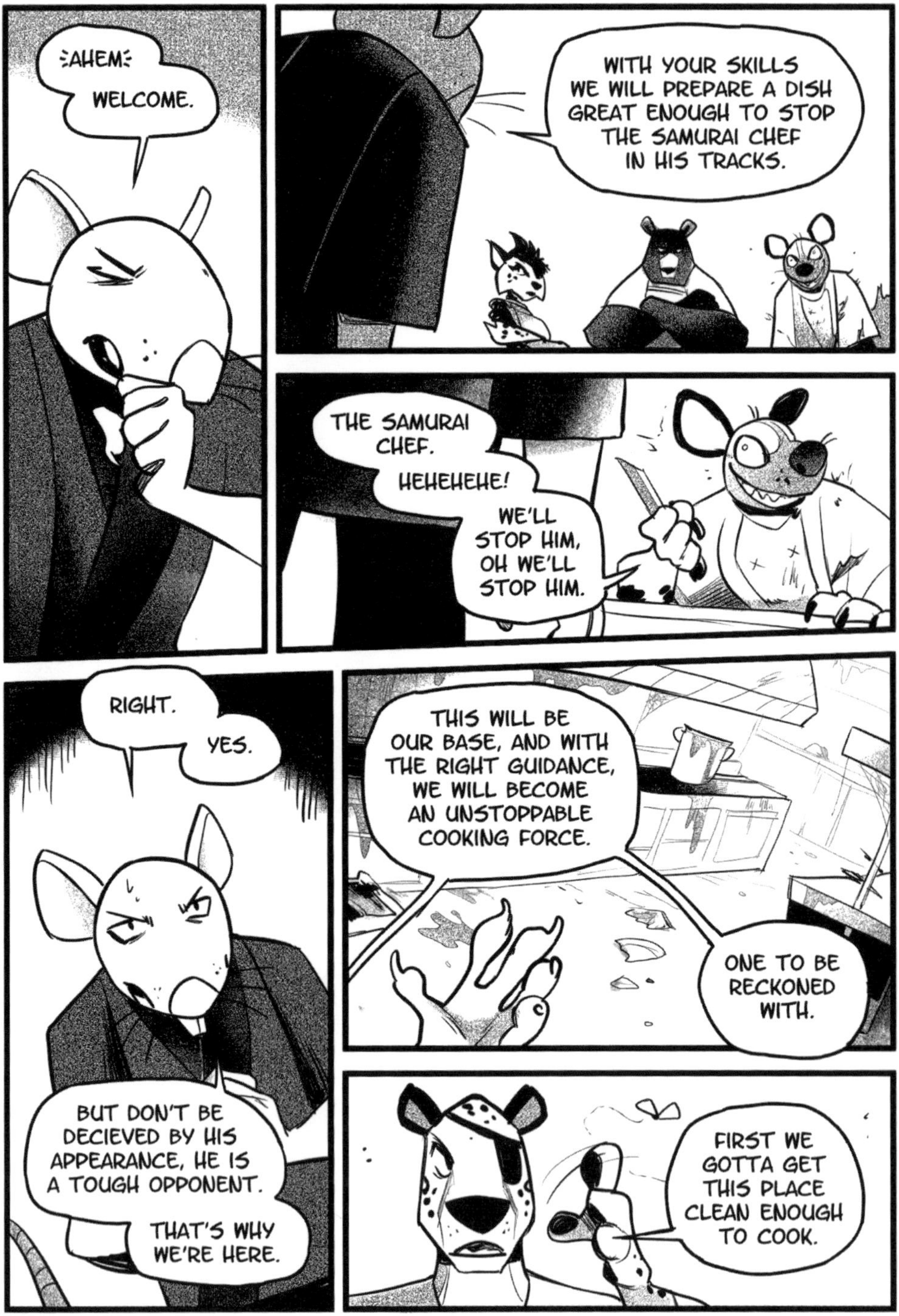
AHEM
WELCOME.
WITH YOUR SKILLS WE WILL PREPARE A DISH GREAT ENOUGH TO STOP THE SAMURAI CHEF IN HIS TRACKS.
THE SAMURAI CHEF.
HEHEHEHE!
WE'LL STOP HIM, OH WE'LL STOP HIM.
RIGHT.
YES.
BUT DON'T BE DECIEVED BY HIS APPEARANCE, HE IS A TOUGH OPPONENT.
THAT'S WHY WE'RE HERE.
THIS WILL BE OUR BASE, AND WITH THE RIGHT GUIDANCE, WE WILL BECOME AN UNSTOPPABLE COOKING FORCE.
ONE TO BE RECKONED WITH.
FIRST WE GOTTA GET THIS PLACE CLEAN ENOUGH TO COOK.

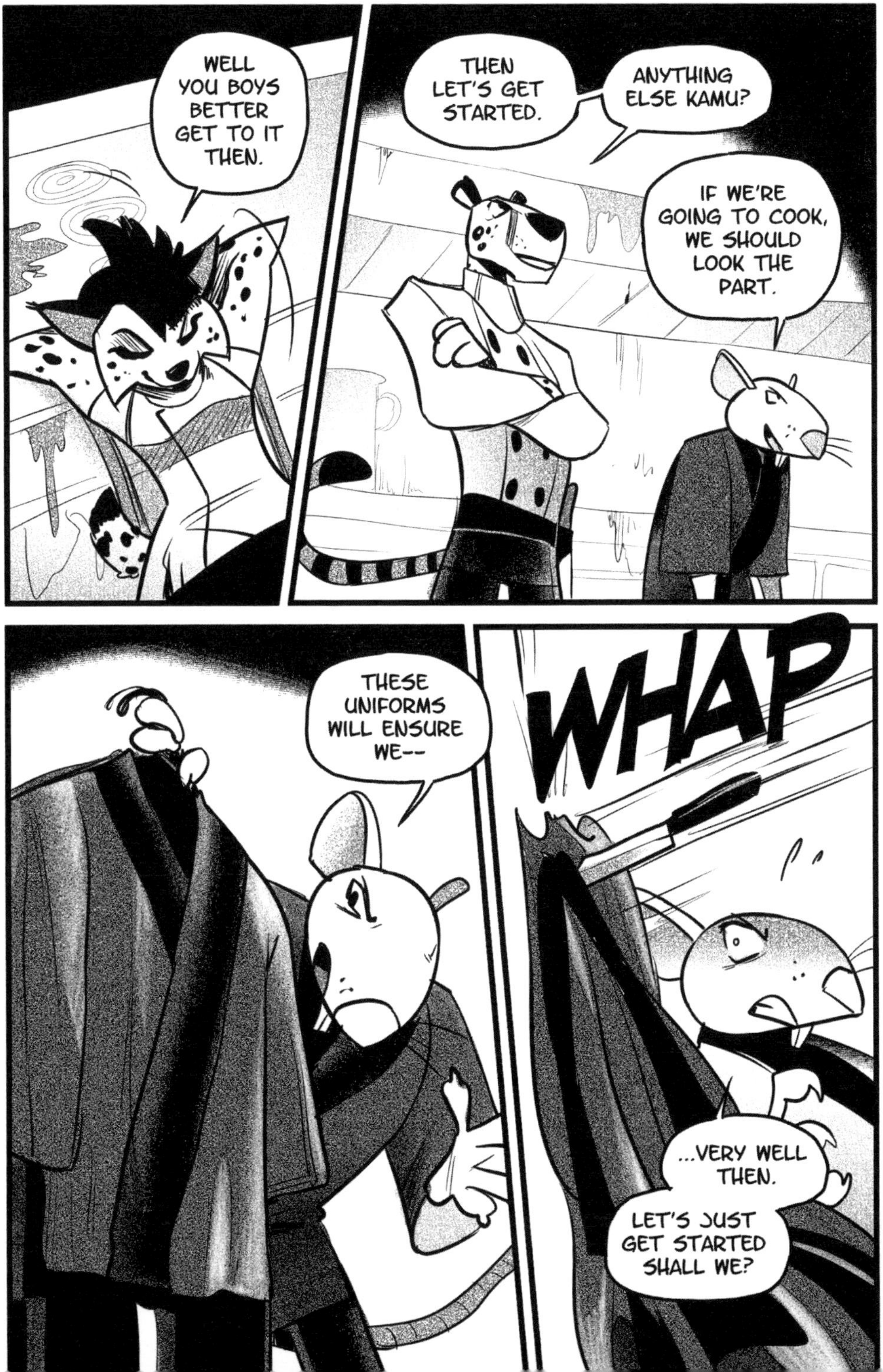
WELL YOU BOYS BETTER GET TO IT THEN.
THEN LET'S GET STARTED.
ANYTHING ELSE KAMU?
IF WE'RE GOING TO COOK, WE SHOULD LOOK THE PART.
THESE UNIFORMS WILL ENSURE WE--
WHAP
...VERY WELL THEN.
LET'S JUST GET STARTED SHALL WE?

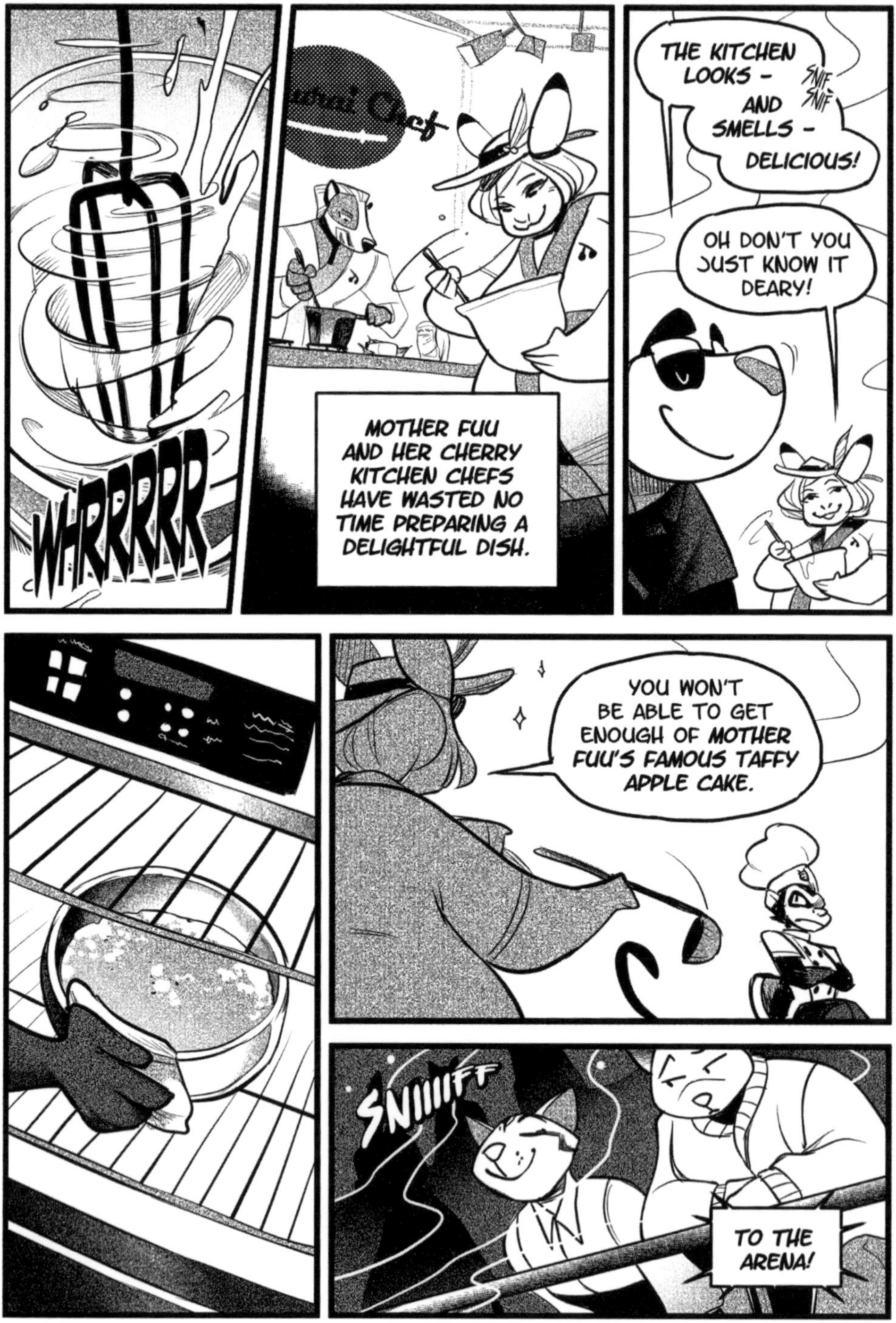
WHRRRRR
MOTHER FUU AND HER CHERRY KITCHEN CHEFS HAVE WASTED NO TIME PREPARING A DELIGHTFUL DISH.
THE KITCHEN LOOKS - AND SMELLS - DELICIOUS!
SNIF SNIF
OH DON'T YOU JUST KNOW IT DEARY!
YOU WON'T BE ABLE TO GET ENOUGH OF MOTHER FUU'S FAMOUS TAFFY APPLE CAKE.
SNIIIIFF
TO THE ARENA!

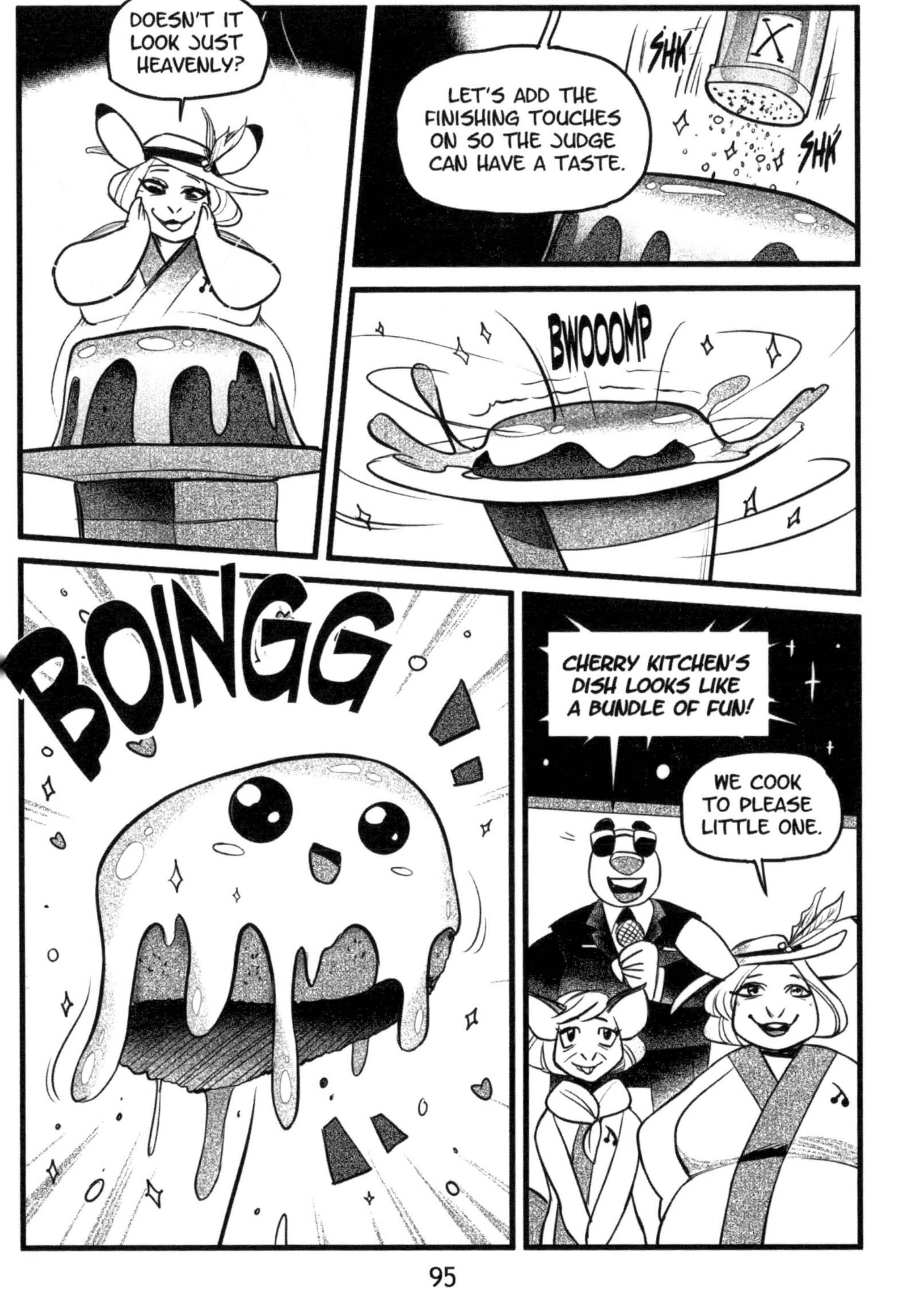
DOESN'T IT LOOK JUST HEAVENLY?
LET'S ADD THE FINISHING TOUCHES ON SO THE JUDGE CAN HAVE A TASTE.
SHK
SHK
BWOOOMP
BOINGG
CHERRY KITCHEN'S DISH LOOKS LIKE A BUNDLE OF FUN!
WE COOK TO PLEASE LITTLE ONE.

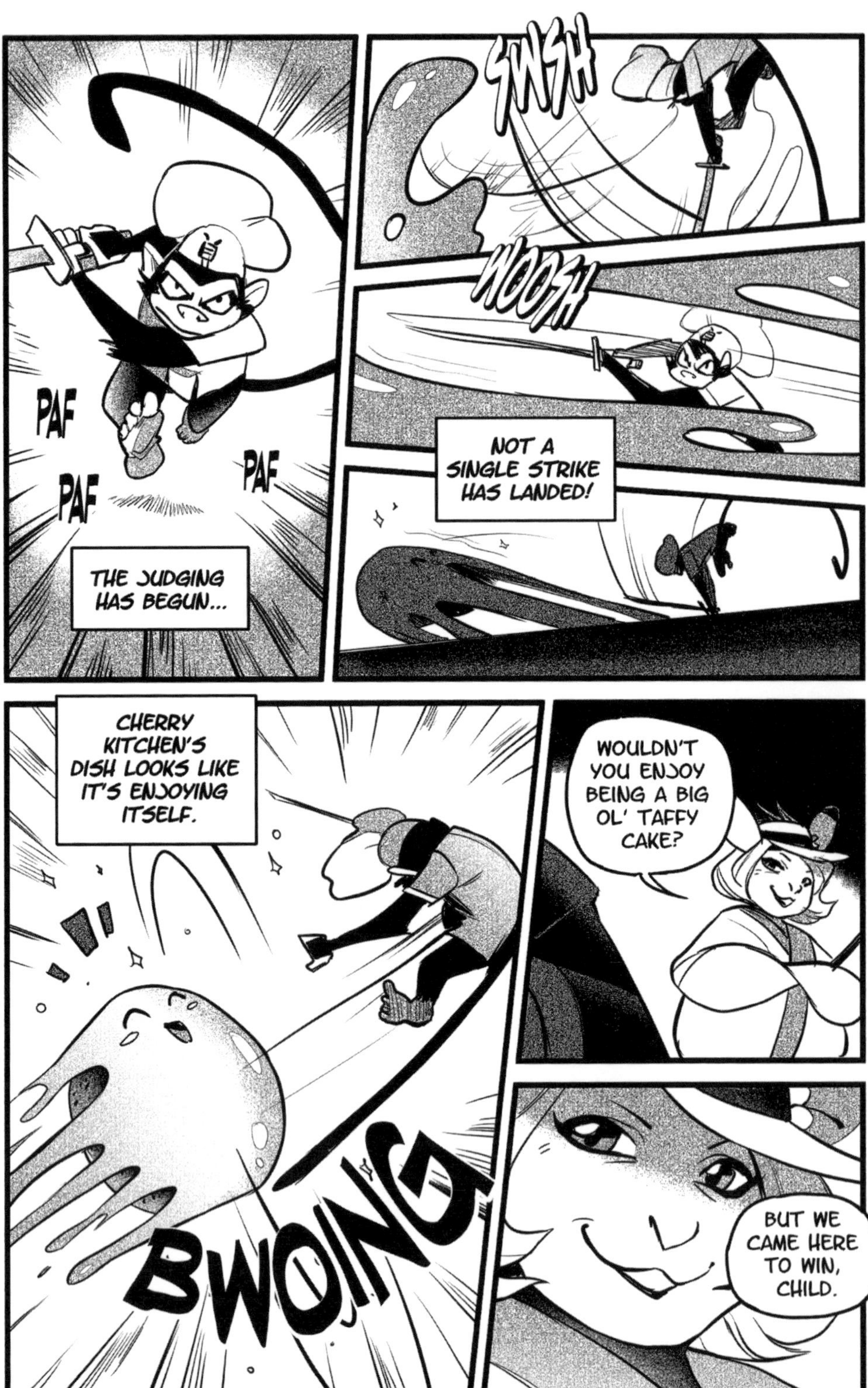
PAF
PAF
PAF
THE JUDGING HAS BEGUN...
SWSH
WOOSH
NOT A SINGLE STRIKE HAS LANDED!
CHERRY KITCHEN'S DISH LOOKS LIKE IT'S ENJOYING ITSELF.
BWOING
WOULDN'T YOU ENJOY BEING A BIG OL' TAFFY CAKE?
BUT WE CAME HERE TO WIN, CHILD.

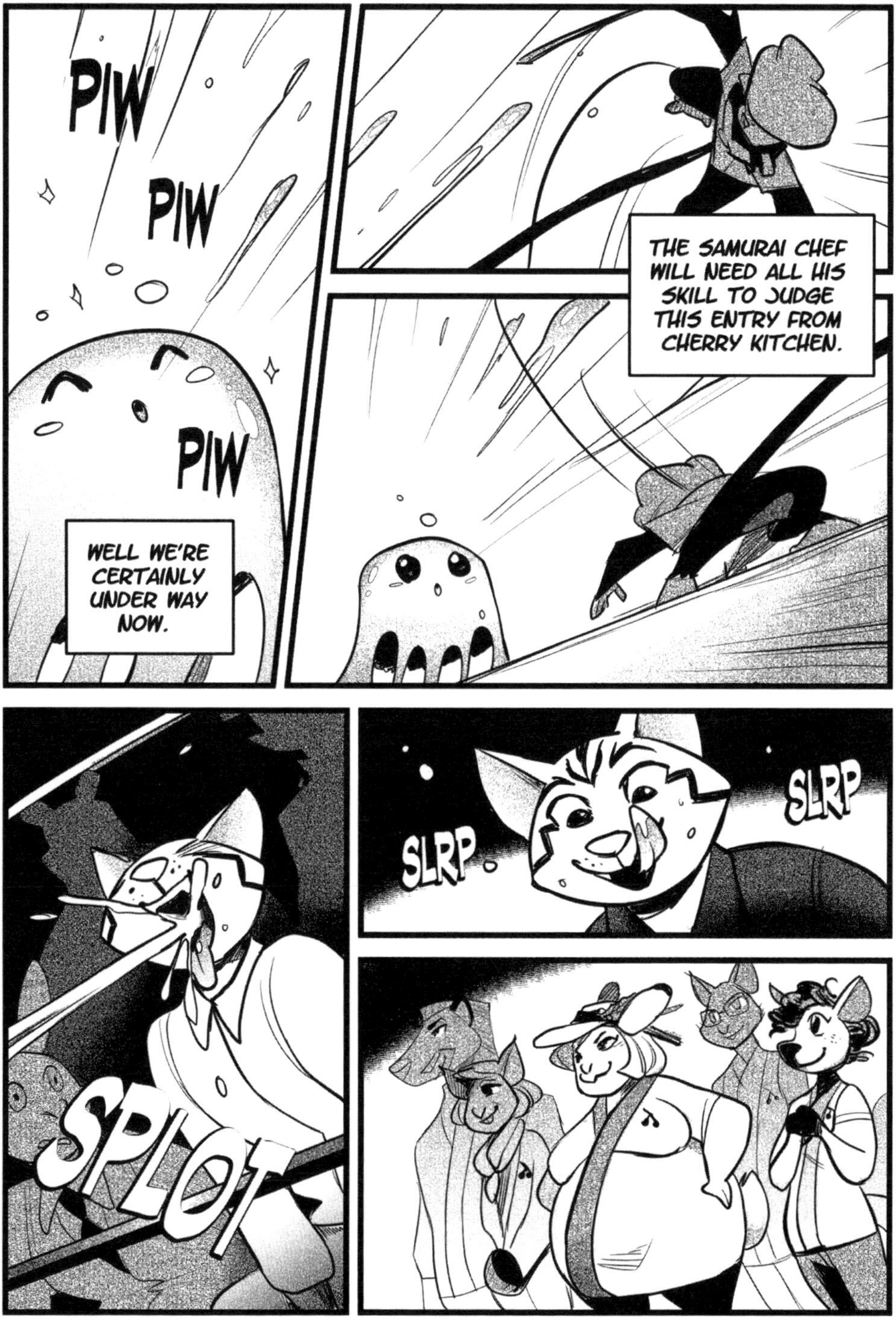
PIW
PIW
PIW
WELL WE'RE CERTAINLY UNDER WAY NOW.
THE SAMURAI CHEF WILL NEED ALL HIS SKILL TO JUDGE THIS ENTRY FROM CHERRY KITCHEN.
SPLOT
SLRP
SLRP

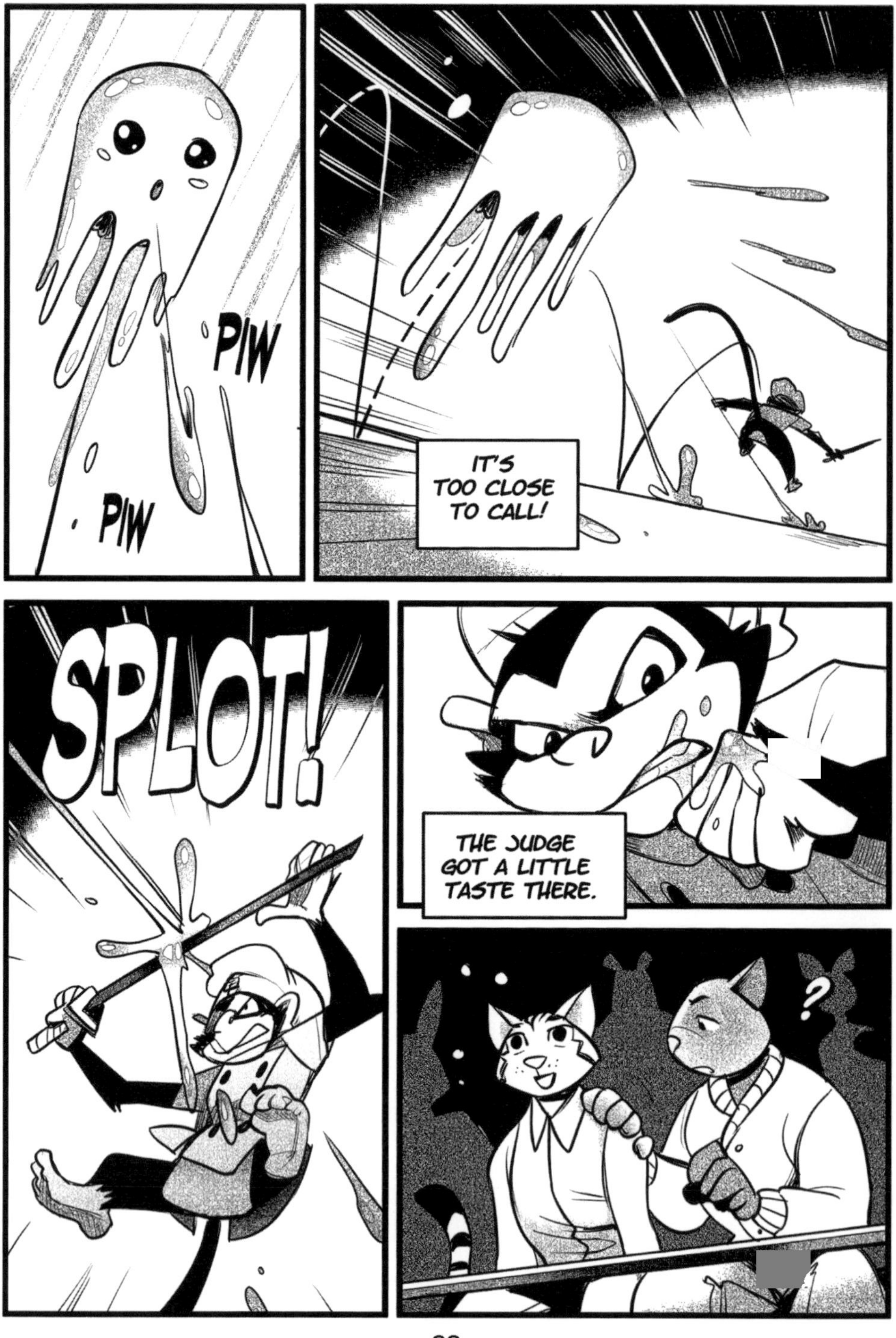
PIW
PIW
IT'S TOO CLOSE TO CALL!
SPLOT!
THE JUDGE GOT A LITTLE TASTE THERE.
?

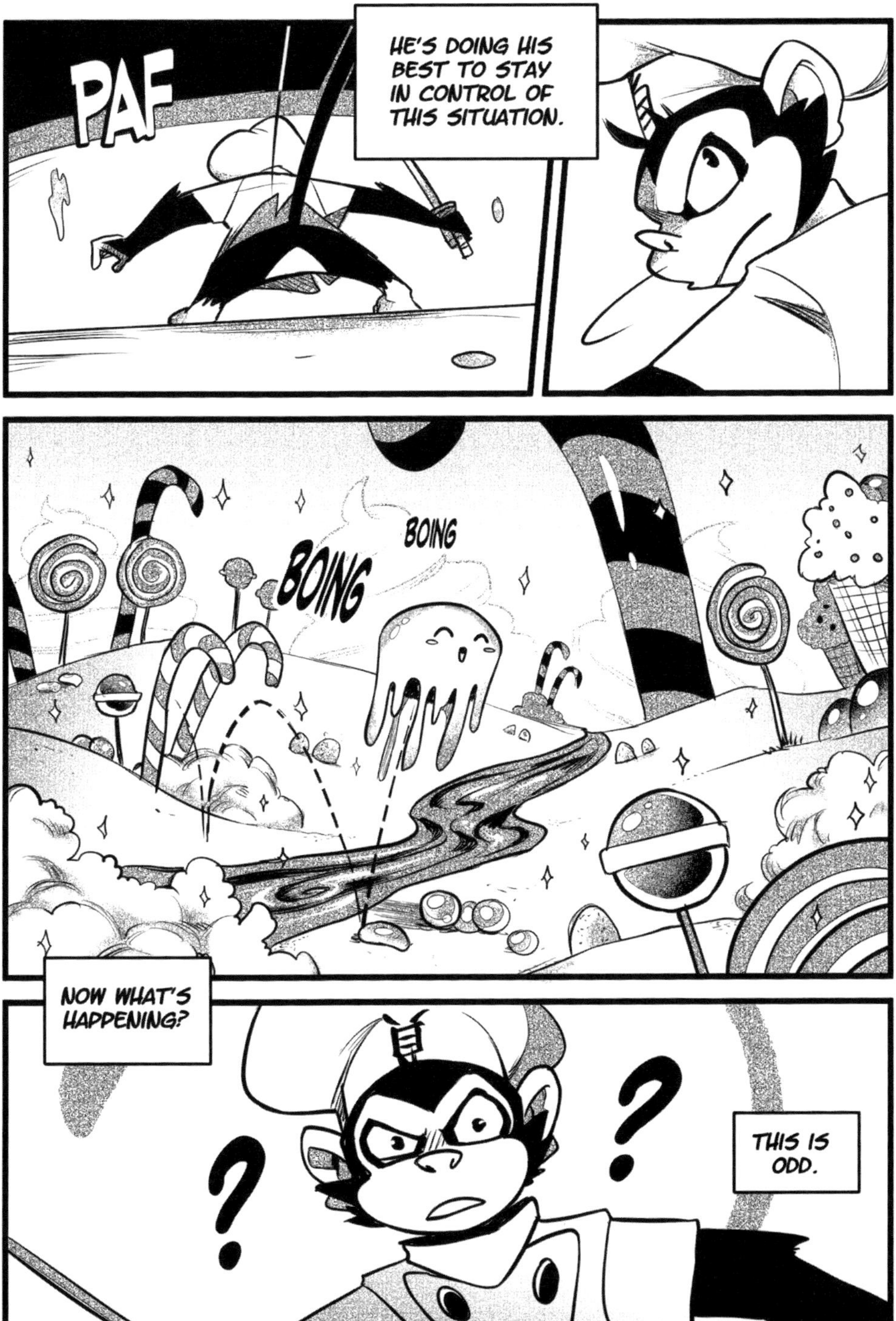
PAF
HE'S DOING HIS BEST TO STAY IN CONTROL OF THIS SITUATION.
BOING
BOING
NOW WHAT'S HAPPENING?
THIS IS ODD.

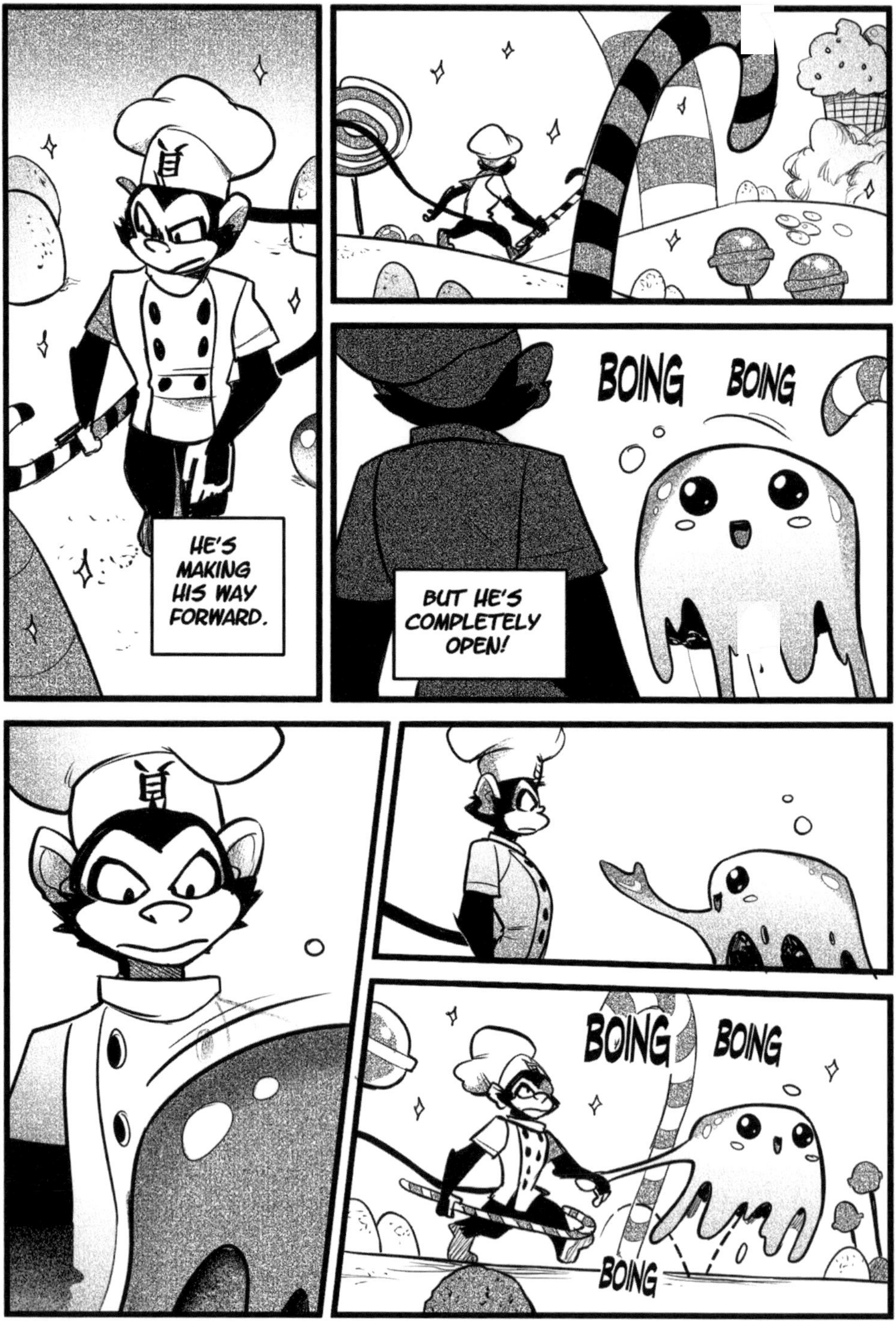
HE'S MAKING HIS WAY FORWARD.
BOING BOING
BUT HE'S COMPLETELY OPEN!
BOING BOING
BOING

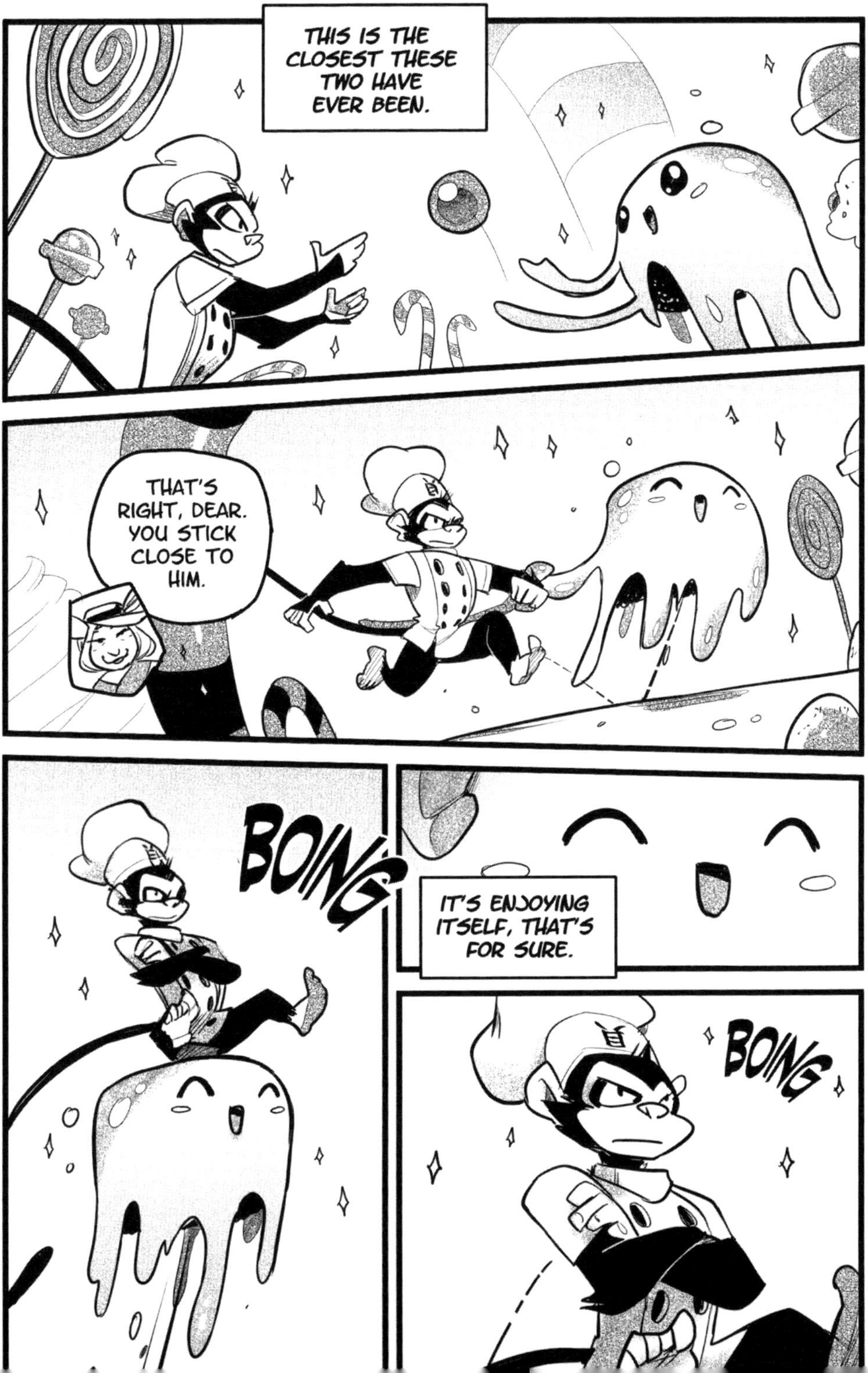
THIS IS THE CLOSEST THESE TWO HAVE EVER BEEN.
THAT'S RIGHT, DEAR. YOU STICK CLOSE TO HIM.
BOING
IT'S ENJOYING ITSELF, THAT'S FOR SURE.
BOING

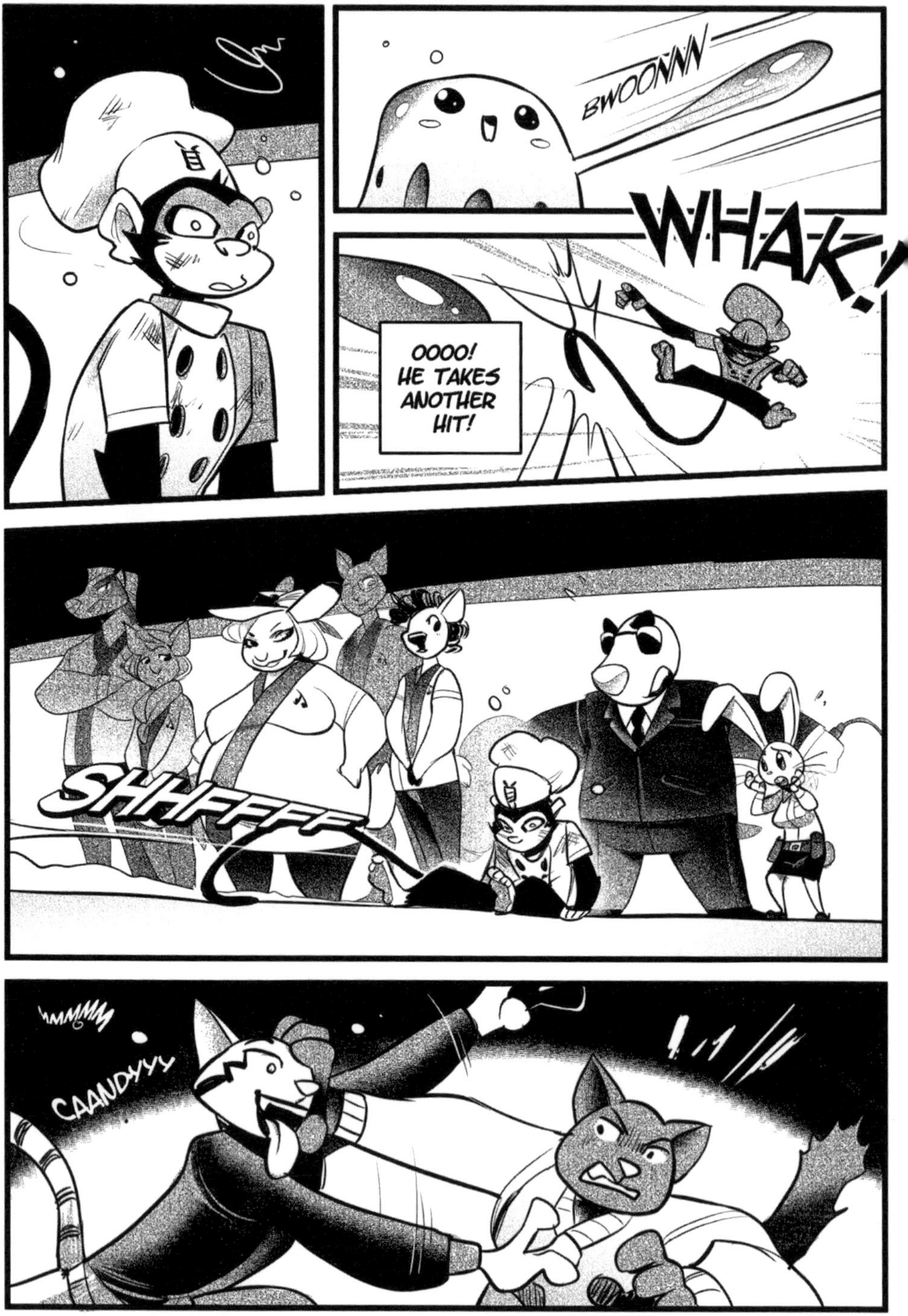
BWOONNN
WHAK!
OOOO! HE TAKES ANOTHER HIT!
SHHFFFF
MMMMM
CAANDYYY

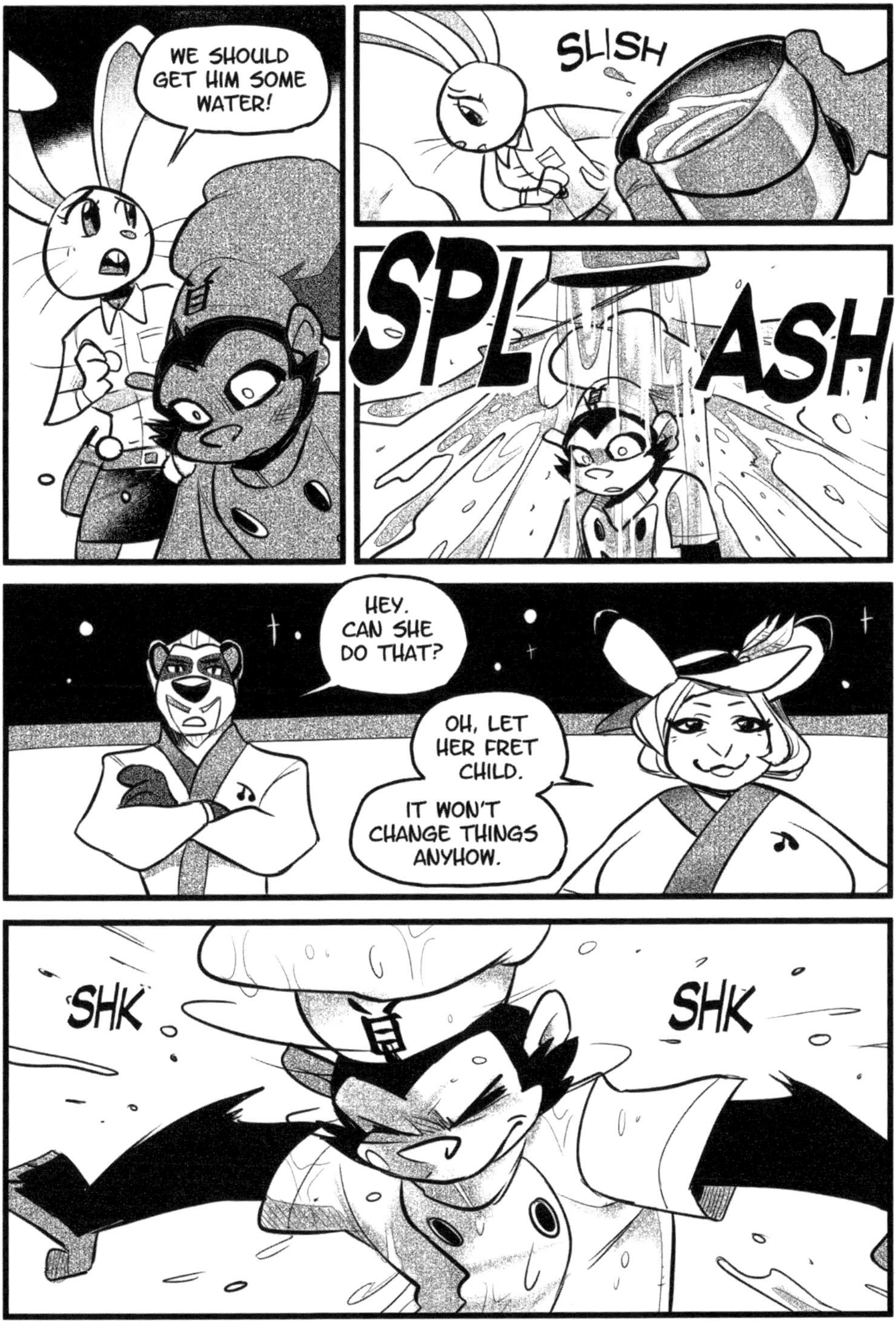
WE SHOULD GET HIM SOME WATER!
SLISH
SPLASH
HEY. CAN SHE DO THAT?
OH, LET HER FRET CHILD.
IT WON'T CHANGE THINGS ANYHOW.
SHK
SHK

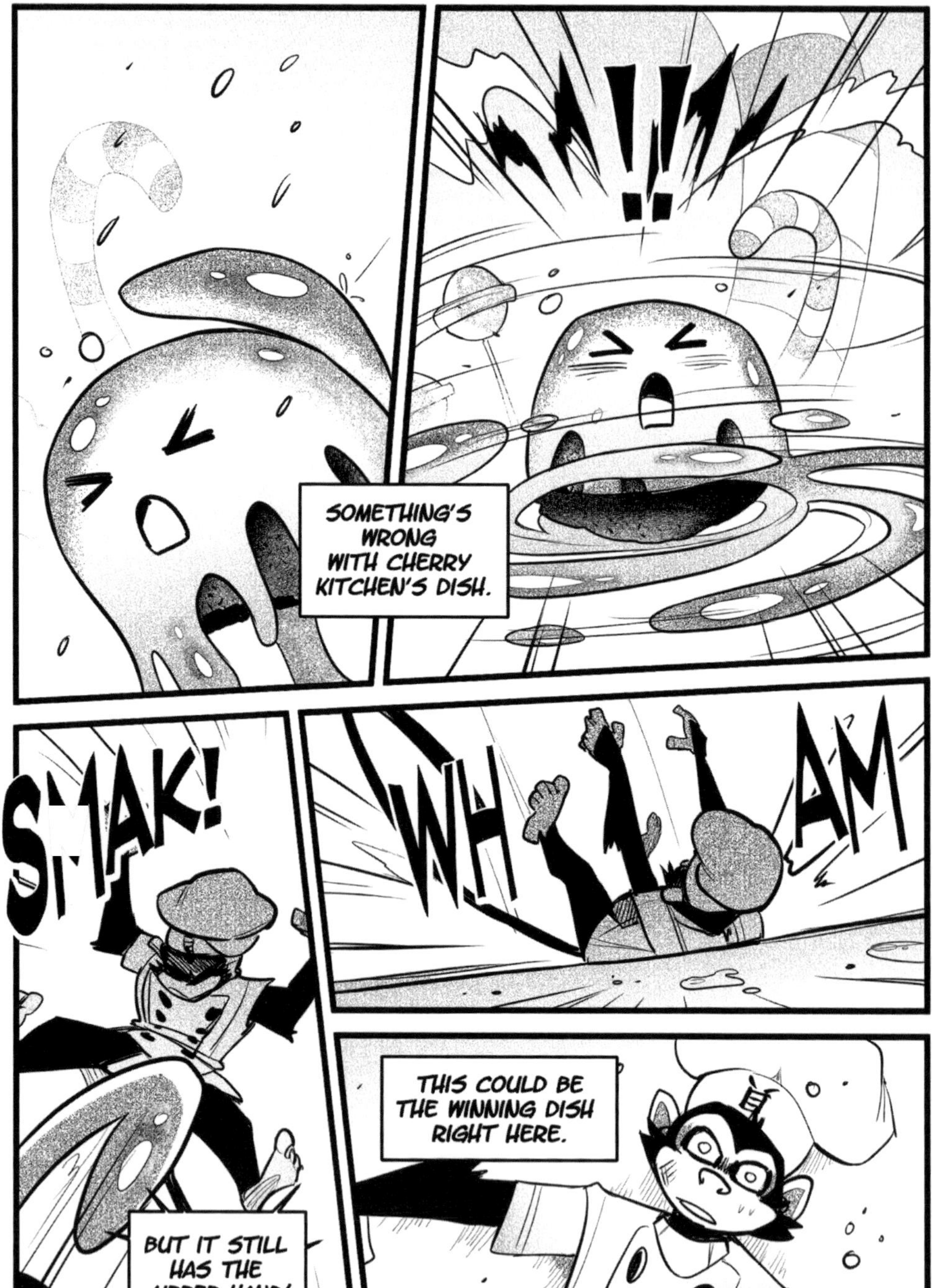
SOMETHING'S WRONG WITH CHERRY KITCHEN'S DISH.
!!
SMAK!
BUT IT STILL HAS THE UPPER HAND!
WHAM
THIS COULD BE THE WINNING DISH RIGHT HERE.

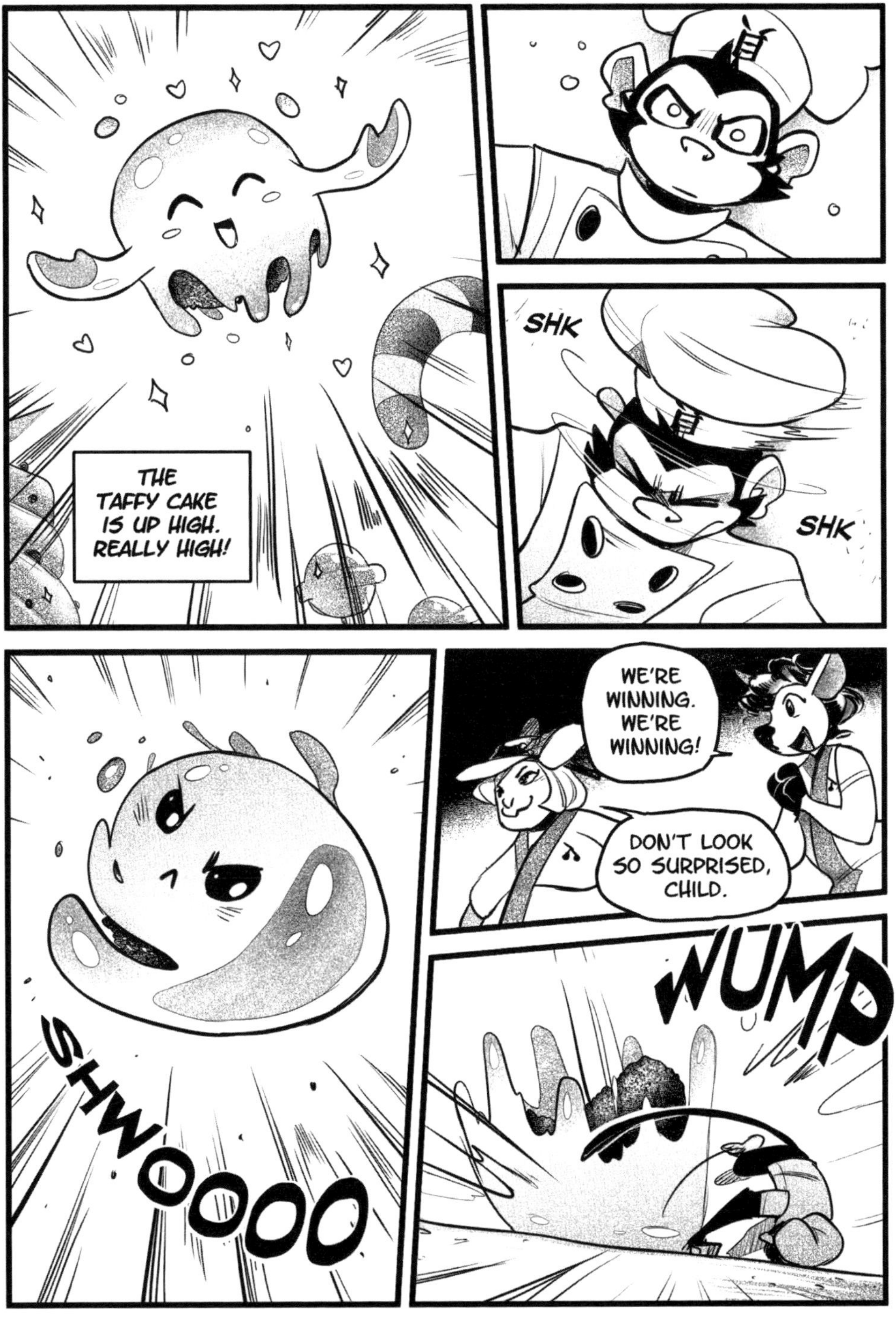
THE TAFFY CAKE IS UP HIGH. REALLY HIGH!
SHK
SHK
SHWOOOO
WE'RE WINNING. WE'RE WINNING!
DON'T LOOK SO SURPRISED, CHILD.
WUMP

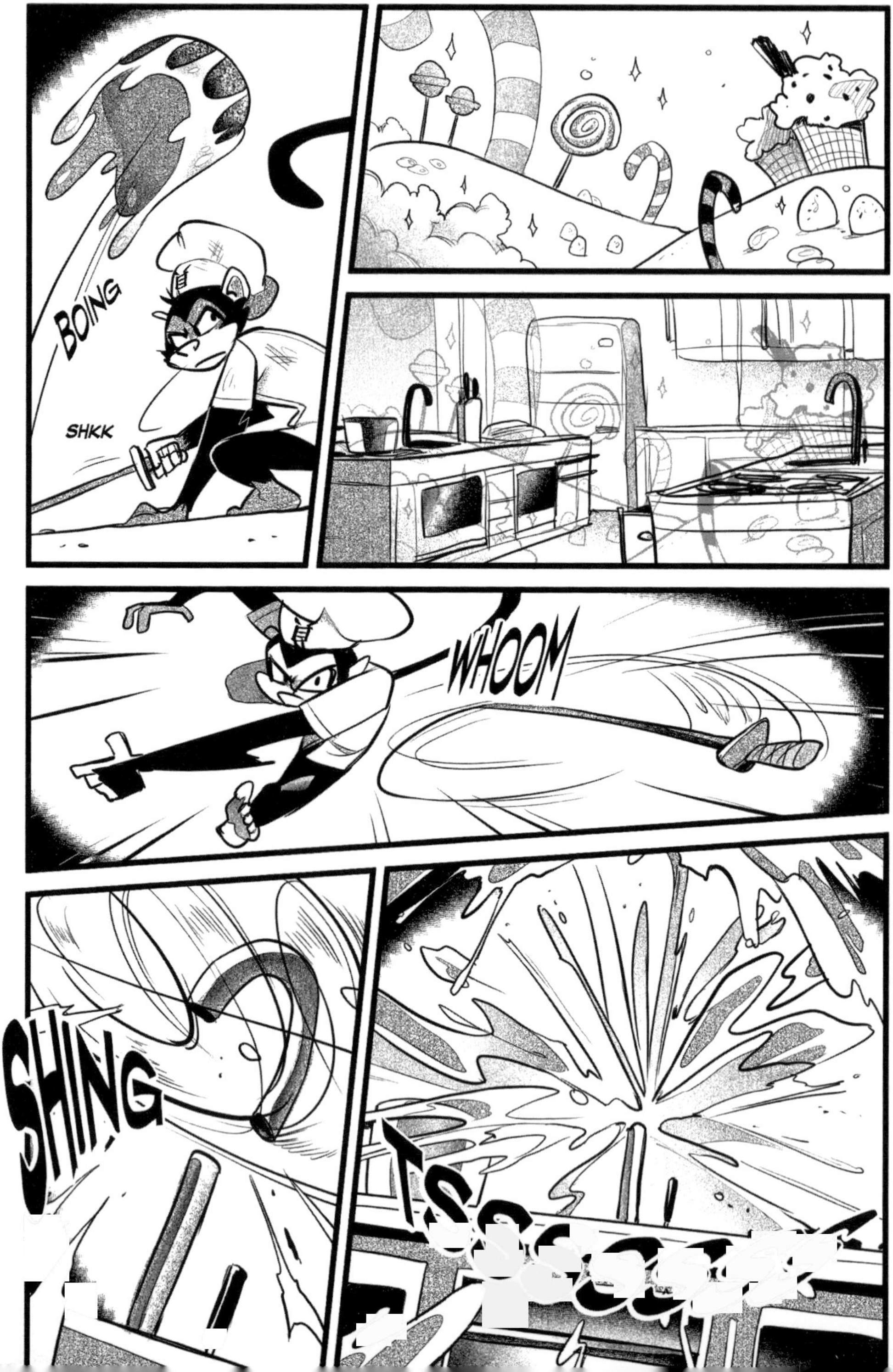
BOING
SHKK
WHOOM
SHING

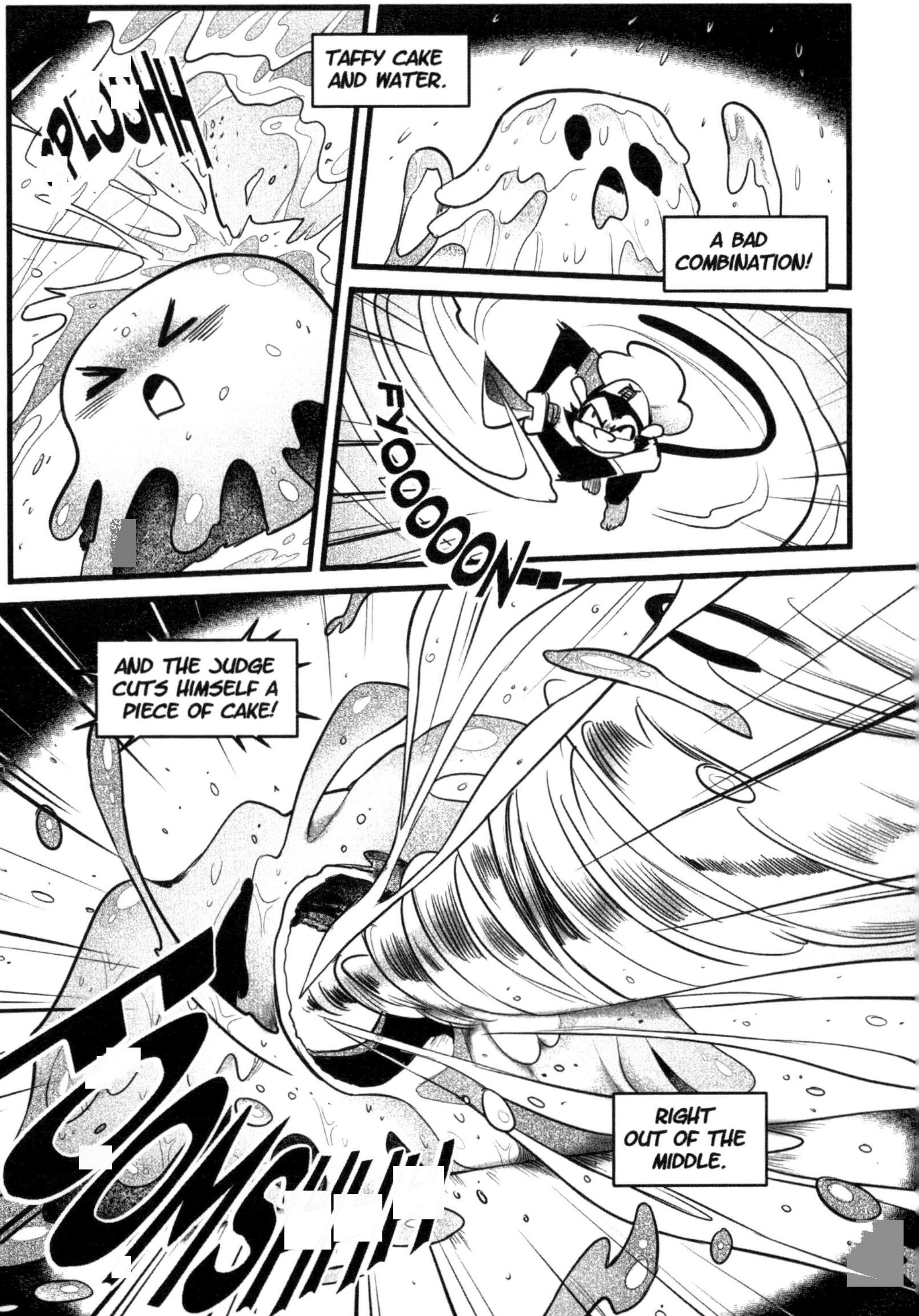
TAFFY CAKE AND WATER.
A BAD COMBINATION!
FYOOOOON--
AND THE JUDGE CUTS HIMSELF A PIECE OF CAKE!
RIGHT OUT OF THE MIDDLE.

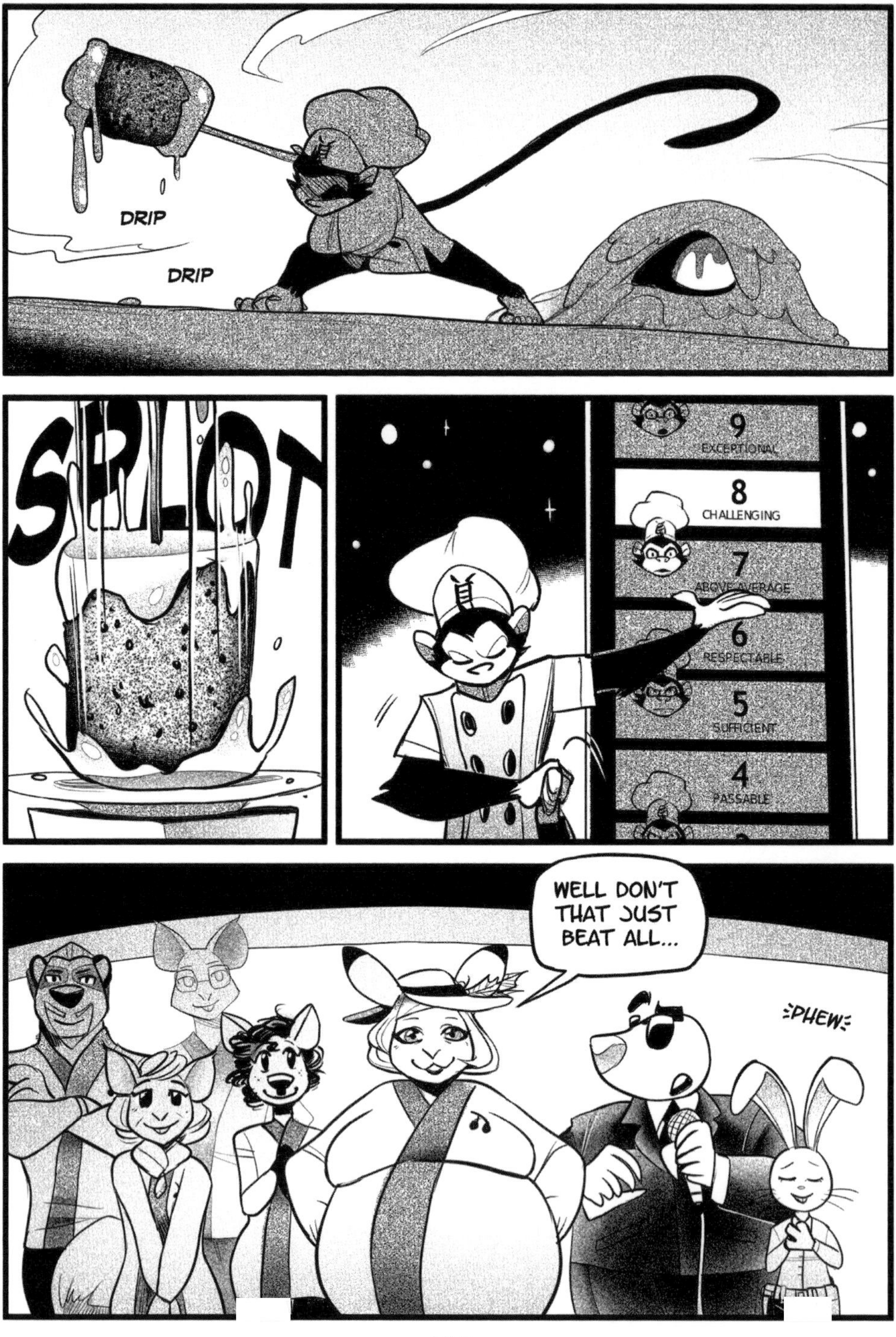
DRIP
DRIP
SPLOT
9
EXCEPTIONAL
8
CHALLENGING
7
ABOVE AVERAGE
6
RESPECTABLE
5
SUFFICIENT
4
PASSABLE
WELL DON'T THAT JUST BEAT ALL...
PHEW

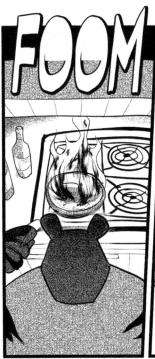

FOOM

THE HEAT HAS TO BE RIGHT!

sssss

sssss

THE HEAT IS RIGHT.

WE'VE DONE THIS ENOUGH TIMES.

AND WE'LL DO IT AGAIN!

THE QUALITY OF THE FINAL DISH DEPENDS ON THE QUALITY OF THE INGREDIENTS AND THE CARE TAKEN DURING COOKING.

AND IT'S ONE PART FLOUR TO TWO PARTS CURRY POWDER.

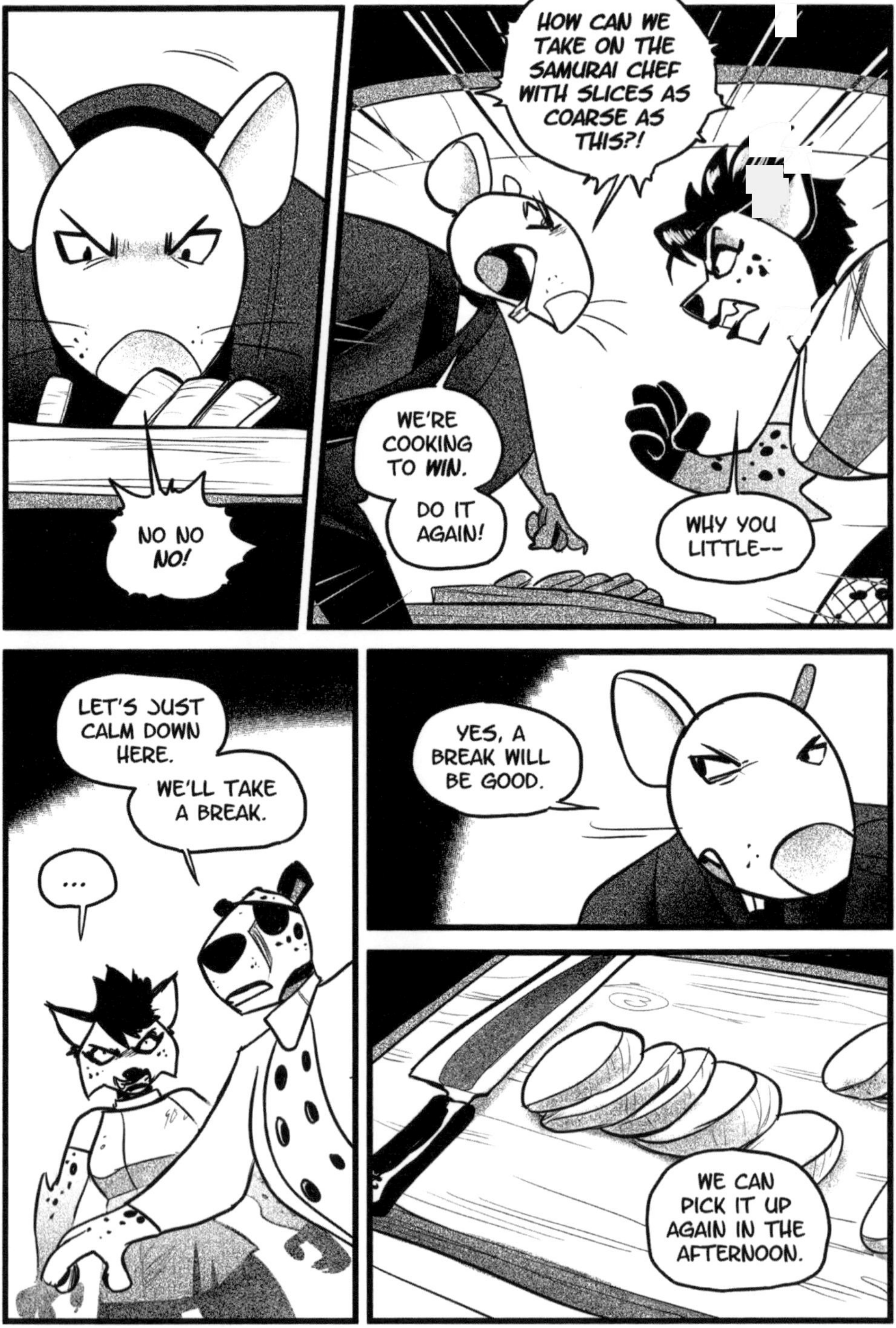
NO NO NO!
HOW CAN WE TAKE ON THE SAMURAI CHEF WITH SLICES AS COARSE AS THIS?!
WE'RE COOKING TO WIN.
DO IT AGAIN!
WHY YOU LITTLE--
LET'S JUST CALM DOWN HERE.
WE'LL TAKE A BREAK.
...
YES, A BREAK WILL BE GOOD.
WE CAN PICK IT UP AGAIN IN THE AFTERNOON.

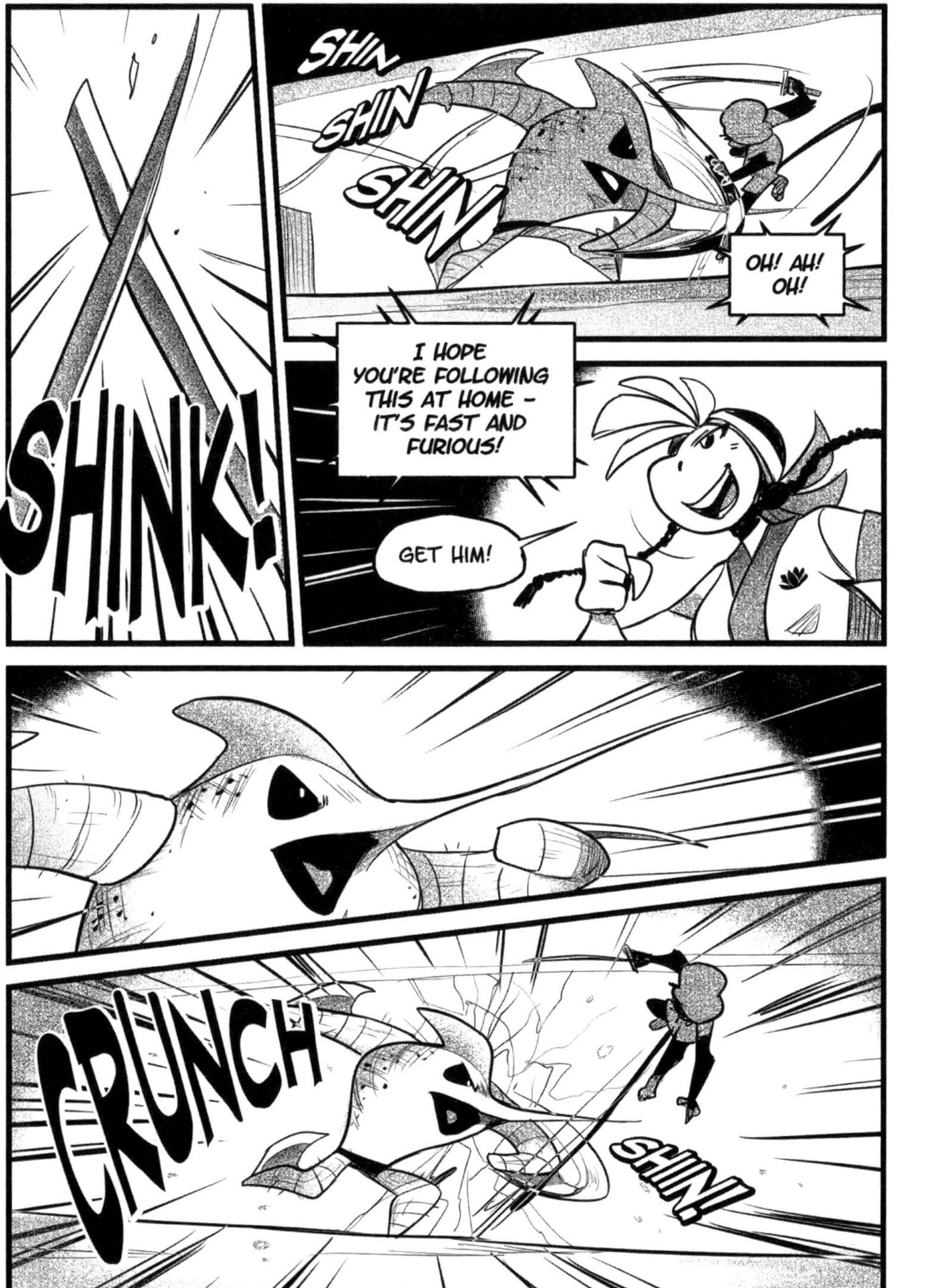
SHINK!
SHIN
SHIN
SHIN
OH! AH! OH!
I HOPE YOU'RE FOLLOWING THIS AT HOME - IT'S FAST AND FURIOUS!
GET HIM!
CRUNCH
SHIN!

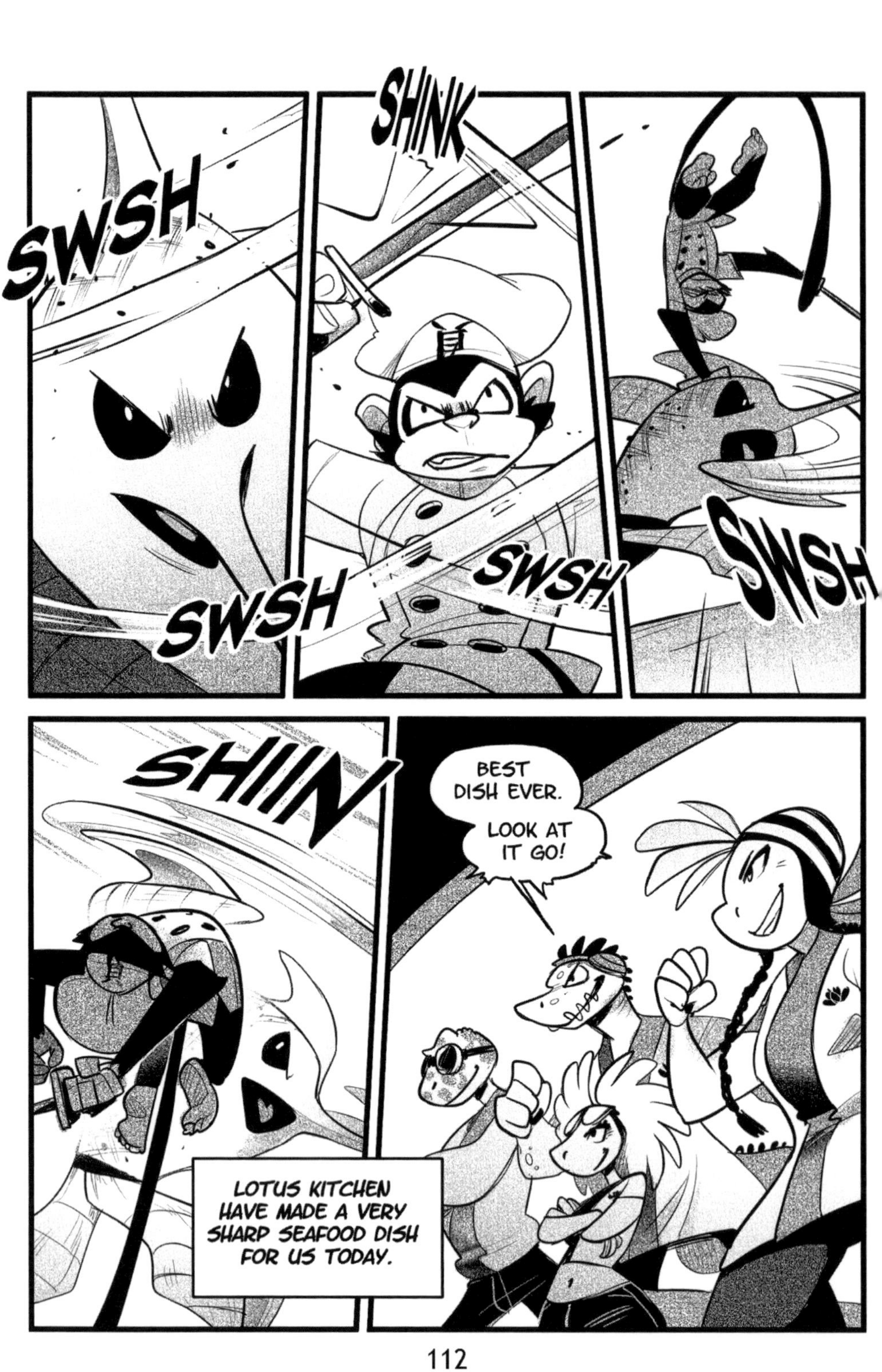
SWSH
SWSH
SHINK
SWSH
SWSH
SHIIN
LOTUS KITCHEN HAVE MADE A VERY SHARP SEAFOOD DISH FOR US TODAY.
BEST DISH EVER.
LOOK AT IT GO!

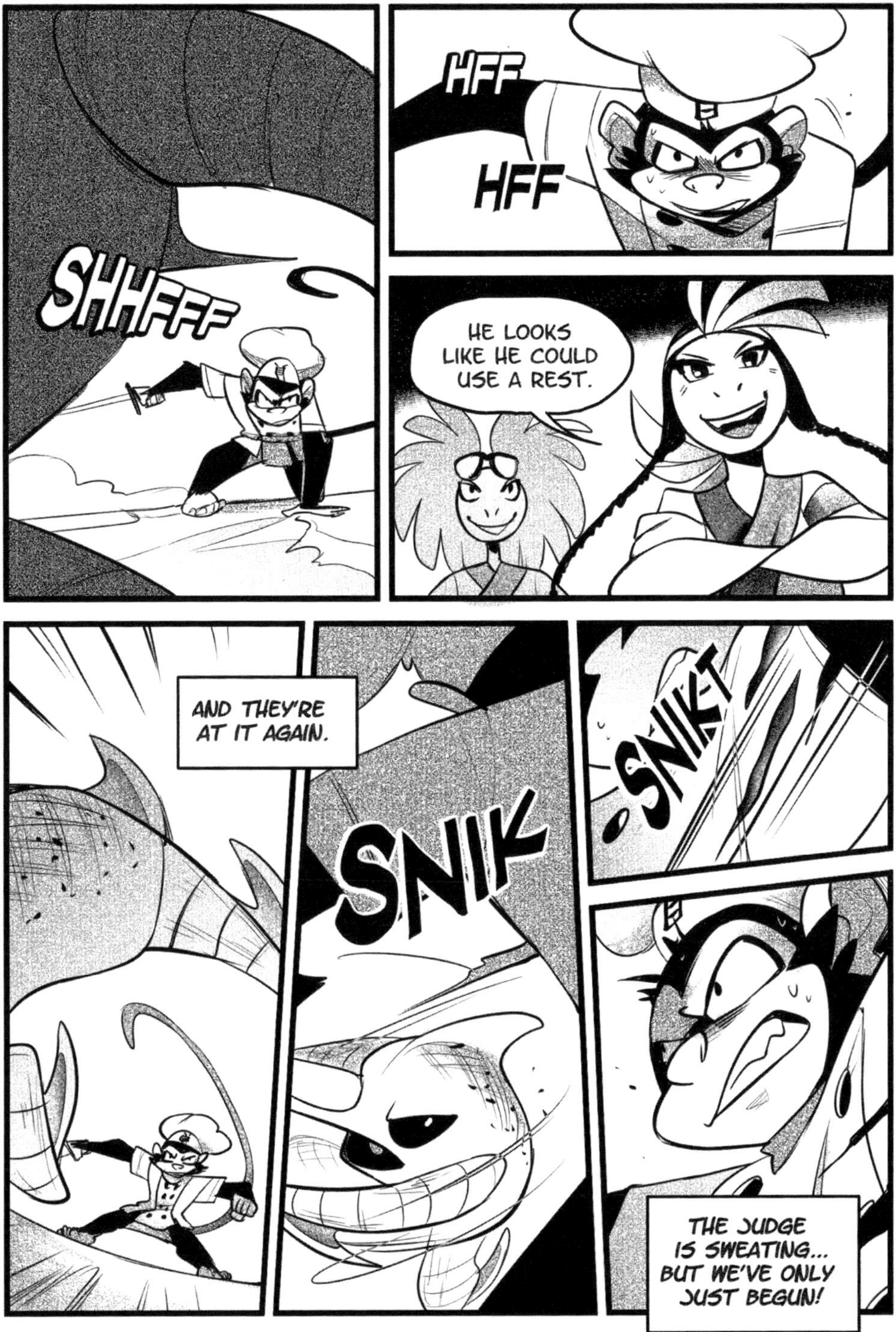
SHHFFFF
HFF
HFF
HE LOOKS LIKE HE COULD USE A REST.
AND THEY'RE AT IT AGAIN.
SNIK
SNIKT
THE JUDGE IS SWEATING... BUT WE'VE ONLY JUST BEGUN!

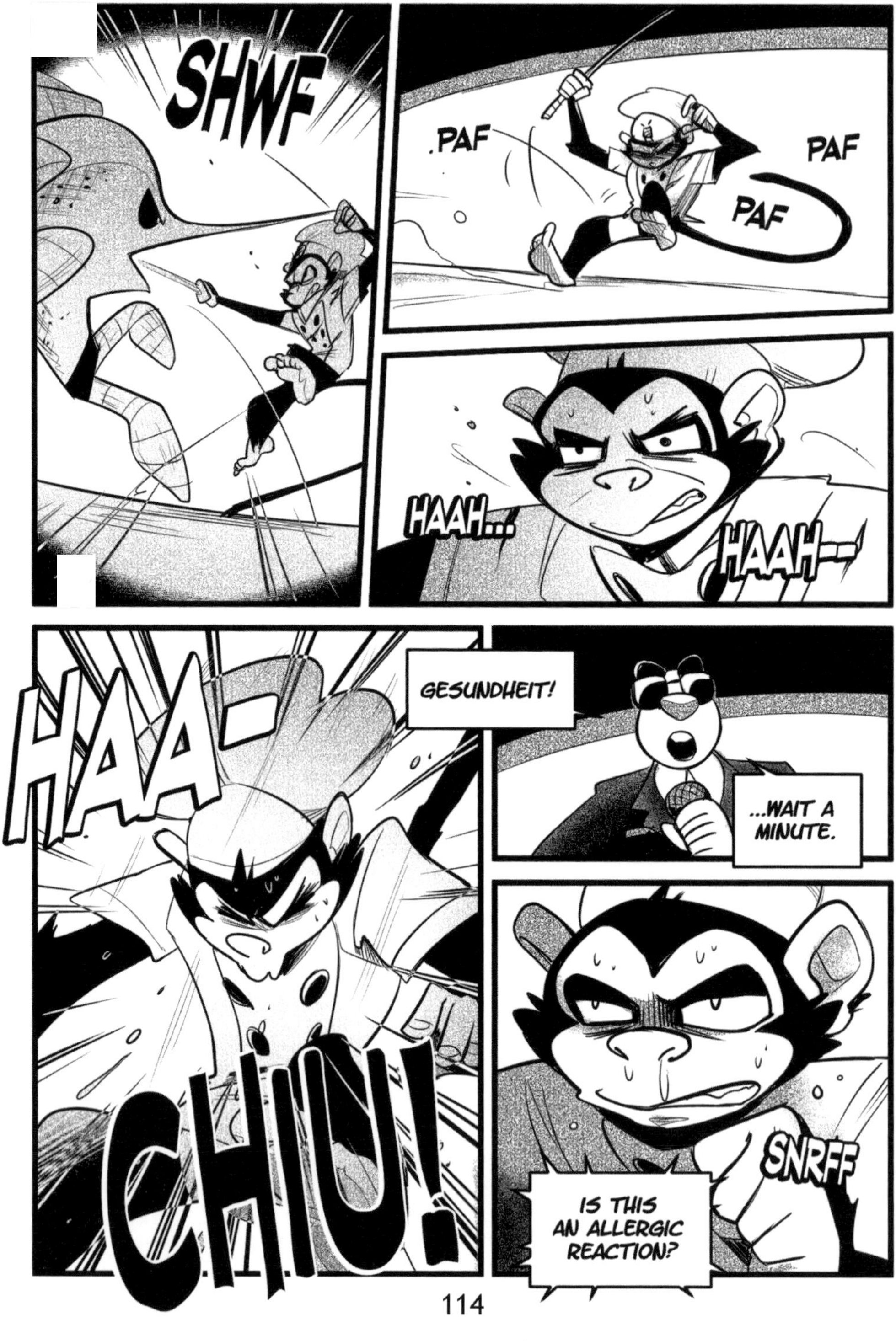
SHWF
PAF
PAF
PAF
HAAH...
HAAH--
HAA-
CHIU!
GESUNDHEIT!
...WAIT A MINUTE.
SNRFF
IS THIS AN ALLERGIC REACTION?

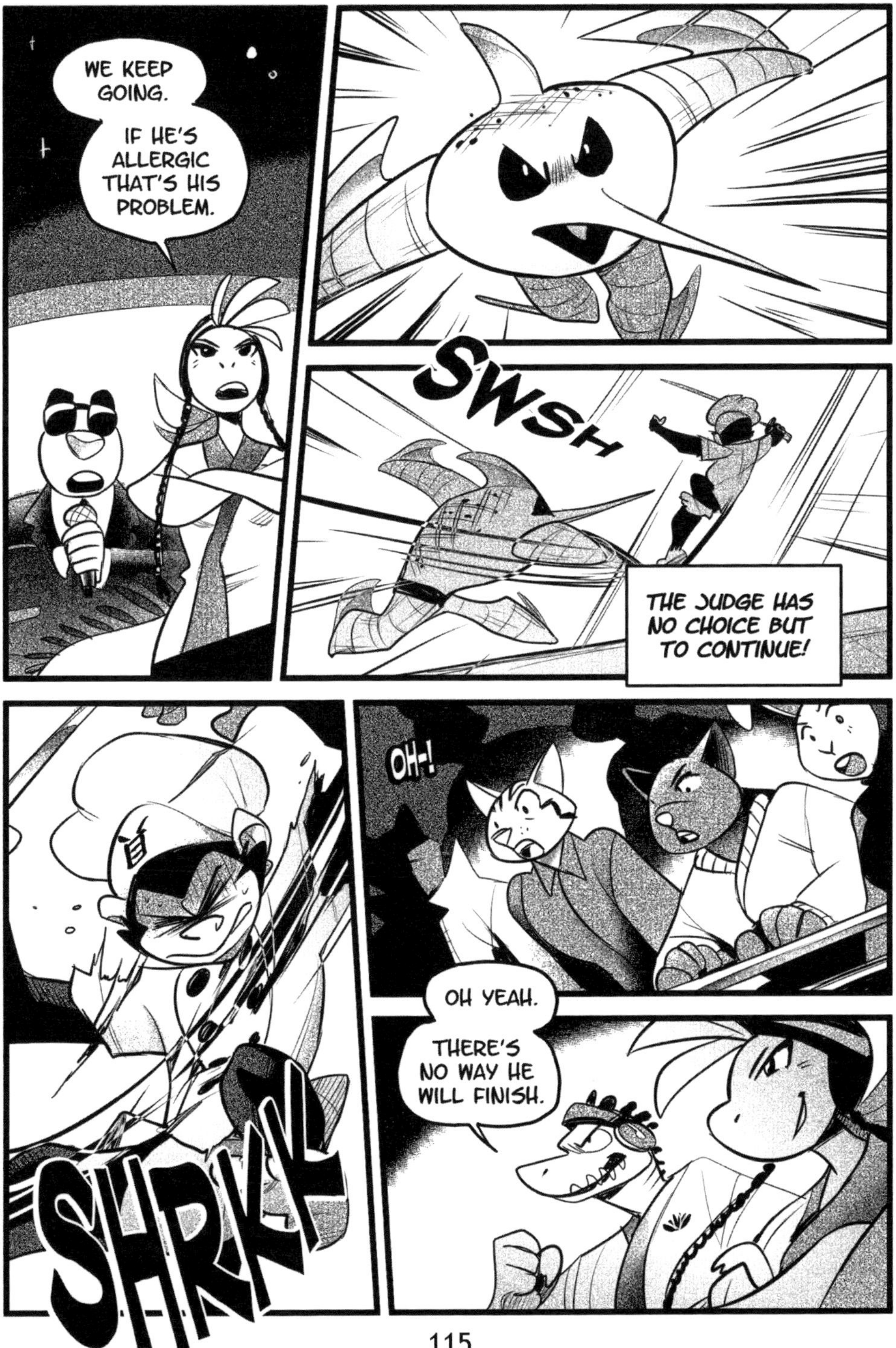
WE KEEP GOING.
IF HE'S ALLERGIC THAT'S HIS PROBLEM.
SWSH
THE JUDGE HAS NO CHOICE BUT TO CONTINUE!
SHRKK
OH-!
OH YEAH.
THERE'S NO WAY HE WILL FINISH.

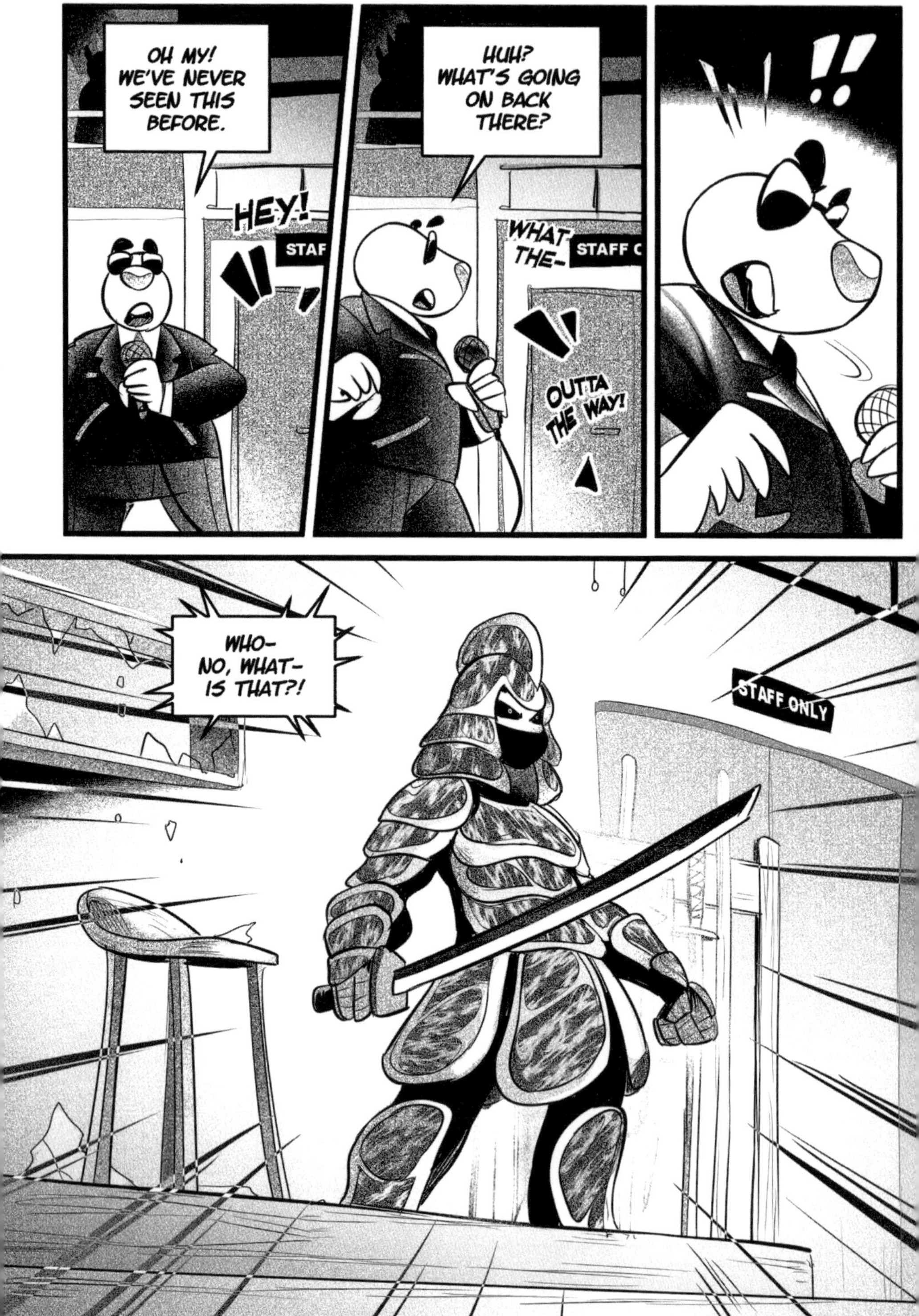
OH MY! WE'VE NEVER SEEN THIS BEFORE.
HEY!
STAFF
HUH? WHAT'S GOING ON BACK THERE?
WHAT THE-
STAFF
OUTTA THE WAY!
!!
WHO- NO, WHAT- IS THAT?!
STAFF ONLY

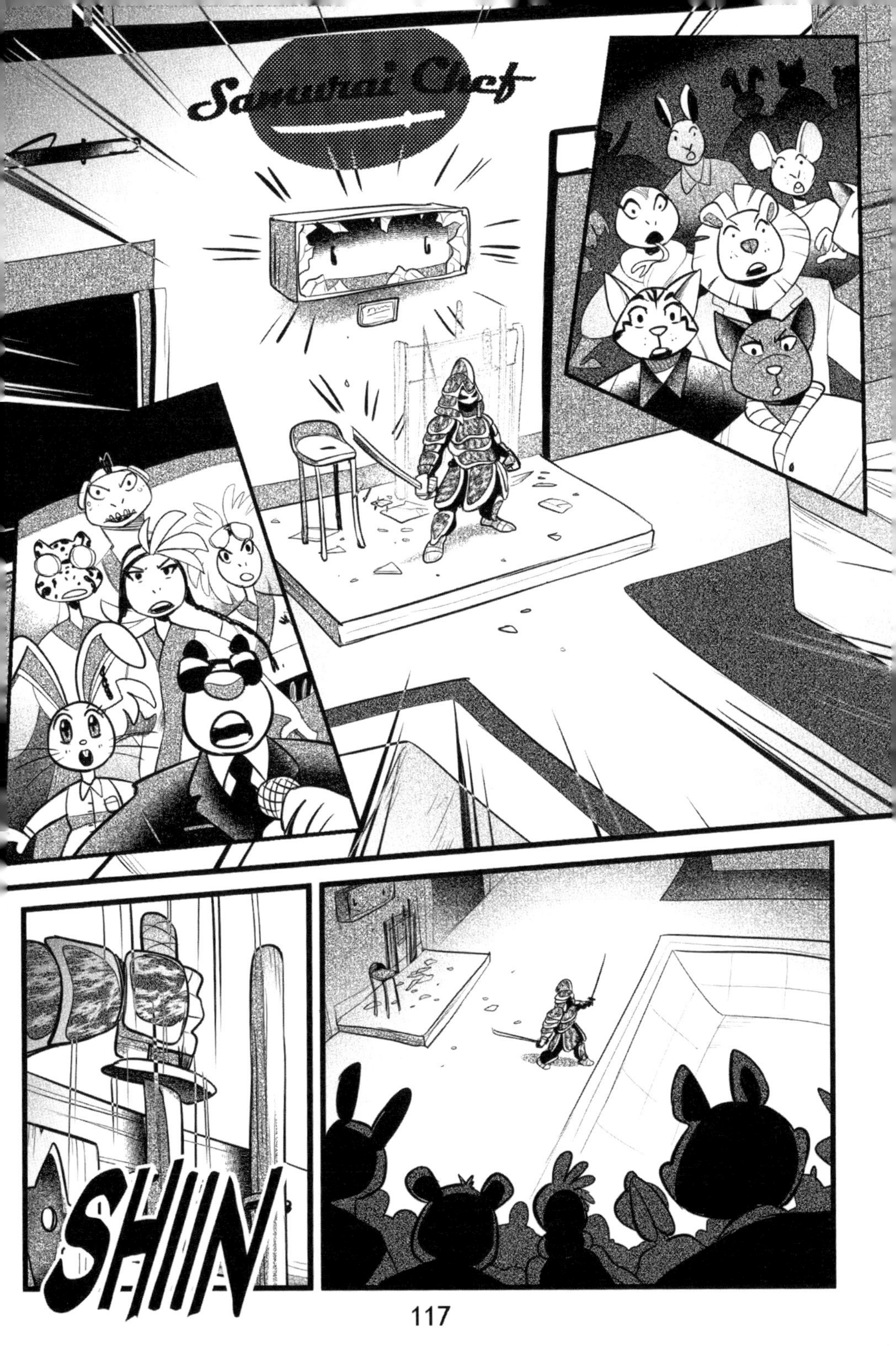
Samurai Chef
SHIIN

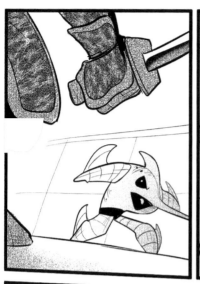

SHIIN!

NOOOO!

WHO DID THIS?!

THAT WOULD BE ME.

STAFF ONLY

WHO THE HECK ARE YOU?!

YOU DON'T NEED TO WORRY ABOUT THAT...

...SINCE YOU'LL BE LEAVING NOW.

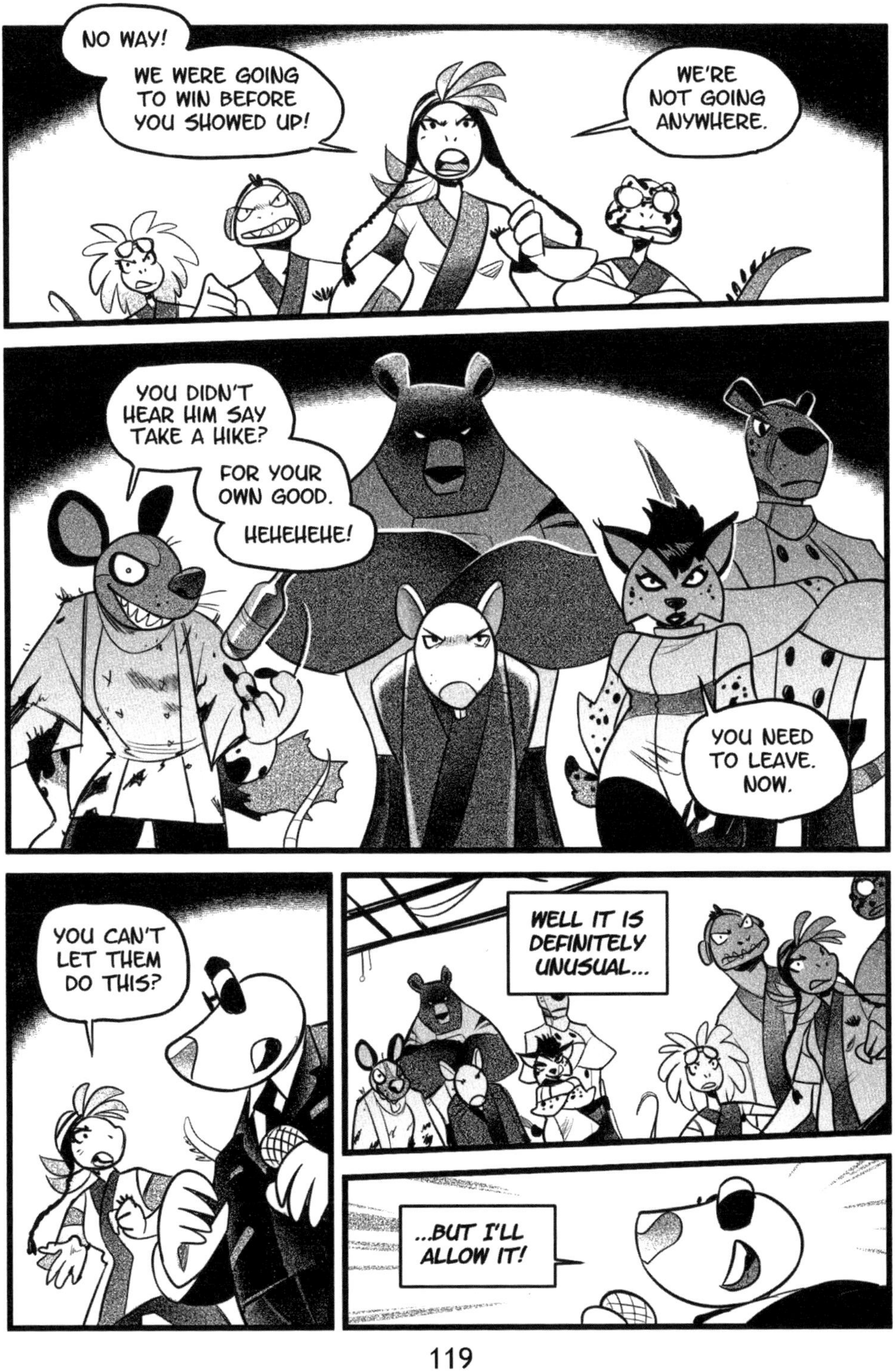
NO WAY!
WE WERE GOING TO WIN BEFORE YOU SHOWED UP!
WE'RE NOT GOING ANYWHERE.
YOU DIDN'T HEAR HIM SAY TAKE A HIKE?
FOR YOUR OWN GOOD.
HEHEHEHE!
YOU NEED TO LEAVE. NOW.
YOU CAN'T LET THEM DO THIS?
WELL IT IS DEFINITELY UNUSUAL...
...BUT I'LL ALLOW IT!

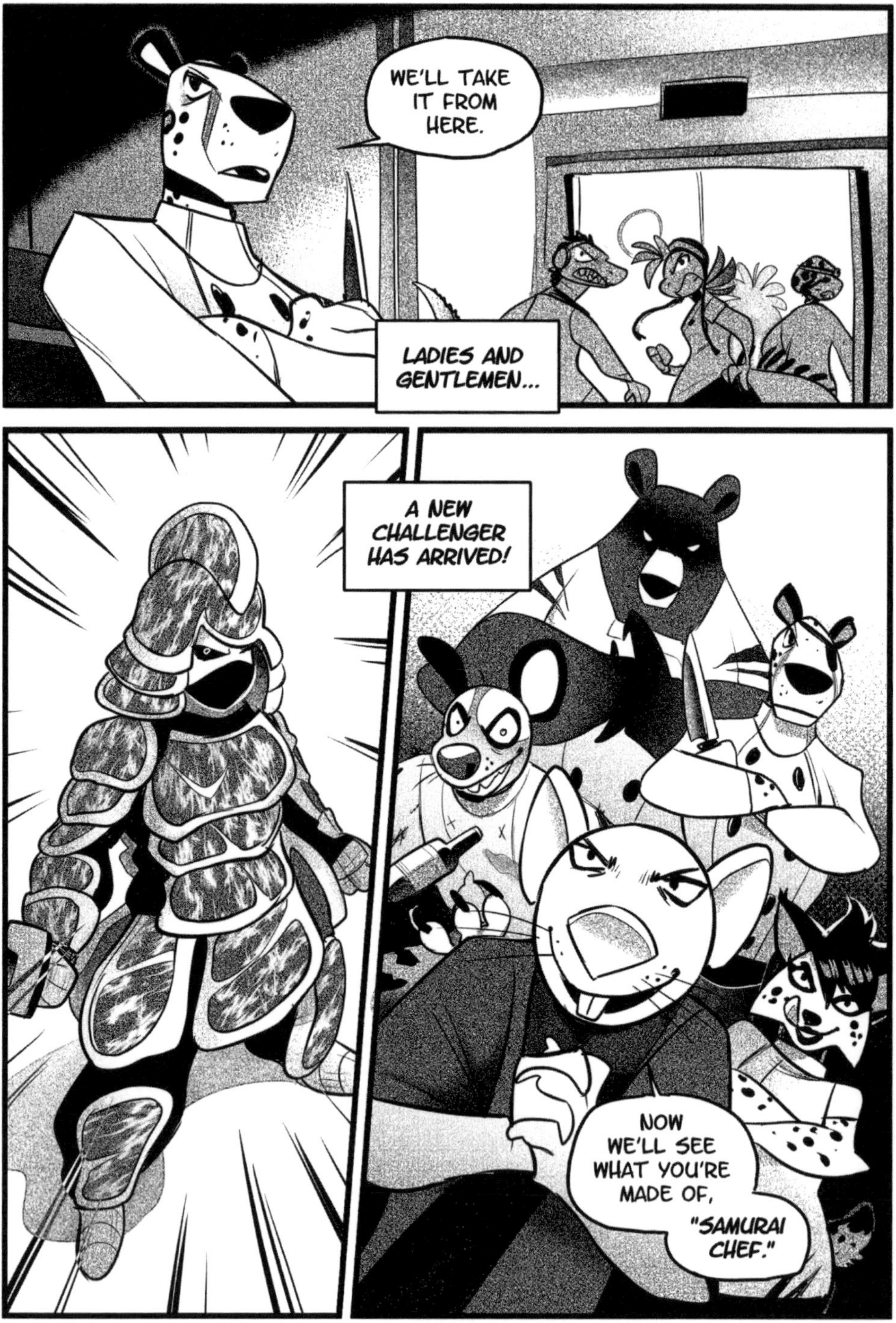
WE'LL TAKE IT FROM HERE.
LADIES AND GENTLEMEN...
A NEW CHALLENGER HAS ARRIVED!
NOW WE'LL SEE WHAT YOU'RE MADE OF, "SAMURAI CHEF."

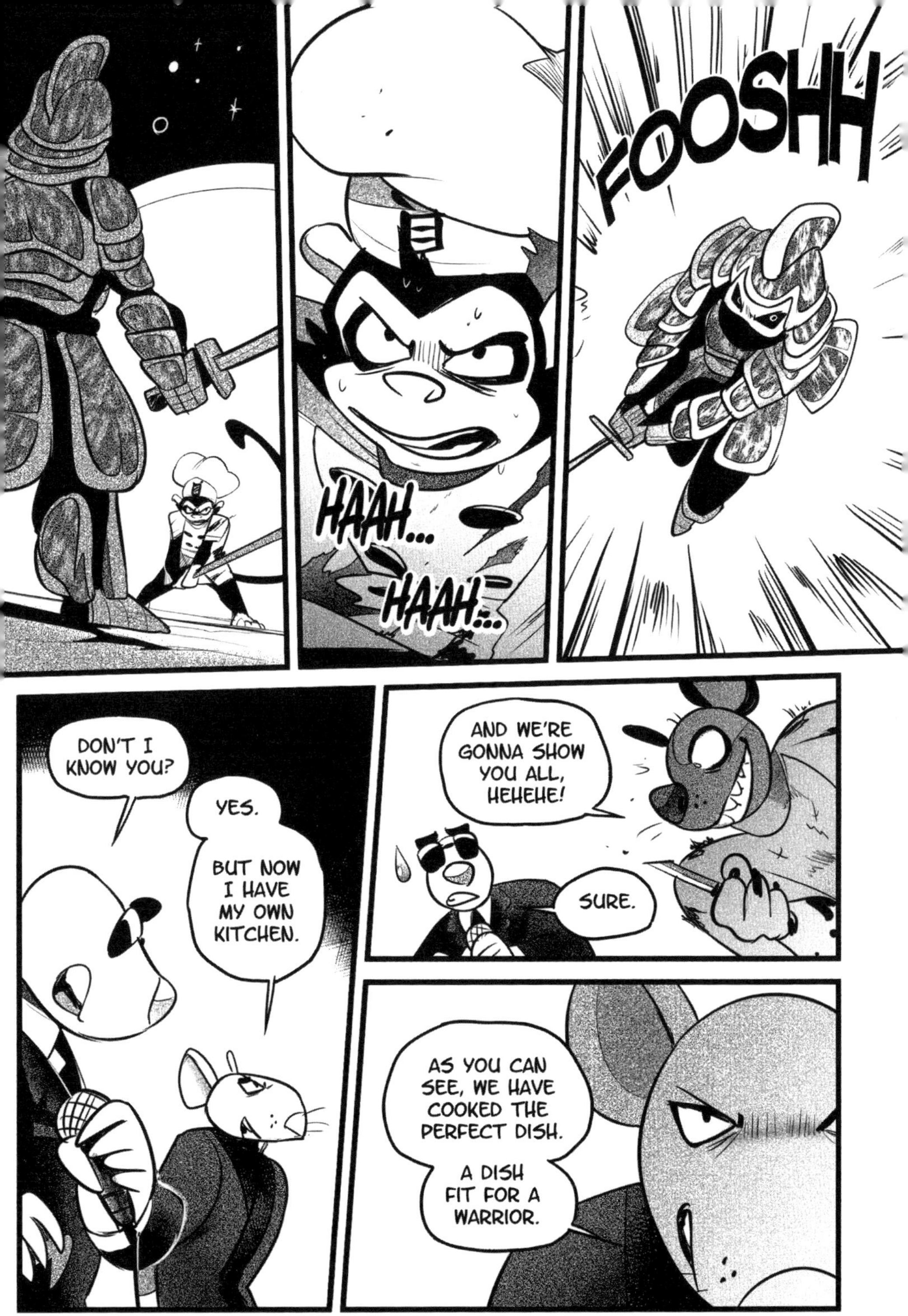
HAAH...
HAAH...
FOOSHH
DON'T I KNOW YOU?
YES.
BUT NOW I HAVE MY OWN KITCHEN.
AND WE'RE GONNA SHOW YOU ALL, HEHEHE!
SURE.
AS YOU CAN SEE, WE HAVE COOKED THE PERFECT DISH.
A DISH FIT FOR A WARRIOR.

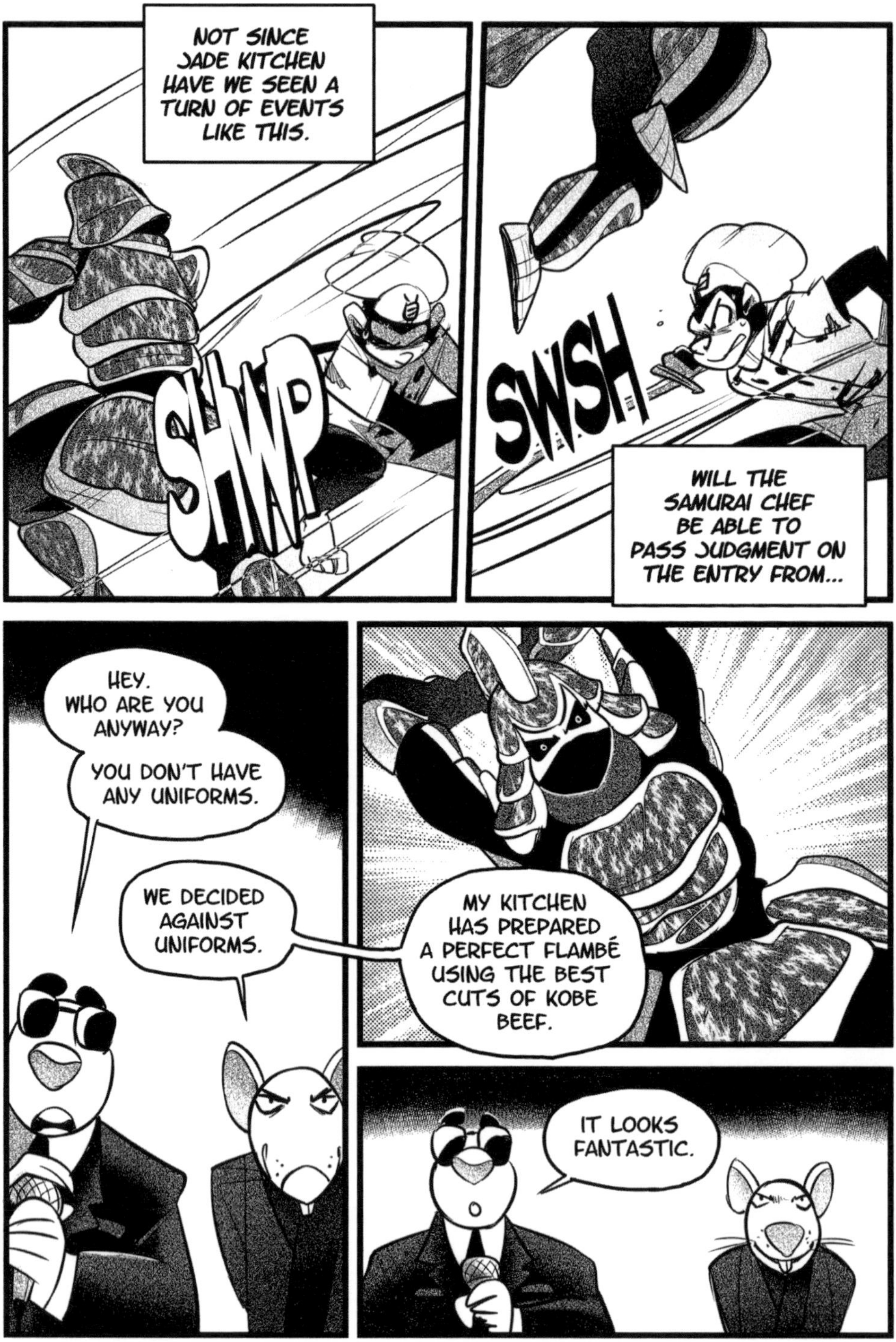
NOT SINCE JADE KITCHEN HAVE WE SEEN A TURN OF EVENTS LIKE THIS.
SHWP
SWSH
WILL THE SAMURAI CHEF BE ABLE TO PASS JUDGMENT ON THE ENTRY FROM...
HEY. WHO ARE YOU ANYWAY?
YOU DON'T HAVE ANY UNIFORMS.
WE DECIDED AGAINST UNIFORMS.
MY KITCHEN HAS PREPARED A PERFECT FLAMBÉ USING THE BEST CUTS OF KOBE BEEF.
IT LOOKS FANTASTIC.

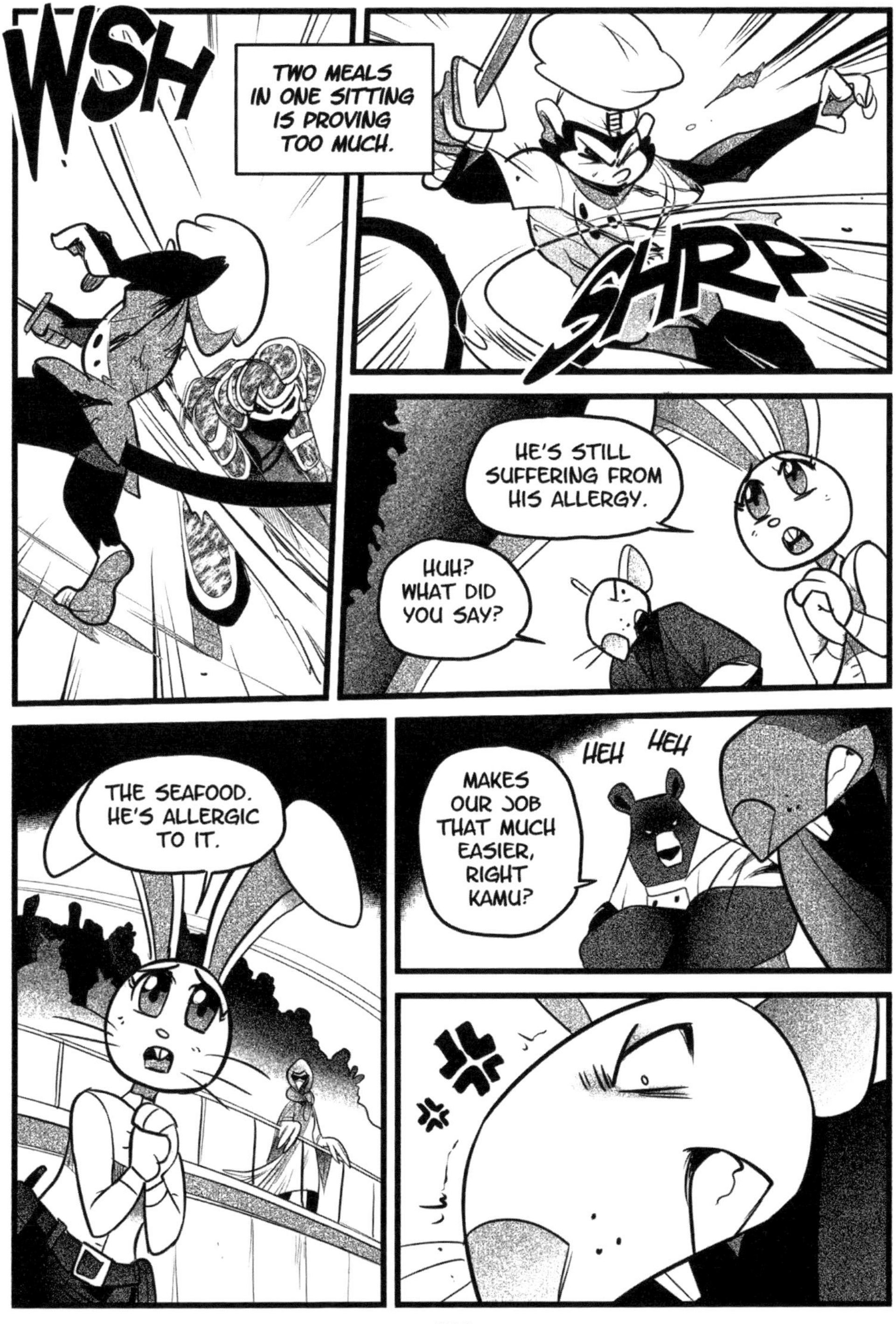
WSH
TWO MEALS IN ONE SITTING IS PROVING TOO MUCH.
SHRP
HE'S STILL SUFFERING FROM HIS ALLERGY.
HUH? WHAT DID YOU SAY?
THE SEAFOOD. HE'S ALLERGIC TO IT.
HEH HEH
MAKES OUR JOB THAT MUCH EASIER, RIGHT KAMU?

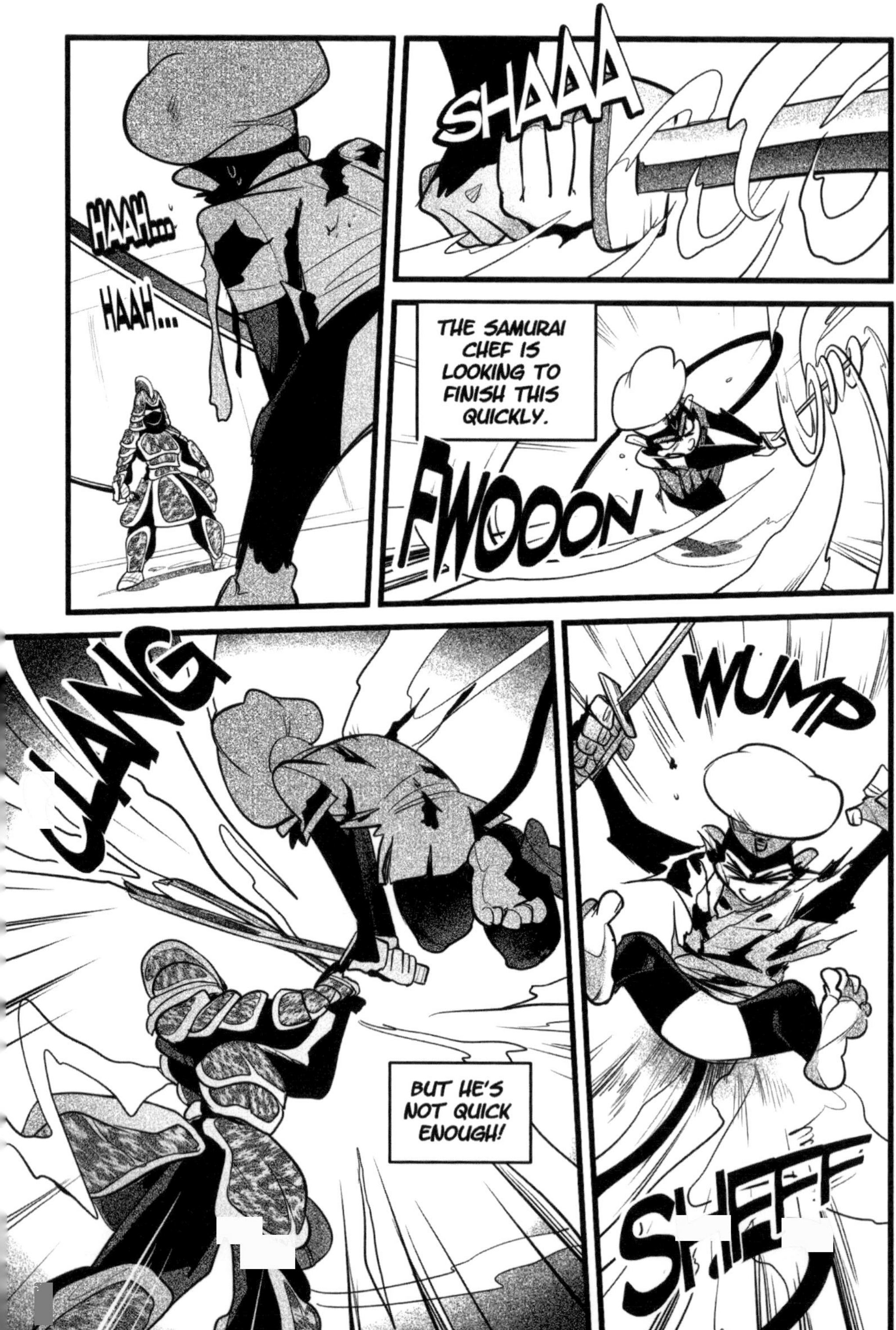
HAAH...
HAAH...
SHAAA
THE SAMURAI CHEF IS LOOKING TO FINISH THIS QUICKLY.
FWOOON
CLANG
BUT HE'S NOT QUICK ENOUGH!
WUMP
SHEFF

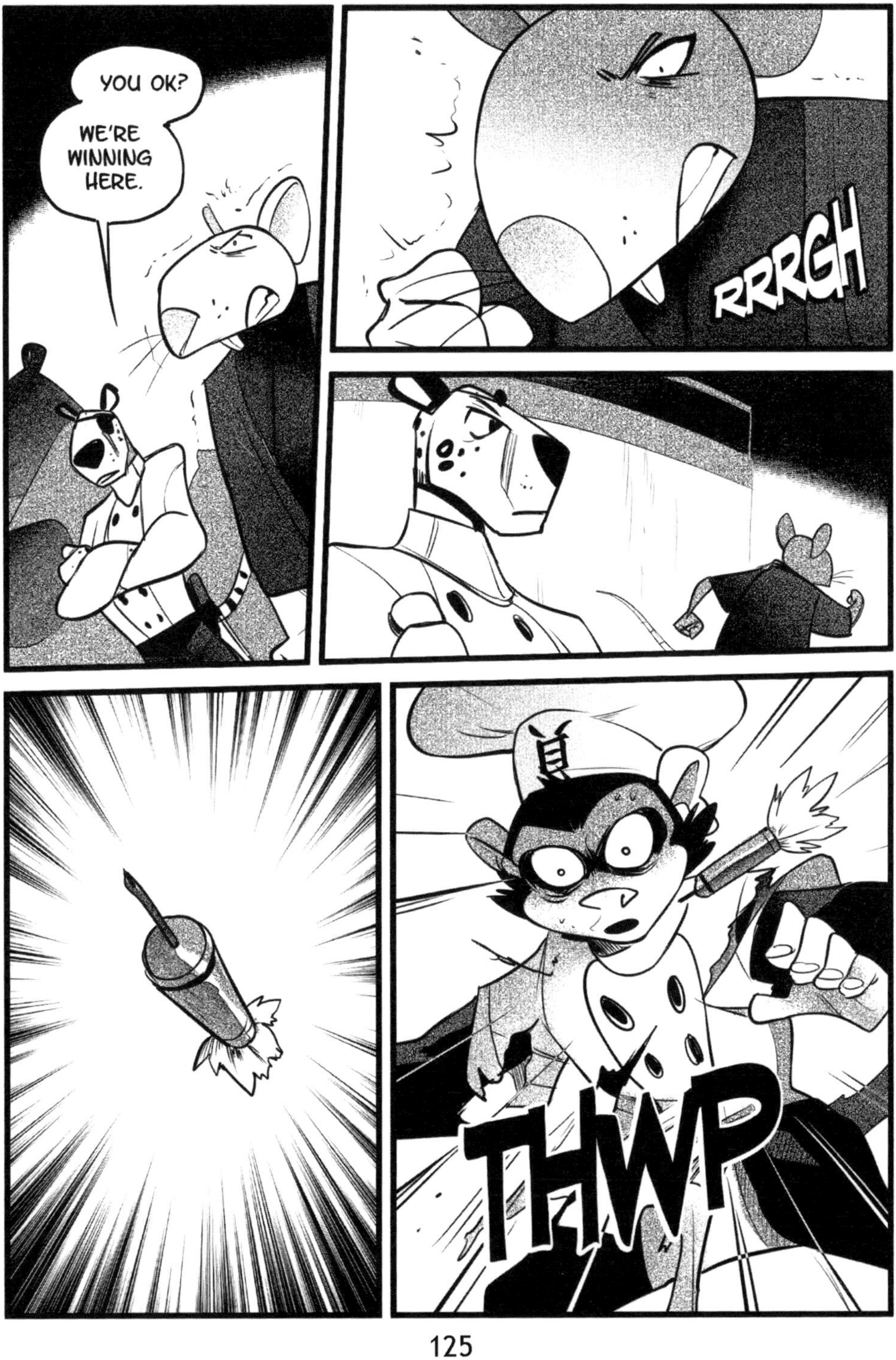
YOU OK?
WE'RE WINNING HERE.
RRRGH
THWP

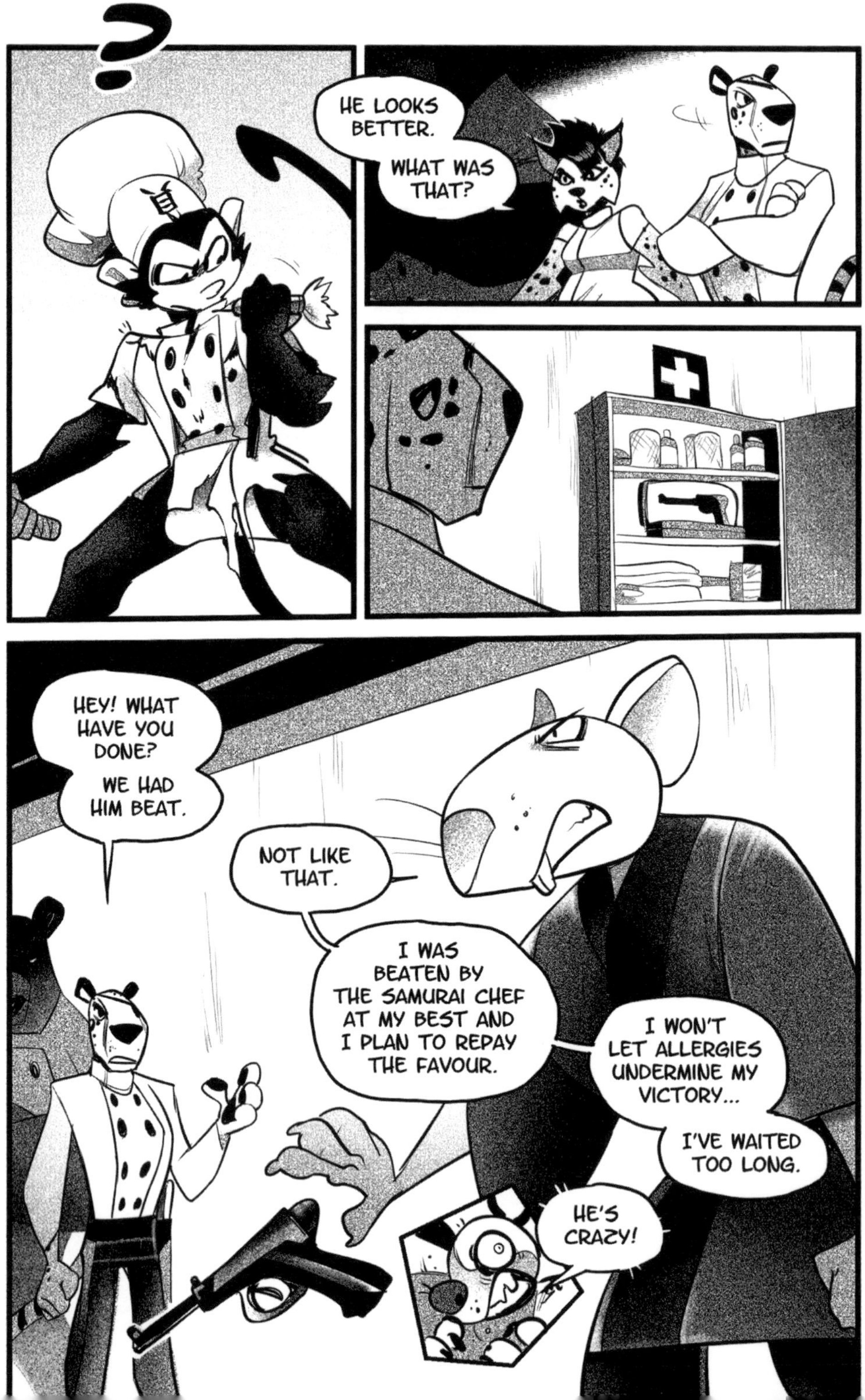
?
HE LOOKS BETTER.
WHAT WAS THAT?
HEY! WHAT HAVE YOU DONE?
WE HAD HIM BEAT.
NOT LIKE THAT.
I WAS BEATEN BY THE SAMURAI CHEF AT MY BEST AND I PLAN TO REPAY THE FAVOUR.
I WON'T LET ALLERGIES UNDERMINE MY VICTORY...
I'VE WAITED TOO LONG.
HE'S CRAZY!

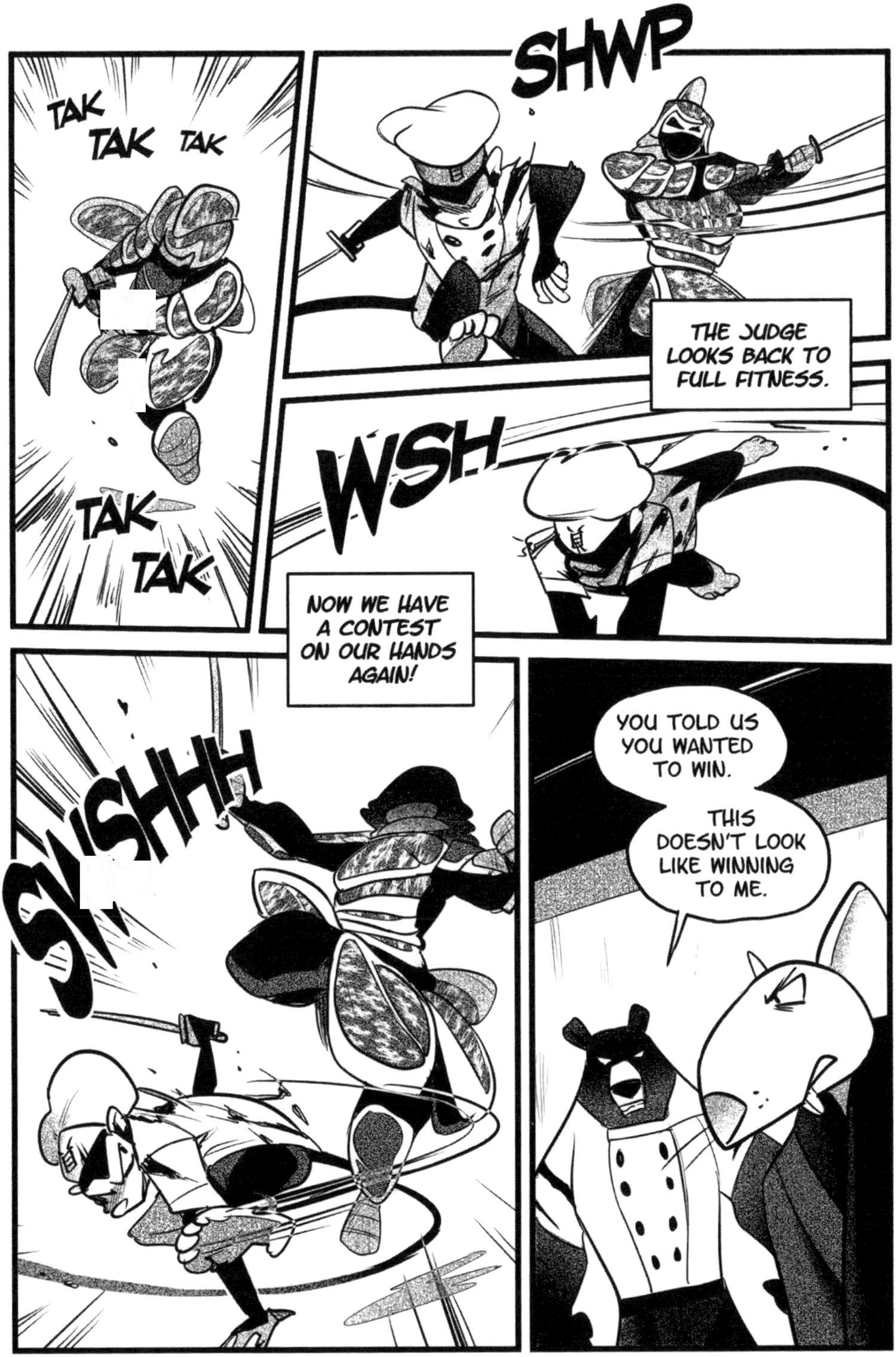
TAK
TAK TAK
TAK
TAK
SHWP
THE JUDGE LOOKS BACK TO FULL FITNESS.
WSH
NOW WE HAVE A CONTEST ON OUR HANDS AGAIN!
SWISHHH
YOU TOLD US YOU WANTED TO WIN.
THIS DOESN'T LOOK LIKE WINNING TO ME.

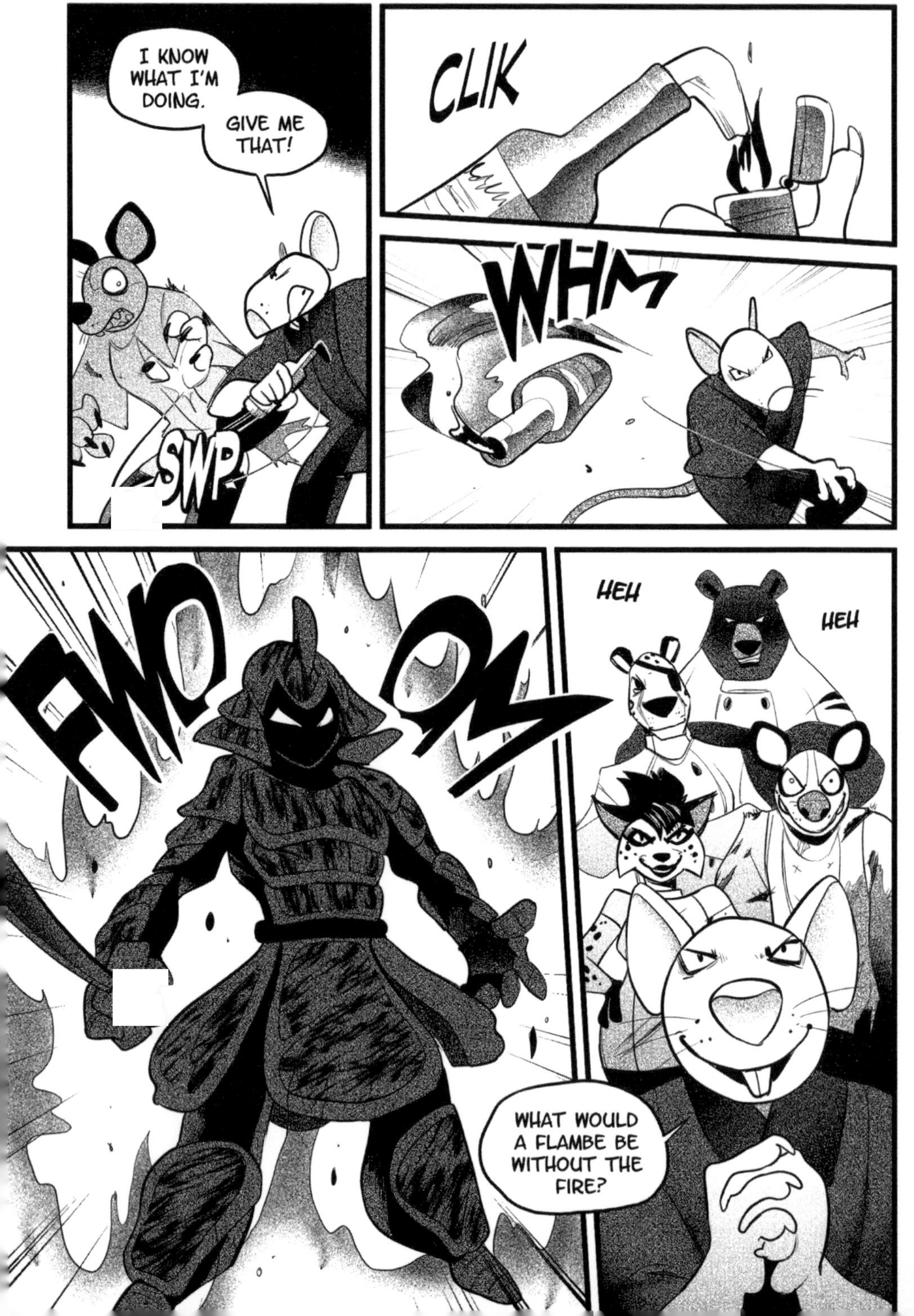
I KNOW WHAT I'M DOING.
GIVE ME THAT!
SWP
CLIK
WHM
FWOOM
HEH
HEH
WHAT WOULD A FLAMBE BE WITHOUT THE FIRE?

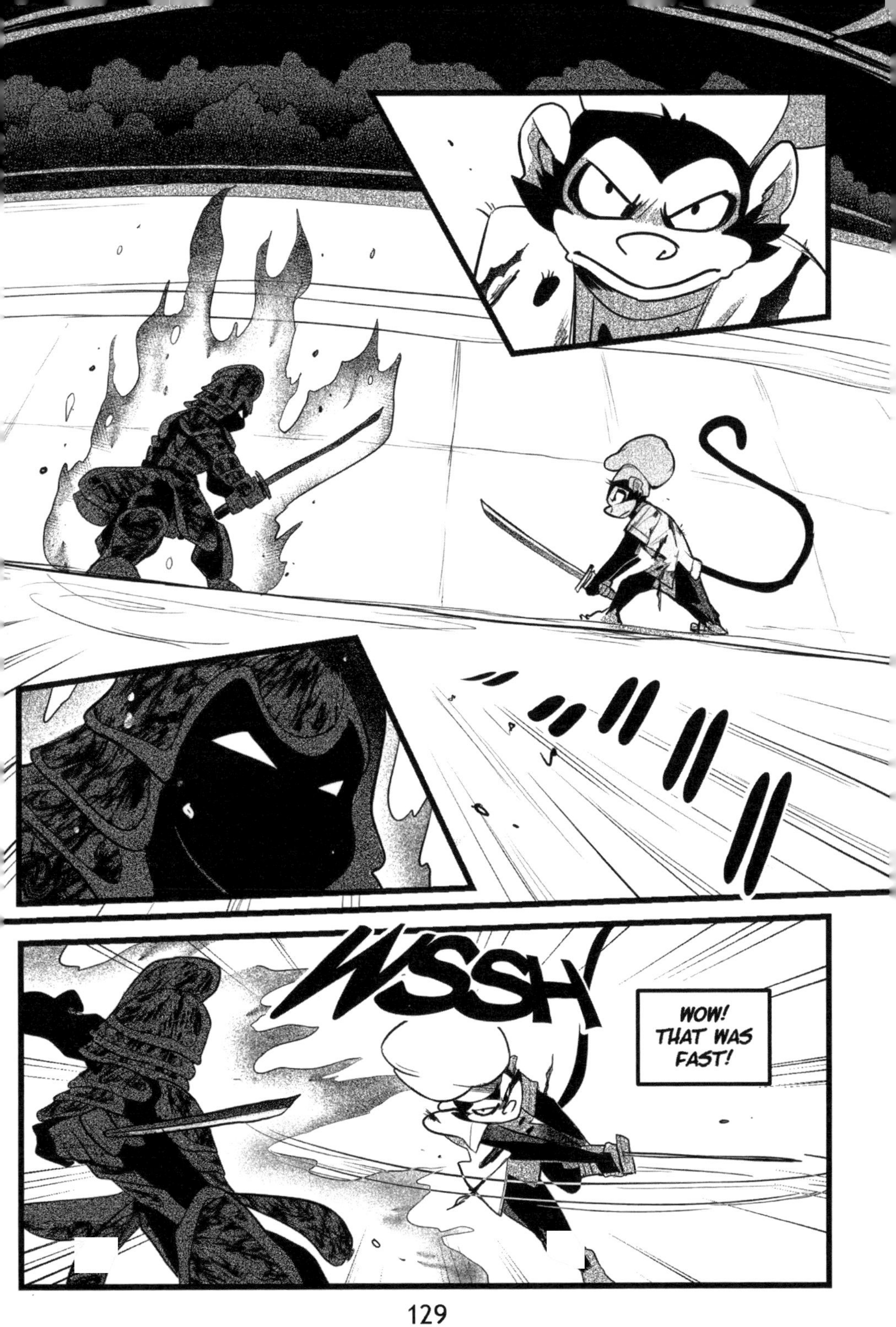
WSSH
WOW! THAT WAS FAST!

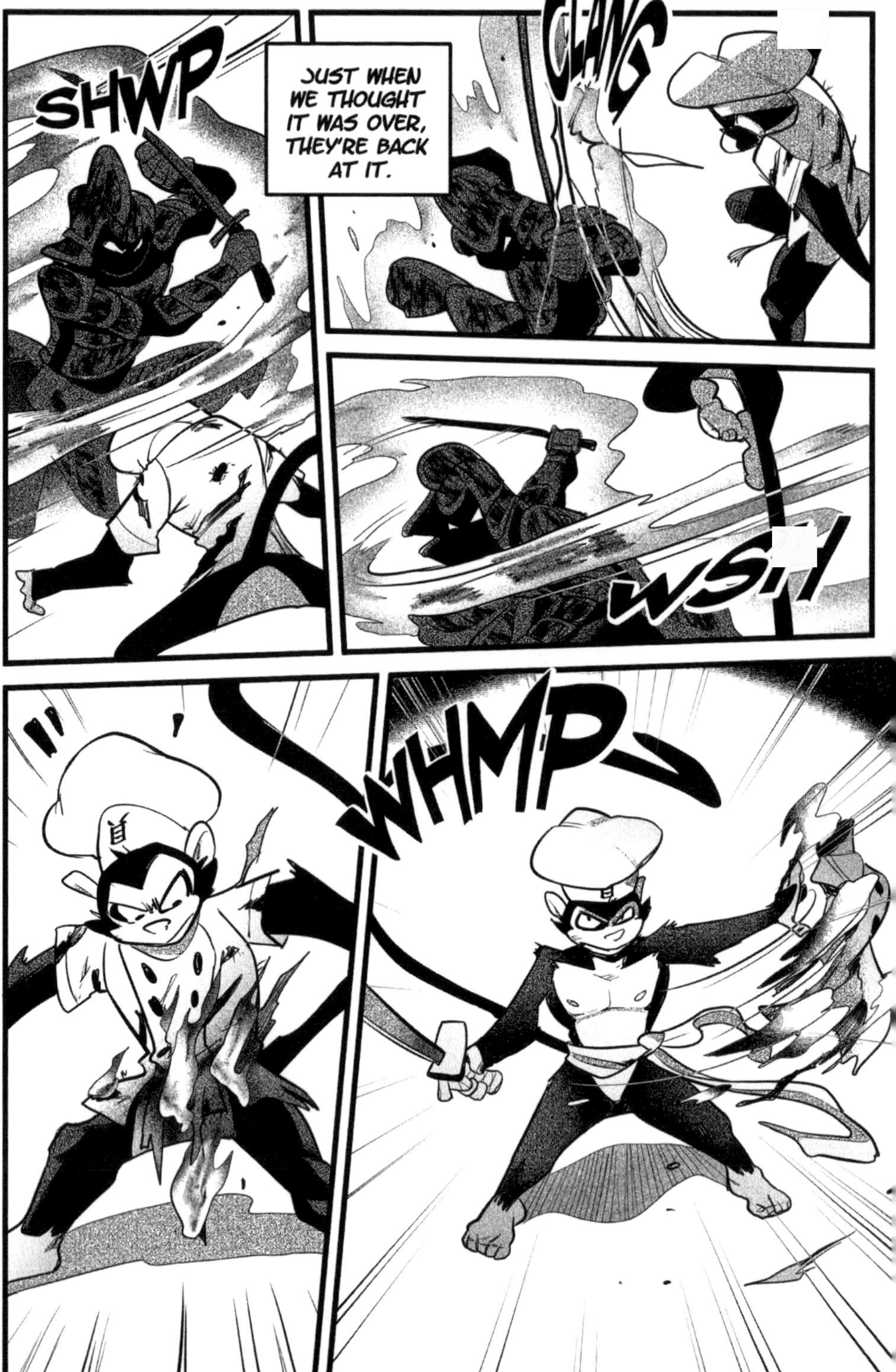
SHWP
JUST WHEN WE THOUGHT IT WAS OVER, THEY'RE BACK AT IT.
CLANG
WSH
WHMP

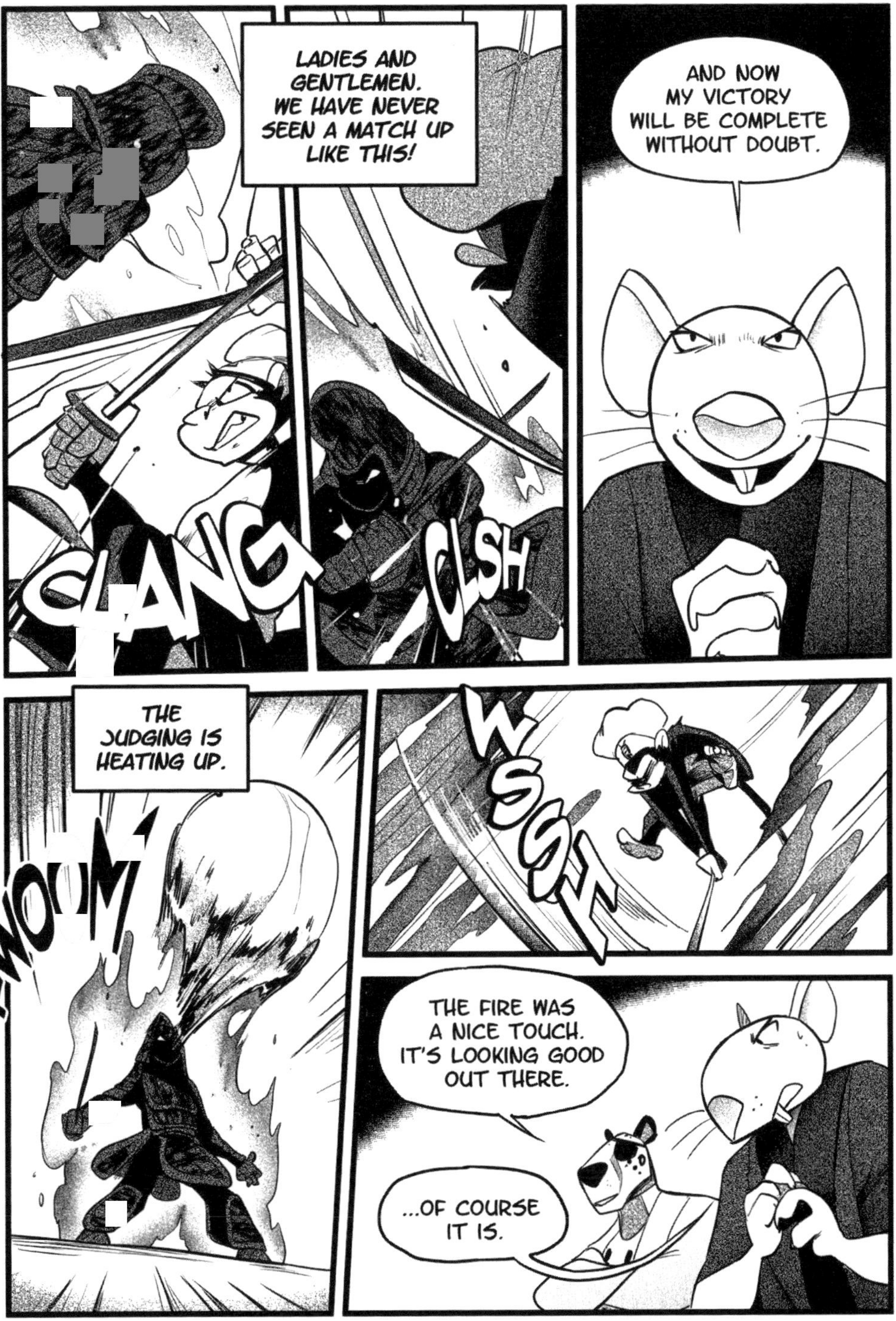
CLANG
LADIES AND GENTLEMEN. WE HAVE NEVER SEEN A MATCH UP LIKE THIS!
CLSH
AND NOW MY VICTORY WILL BE COMPLETE WITHOUT DOUBT.
THE JUDGING IS HEATING UP.
FWOOM
WSSH
THE FIRE WAS A NICE TOUCH. IT'S LOOKING GOOD OUT THERE.
...OF COURSE IT IS.

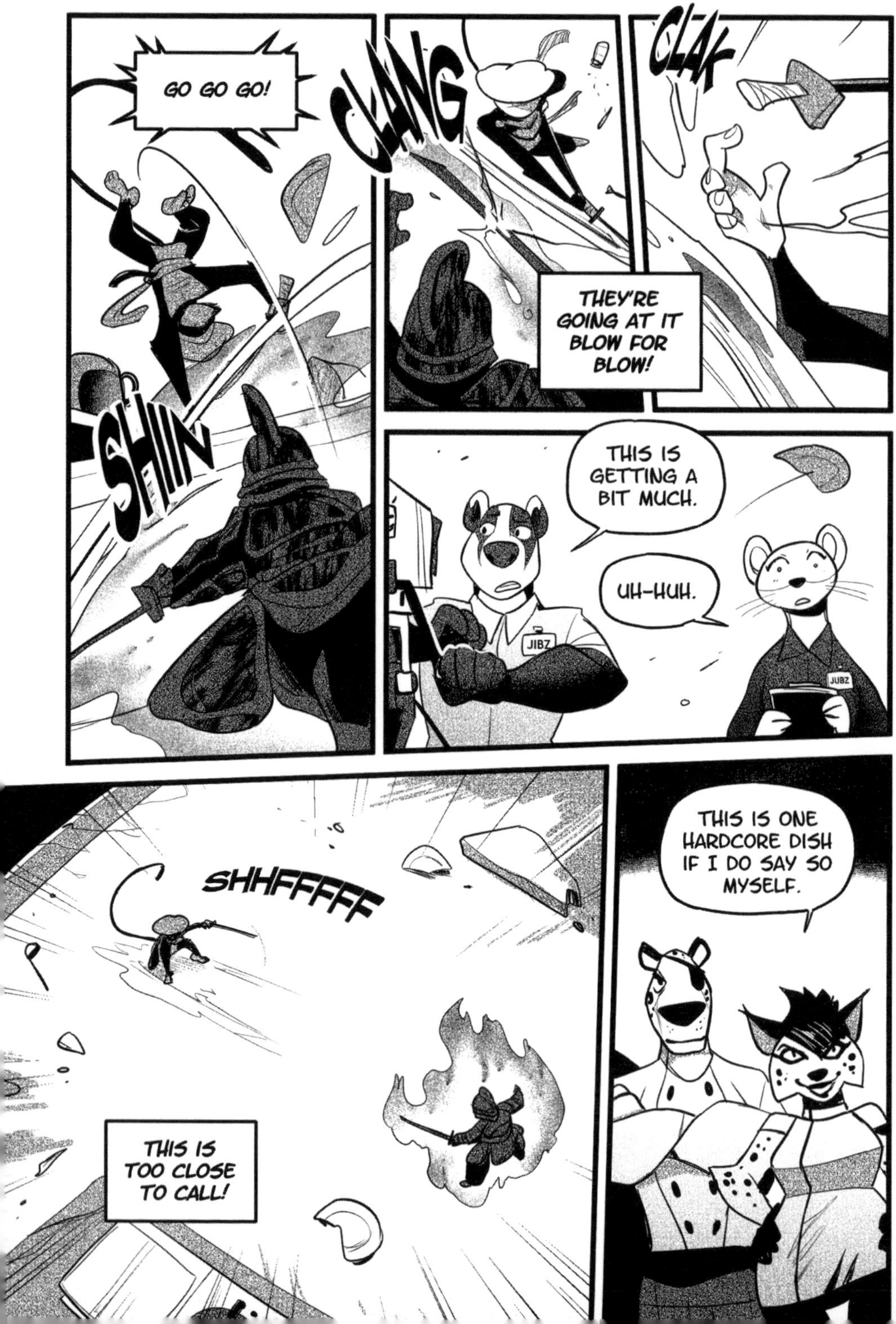
GO GO GO!
SHIIN
CLANG
THEY'RE GOING AT IT BLOW FOR BLOW!
CLAK
THIS IS GETTING A BIT MUCH.
UH-HUH.
JIBZ
JUBZ
SHHFFFFF
THIS IS TOO CLOSE TO CALL!
THIS IS ONE HARDCORE DISH IF I DO SAY SO MYSELF.

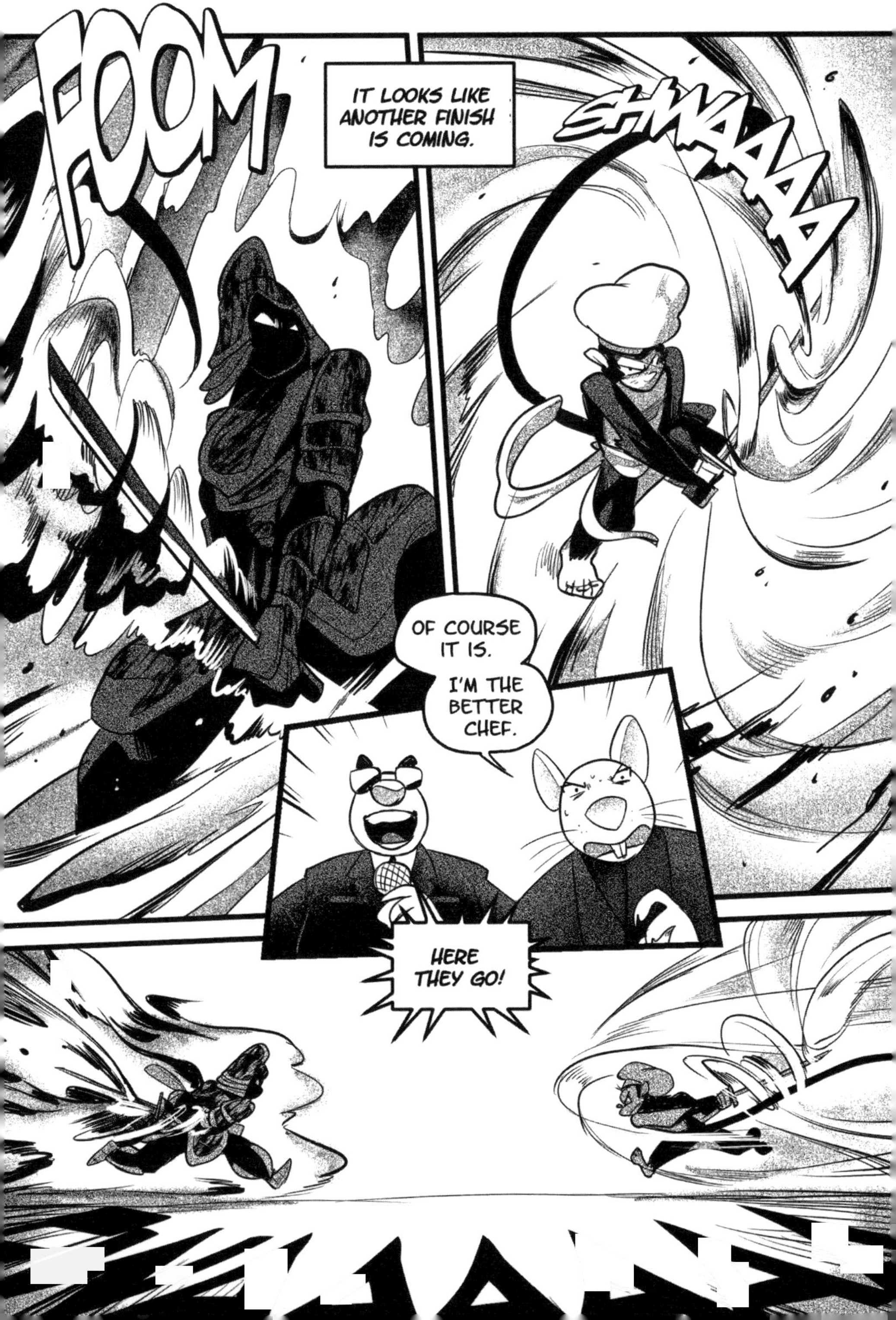
FOOM
IT LOOKS LIKE ANOTHER FINISH IS COMING.
SHWAAAAA
OF COURSE IT IS.
I'M THE BETTER CHEF.
HERE THEY GO!

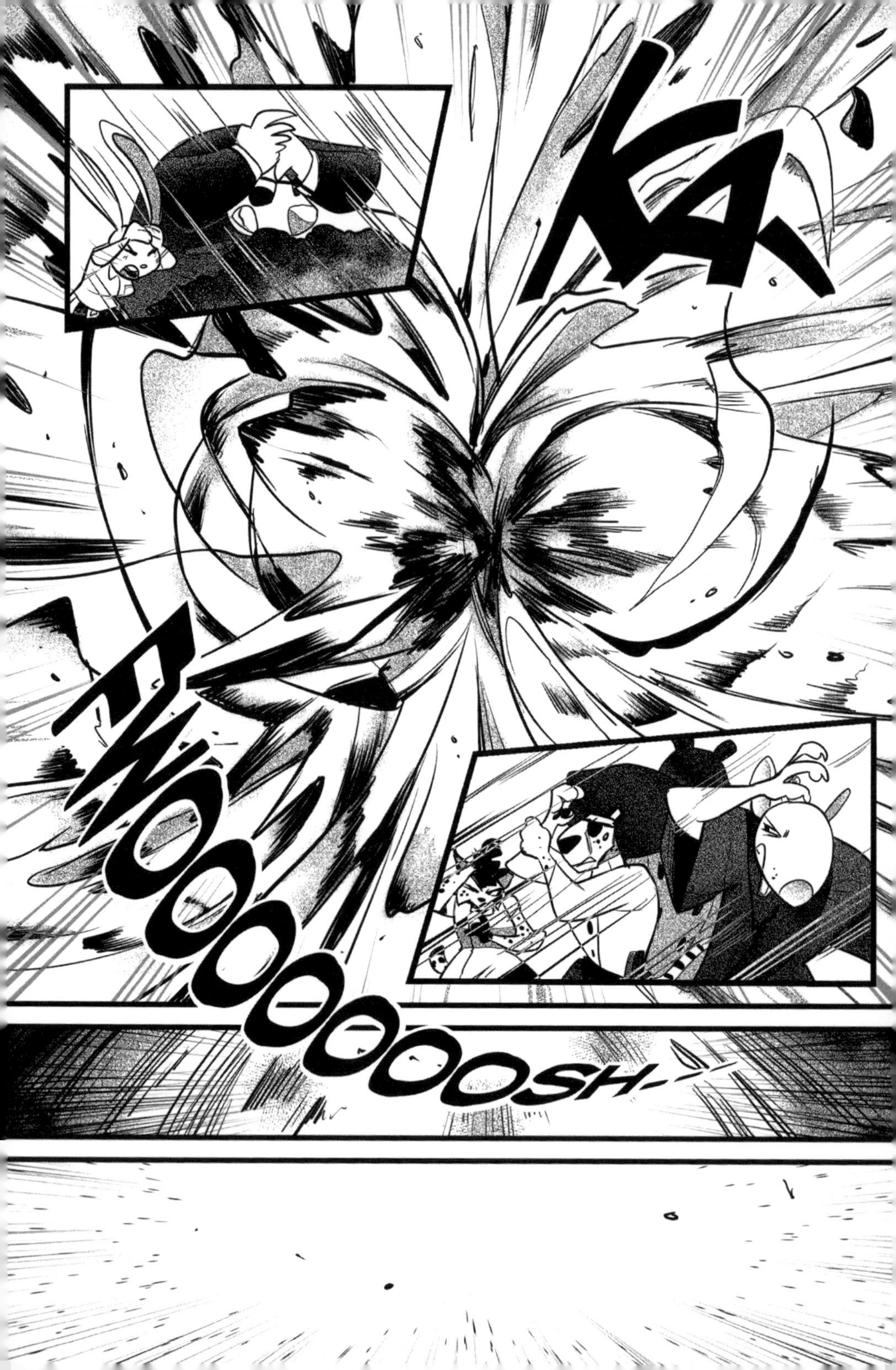
KA
FWOOOOOOOOSH--

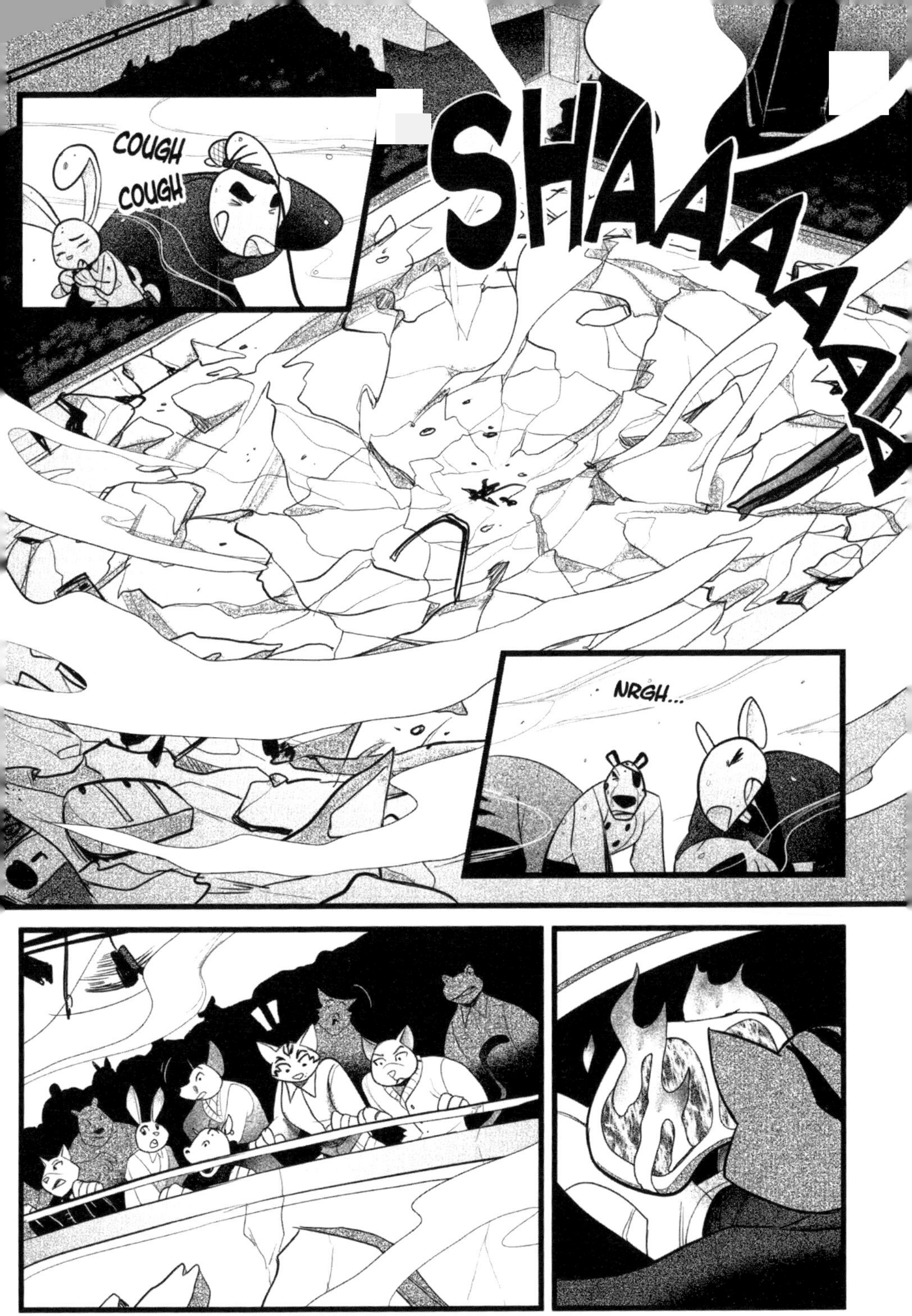
COUGH
COUGH
SHAAAAAAAA
NRGH...

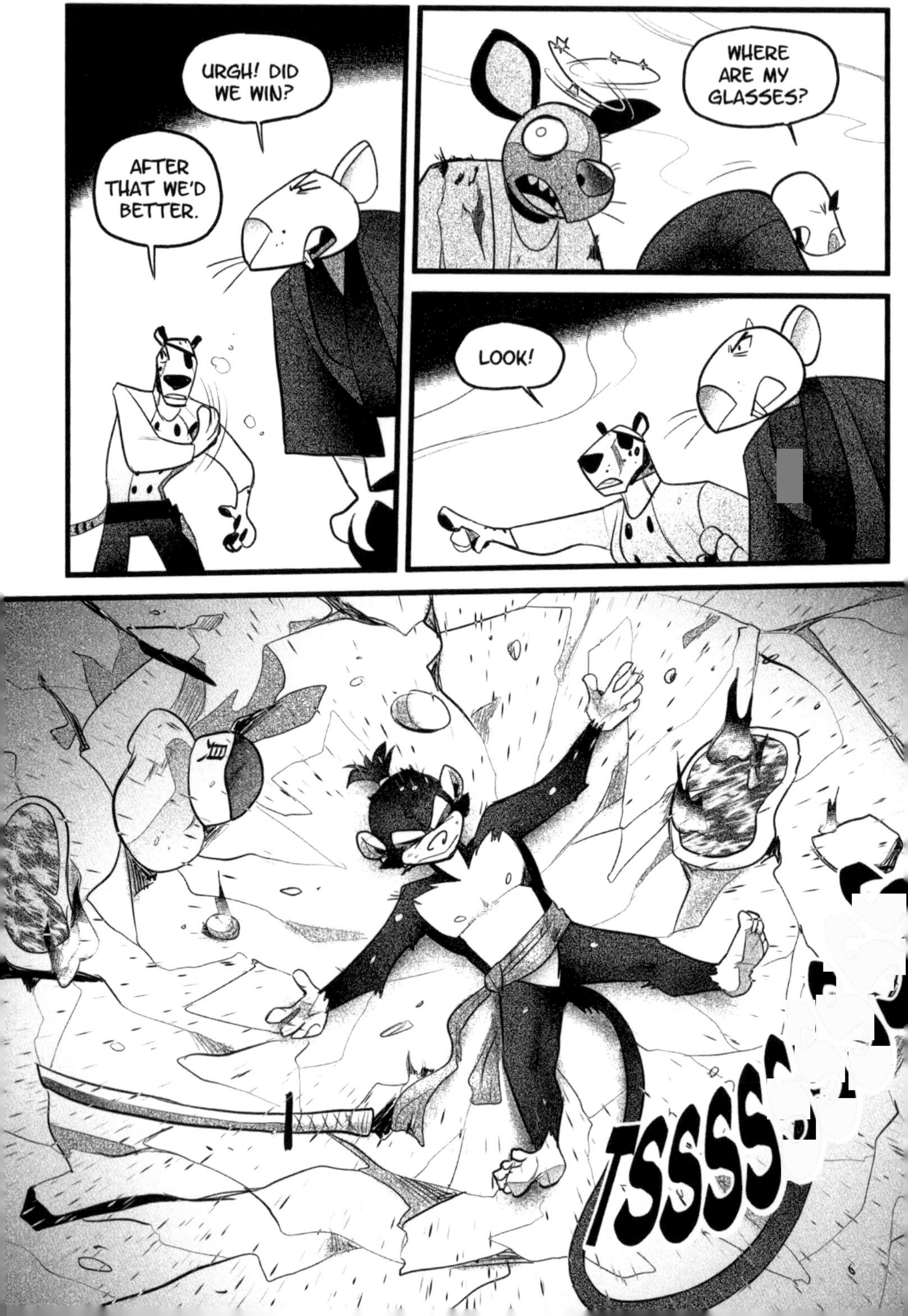
URGH! DID WE WIN?
AFTER THAT WE'D BETTER.
WHERE ARE MY GLASSES?
LOOK!
TSSSS

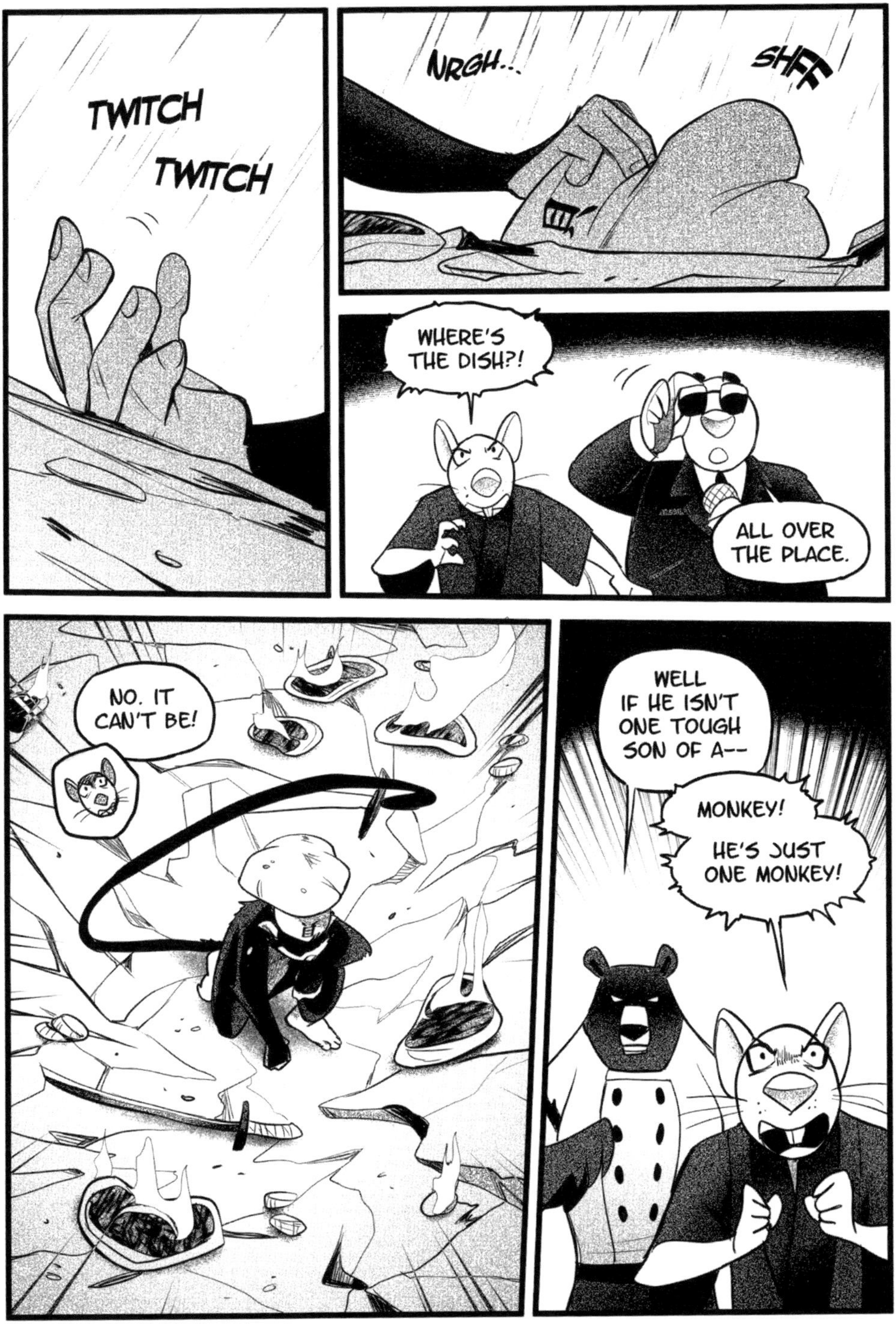
TWITCH
TWITCH
NRGH...
SHFF
WHERE'S THE DISH?!
ALL OVER THE PLACE.
NO. IT CAN'T BE!
WELL IF HE ISN'T ONE TOUGH SON OF A--
MONKEY!
HE'S JUST ONE MONKEY!

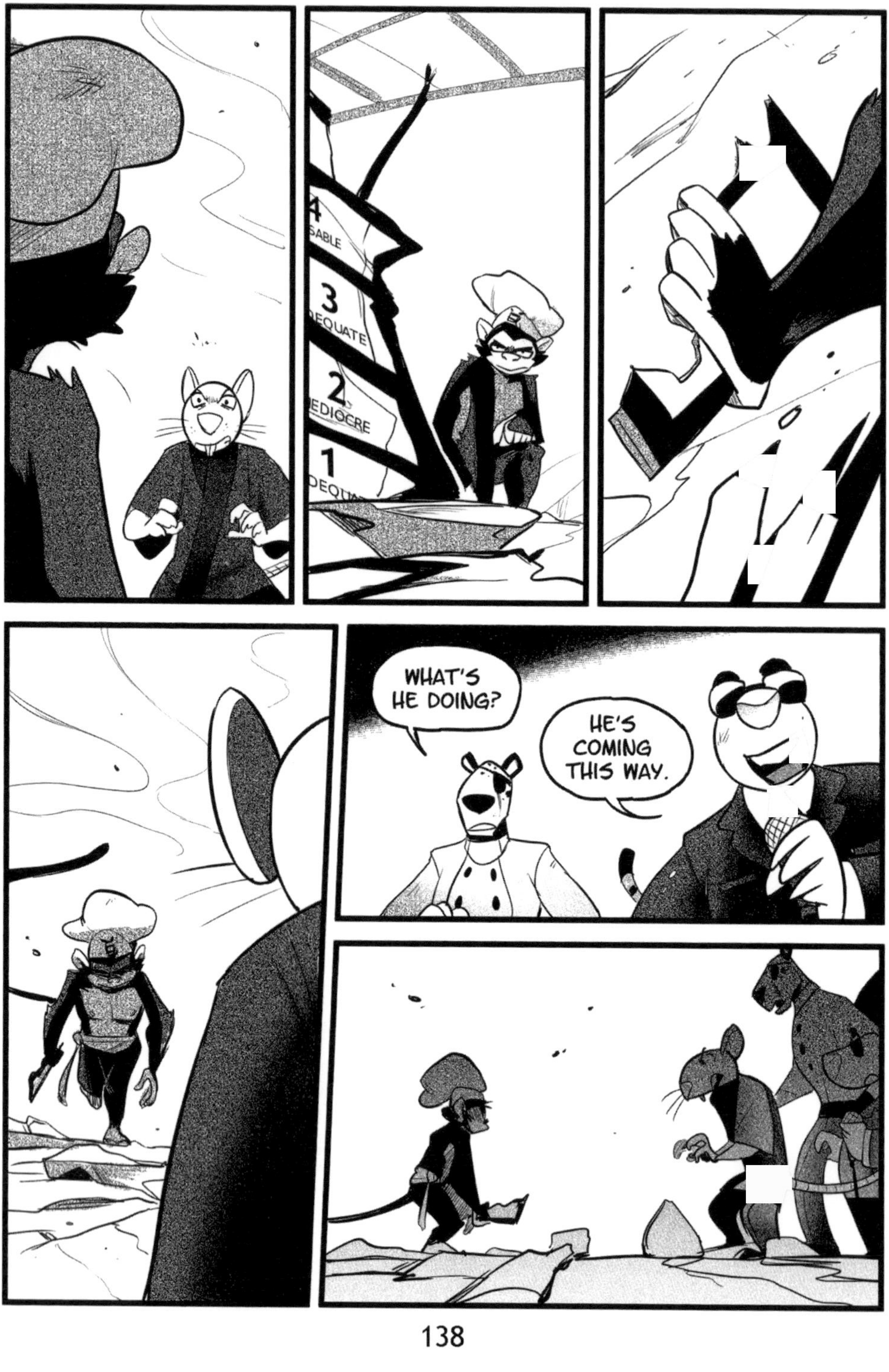
4
SABLE
3
DEQUATE
2
EDIOCRE
1
DEQUA
WHAT'S HE DOING?
HE'S COMING THIS WAY.

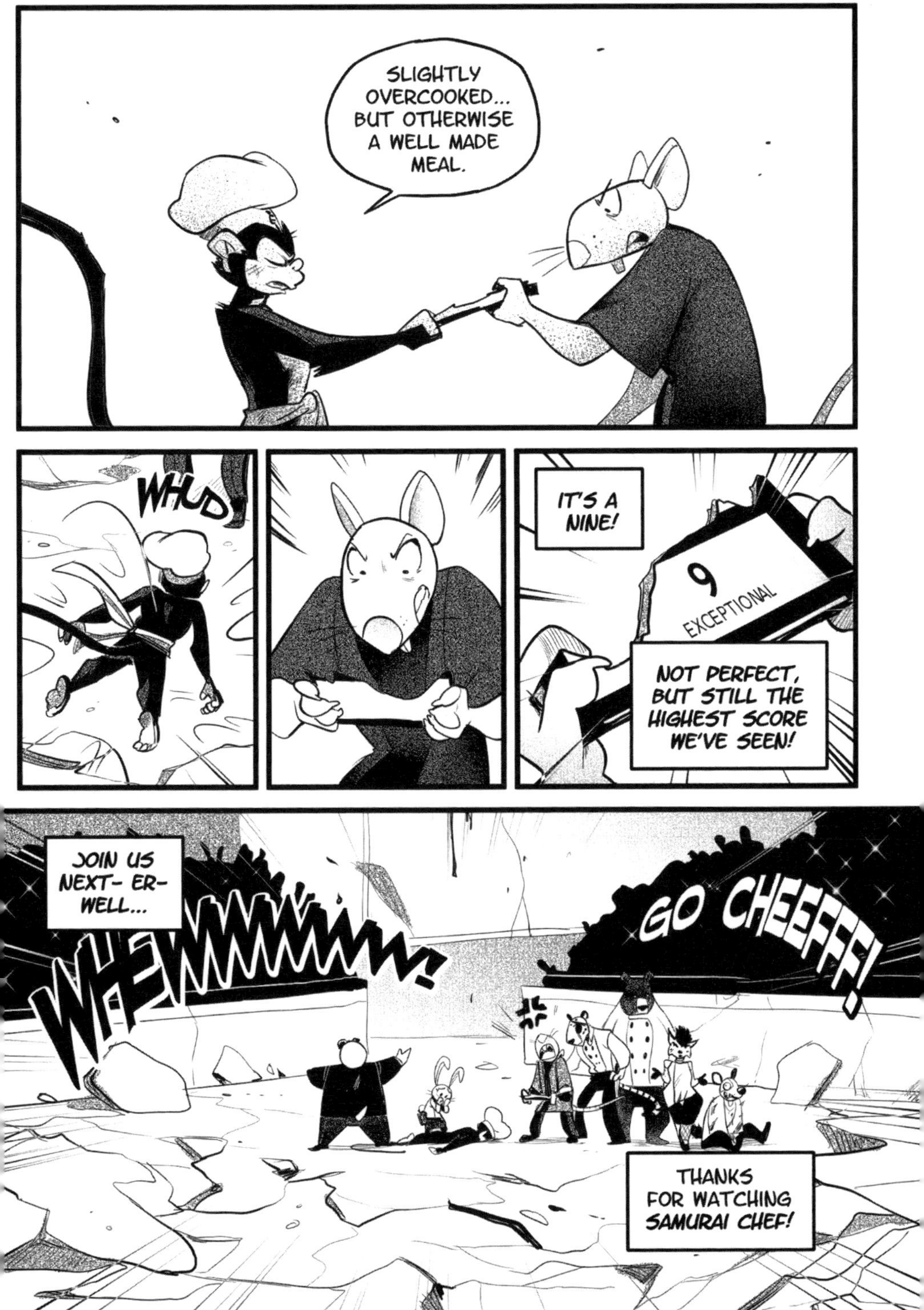
SLIGHTLY OVERCOOKED... BUT OTHERWISE A WELL MADE MEAL.
WHUD
IT'S A NINE!
9
EXCEPTIONAL
NOT PERFECT, BUT STILL THE HIGHEST SCORE WE'VE SEEN!
JOIN US NEXT- ER- WELL...
WHEWWWWWW!
GO CHEEFFF!
THANKS FOR WATCHING SAMURAI CHEF!

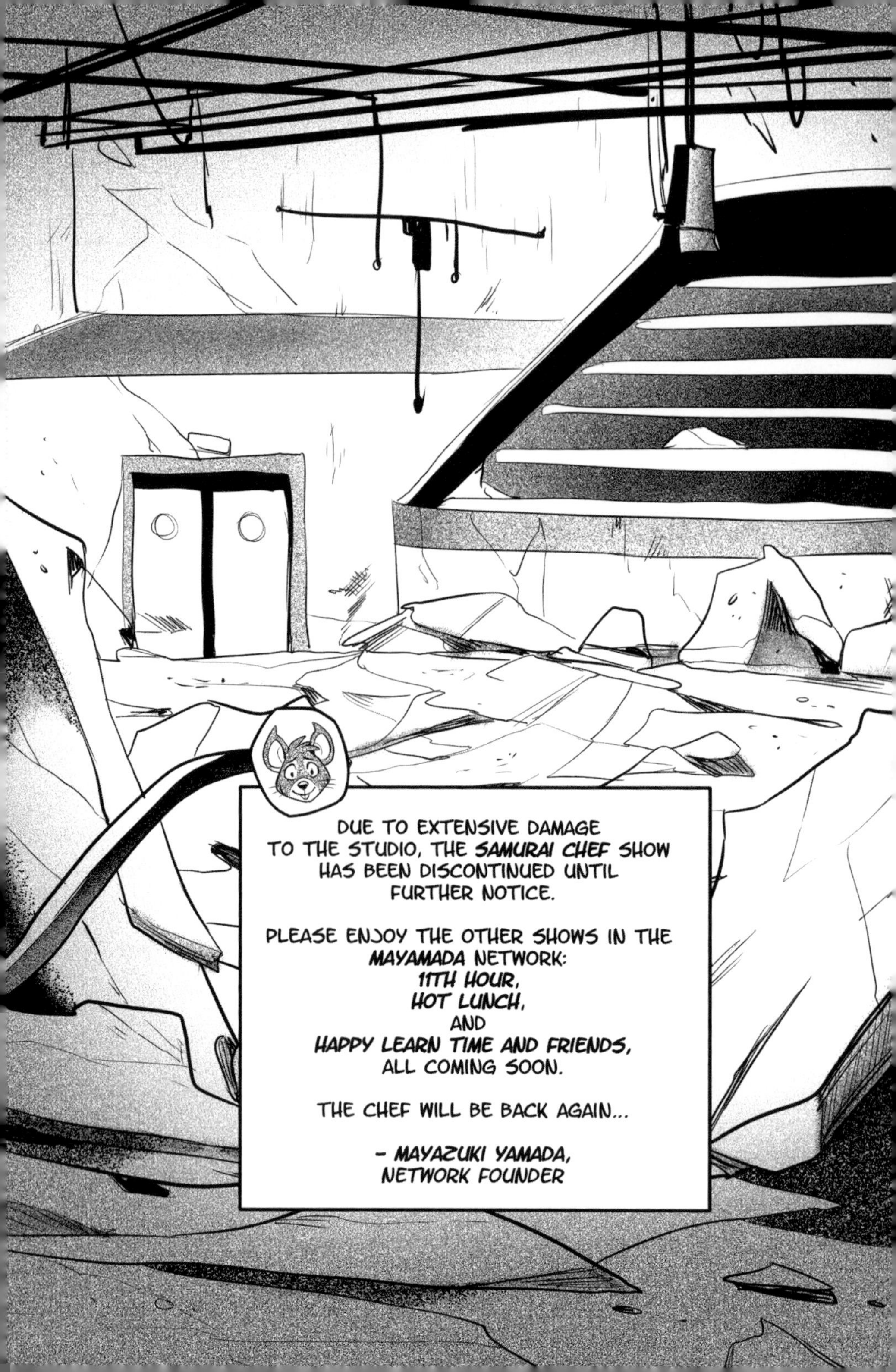
DUE TO EXTENSIVE DAMAGE TO THE STUDIO, THE *SAMURAI CHEF* SHOW HAS BEEN DISCONTINUED UNTIL FURTHER NOTICE.
PLEASE ENJOY THE OTHER SHOWS IN THE *MAYAMADA* NETWORK: *11TH HOUR*, *HOT LUNCH*, AND *HAPPY LEARN TIME AND FRIENDS*, ALL COMING SOON.
THE CHEF WILL BE BACK AGAIN...
- *MAYAZUKI YAMADA*, NETWORK FOUNDER

TO THE AMAZING PEOPLE THAT MADE THIS BOOK POSSIBLE

JABRIL MUSE JAY LOFSTEAD REMI PERRON
MATTHEW DAVID ELIZABETH CRISSEY
JOHN ALLEN STEVEN LORD
DATTAS MOONCHASER
JAMAS ENRIGHT WILL HALL
JOSEPH JIMENEZ
LEAH ONYEANUSI SONIA LAI OPE OYELANA
GARETH POWELL
PRESTON COUTTS EMIR ATTIG GARY THORTON BOBBIE KIRBY DANIEL LIPSCOMBE CATHERINE KENYATTA
HENRIK LINDHE ANTHONY GASCON MARKUSMERGARD
SAMUEL BANKOLE LOUISE HARDEEP REX OSAFO-ASARE ILLY RADDERS BARBARA
JOHN MACLEOD ELISABETH PANZENBOECK EVAN RITCHIE EDERSON MAPELLI DOS SANTOS
REVEK SCOTT EARLY JEREMY ROWLAND KLH JOSEPH D. BLISKA KRENIZ CHEDEE ALEXANDER
CUDDLY TIGER SAM ROBERTS STUDIO CUTE TOBIAS LEHMEIER ERICH SHEOGORATH PAUL TREW
MAGNUS H. BLYSTAD RICHARD NEY ZAK ANTILLA TIM MEAKINS JOSE SAMUELS
ALAN 'MANIAC32' BANKS ROSS PATTERSON VINCENT BAIDOO ROBERT COOT
ASHAN DHARMAKIRTHI JAMES RAMIREZ MELISSA BOLUS ANDREW DONKOR
MIKE CATRIS CRAIG L WITTLER REBECCA RAJENDRA ZEBAK LONG FANG ANASTASIA CATRIS
PAUL MACGREGOR
ANDREW DICKMAN
SAMUEL SOPHIE SHARVAN A. UWAIS HILDA MILLICENT SOPHIE ANTWI
DAMILOLA ALERO AJAYI FISAYO KARUNWI
YLVA LINDSKOG ROB FELSBURG AARON SAND
FECAL ENCEPHALOPATH MICHAEL KRILIVSKY
GINA GRAINGER-WINDRIDGE J C LOCKE
PRESTON COUTTS HARRY BENTLEY FISI CHAN
ROBERT AVERY VIKAS CHOPRA NICK SALT
PAUL SOLOMON-TURAY AMEETAMBEKAR
A MARGRIE MARCUS NASH ANDREW DONKOR
REX OSAFO-ASARE SAMUEL BANKOLE
GARY THORNTON NIGEL JEYAKUMAR
DAFYDD WATKINS ASHAN DHARMAKIRTHI
ANDREW SMITH MANDEEP BANSAL
PAUL MURPHY TOSIN CHICHI WANG
FLORA VAISH SHETH NISHA REZA
MERCY ANTWI RICKY MITCHELL CHEDEE ALEXANDER
LLOYD HEADBUSH OKIEM WARMANN SHAUN SKERRITT
ANNIE GULLIFORD DIETER GOLDSCHMIDT
ADAM NOAD
MILAN SHAH
KOFI MENSAH
ARIYO GRACE RAHEL T
CHEF-KING JOHN PAUL ZAHARY SHAUNETT HARRIS
MERCY ANTWI RICKY MITCHELL CHEDEE ALEXANDER
MICHELLE LEEWARD PATRICK NKRUMAH SAAJID

THANK YOU

MORE MANGA IS ON THE WAY!

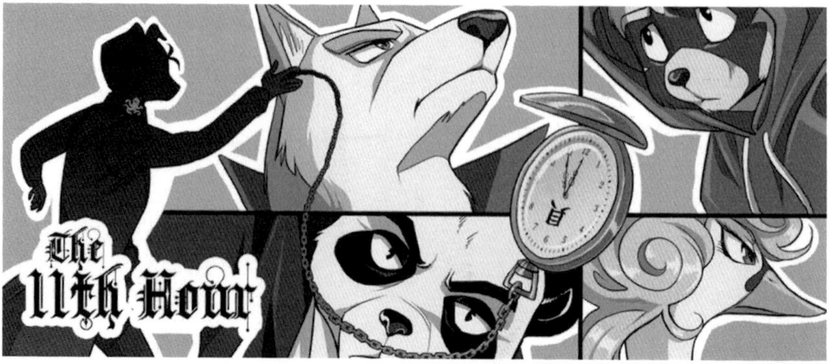
The 11th Hour

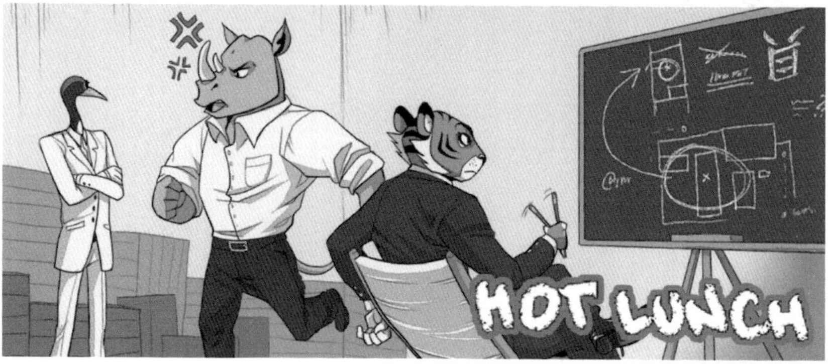
HOT LUNCH

FASHION X COMICS

DID YOU KNOW WE ALSO HAVE A CLOTHING LINE?

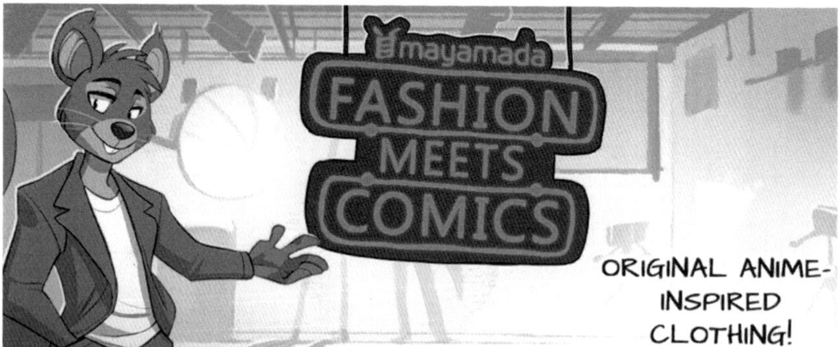
mayamada
FASHION MEETS COMICS
ORIGINAL ANIME-INSPIRED CLOTHING!

SEE IT ALL AT WWW.MAYAMADA.COM